Minding the Machine

The publisher gratefully acknowledges the generous contribution to this book provided by the General Endowment Fund of the University of California Press Associates.

Minding the Machine

Languages of Class in
Early Industrial America

Stephen P. Rice

UNIVERSITY OF CALIFORNIA PRESS
Berkeley · Los Angeles · London

A portion of chapter 2 appeared as "The Mechanics' Institute of the City of New-York and the Conception of Class Authority in Early Industrial America, 1830–1860," *New York History*, 81 (July 2000), 269–99. It appears courtesy of *New York History*, the quarterly journal of the New York State Historical Association.

University of California Press
Berkeley and Los Angeles, California

University of California Press, Ltd.
London, England

Library of Congress Cataloging-in-Publication Data

Rice, Stephen Patrick, 1963–.
    Minding the machine : languages of class in early industrial America / Stephen Patrick Rice.
        p. cm.
    Includes bibliographical references and index.
    ISBN 0-520-22781-6 (cloth)
    1. Social classes—United States—History—19th century.   2. Industrial revolution—United States—History—19th century.   3. Work in literature.
4. Social classes in literature.   I. Title.
HN90.S65R49   2004
305.5'0973'09034—dc22   2003022846

Manufactured in the United States of America

13   12   11   10   09   08   07   06   05   04
10   9   8   7   6   5   4   3   2   1

The paper used in this publication meets the minimum requirements of ANSI/NISO Z39.48-1992 (R 1997) (*Permanence of Paper*).

To the memory of
Viola Eva Rice
(1909–1995)

Contents

Illustrations

Acknowledgments

A number of institutions have generously given their support to the research and writing of this book, and I now have the great pleasure of thanking them: Ramapo College of New Jersey, for two Separately Budgeted Research Grants; the Mrs. Giles Whiting Foundation, for a final-year dissertation fellowship; the American Antiquarian Society, for a Kate B. and Hall J. Peterson Fellowship; the American Philosophical Society, for a Mellon Resident Research Fellowship; the Harvard University Graduate School of Business Administration, for an Alfred D. Chandler, Jr. Traveling Fellowship; the Library Company of Philadelphia, for an Andrew W. Mellon Foundation Fellowship; the Massachusetts Historical Society, for an Andrew W. Mellon Research Fellowship; the Yale University American Studies Program, for a travel grant very early on; and the Yale University Graduate School, for a University Fellowship, an A. Bartlett Giamatti Fellowship in Humanities, and two John F. Enders Research Grants.

In addition, I received immense help from individuals at the research libraries where I spent so many hours gathering material for this book. At the American Antiquarian Society, Joanne Chaison, John Hench, and Caroline Sloat made me feel right at home during my month of research there. Roy E. Goodman at the American Philosophical Society was as generous with his time and knowledge as anyone could hope for. At the Library Company of Philadelphia, James Green, Phil Lapsansky, and Sarah Wetherwax helped me make my way through the library's wonderful collection of material on early-nineteenth-century America. Virginia Smith and Conrad E.

Wright at the Massachusetts Historical Society were both gracious and help-ful as I launched into my research program. My visit to the Lafayette Col-lege archive would not have been nearly as fruitful as it was without the gen-erous help of Diane Windham Shaw. Finally, John Alviti at the Franklin Institute Science Museum kindly allowed me to sift through the institute's rich archive.

This project began as a dissertation in the American Studies Program at Yale University. While at Yale, I received bountiful support from a number of individuals. Jon Butler, my dissertation advisor, guided me at every step in the long process from conceiving a project to turning a dissertation into a book. I am grateful for all his help, and I consider myself fortunate to have had an opportunity to work with him. The other two members of my dis-sertation committee, Jean-Christophe Agnew and Alan Trachtenberg, have also been generous with their comments, advice, and continuing support. Ann Fabian has helped me with this project in so many ways, starting from the inspiring graduate seminar on American cultural history she taught in my first year of graduate school and continuing through numerous readings of my revisions. She truly is an exemplary teacher, scholar, and critic. Finally, David Montgomery, Franny Nudelman, John Harley Warner, and Bryan J. Wolf have given me help and inspiration at different points along the way.

I am grateful to a number of other individuals who, at various stages, read and commented on all or part of this study, in some instances as commen-tators on conference panels: Mary Blewett, Martin Burke, Scott Casper, Julia Ehrhardt, Gary Kornblith, Margaretta Lovell, Timothy Marr, Eileen McWilliam, Kathleen Newman, Nicole Parisier, Daniel Rodgers, Philip Scranton, Diane Simon, Kio Stark, Chris Sterba, Trysh Travis, David Wald-streicher, and Glenn Wallach. I would also like to thank the two readers for the University of California Press, whose comments were very helpful in my final round of revisions. Others who generously helped by providing me with material were Robert E. Bonner, Martha Ecker, F. G. Gosling, and Mark Rice. A portion of chapter 1 appeared in a different form in "Making Way for the Machine: Maelzel's Automaton Chess-Player and Antebellum American Cul-ture," *Proceedings of the Massachusetts Historical Society* 106 (1994), 1–16. Part of chapter 2, also in a different form, appeared in "The Mechanics' Insti-tute of the City of New-York and the Conception of Class Authority in Early Industrial America, 1830–1860," *New York History* 81 (July 2000), 269–99. I am grateful to both journals for permission to use this material again here.

Ramapo College of New Jersey has been a hospitable place to continue working on this project. I have appreciated the college's support of my research and writing, as well as the help and kindness of my colleagues, especially Carol Hovanec, Carter Jones Meyer, Ellen Ross, Peter Scheckner, Alexander Urbiel, and Sydney Weinberg. I would also like to thank my parents, LeRoi Rice and Eleanor Rice, for all their support over the years. At the University of California Press, Monica McCormick has been an encouraging and patient editor.

More than anyone else, I want to thank my wife Jacqueline Lunchick, whose wit and generosity and enthusiasm have been sustaining. Our two children, Sophie and Max, have enlivened the latter stages of this enterprise in ways I could not have imagined when I got started. Finally, this book is dedicated to the memory of my grandmother, who kept the family history and who gently encouraged her grandson's interest in the past.

Introduction

Readers of the *North American Review*, an elite monthly periodical published in Boston, found in the first issue of 1832 an article titled "Effects of Machinery," which set out to examine "the influence of machinery . . . in its effects on society." "The question is," the unidentified author wrote, "is this influence,—confessedly, and beyond calculation, vast,—good or evil?" After acknowledging that there presently was a "conflict of opinions" on this question, the author commenced with his own argument, which was that machinery was a virtually unalloyed benefit. In making this case, he addressed three charges made by those who found "labor-saving machinery" to be a "grievous curse." To the first charge—that labor-saving machines simply replaced people in the workplace, depriving them of employment and causing untold misery—the author admitted that displacements did occur, but he insisted that any consequent suffering would be temporary because new and less toilsome employment would quickly be available in other quarters. The second objection, that machinery tended to "gather wealth into masses, and widen the distance between the rich and the poor," seemed "little less than absurd" to this observer, because workers "not unfrequently" owned stock in the companies that employed them, thereby sharing in whatever wealth was created. Finally, the author dispensed with the charge that mechanization was ruinous to the physical health and moral well-being of machine tenders simply by noting that while such might be the case in England, it was not so in America. "The poet, who should search those districts of our country, where machinery is most extensively employed, for images of wretchedness and want," he wrote, "would return disappointed from his quest." The author concluded with a reflection on the many and varied blessings of machinery: food, clothing, and other needs could be met more easily and cheaply than ever before; people were released from much burdensome toil, free now to pursue higher ends; education was improved, knowledge more quickly and much more widely diffused, and the scope and depth of human achievement extended in ways unimaginable just a generation or two earlier. Indeed, for this observer, the effects of machinery were "almost miraculous."[1]

Before the end of the year, however, a very different assessment of the "effects of machinery" would be published, also in Boston. In *An Address to the Working-Men of New England, on the State of Education, and on the Condition of the Producing Classes in Europe and America*, Seth Luther, who was a carpenter by trade and who would become one of the most radical voices in the antebellum American labor movement, inveighed against the avarice and sheer inhumanity that to his mind thoroughly characterized what was generally called the "factory system of production." Luther mocked those, like the *North American Review* author, who found favor with mechanization, arguing that they were either ignorant of the truth or else moved by simple and heart-hardened greed. He pointed to the long hours of work in textile mills, to the rigid work rules and the reliance on child labor and the vicious use of corporal punishment. Machine operatives, he wrote, were but "slaves of the factory," crushed by the "*tyrannical government*" of the mill owners. "We have seen," Luther concluded after discussing conditions in the textile manufacturing districts of England, "a large body of human beings *ruined* by a neglect of education, rendered miserable in the extreme, and incapable of self government; and this by the grinding of the rich on the faces of the poor, through the operation of cotton and other machinery." Conditions in America were no better, he continued. "The whole system of labor in New England, *more especially in cotton mills*," he wrote, "is a cruel system of exaction on the bodies and minds of the producing classes, destroying the energies of both." So long as manufactories enriched the few while they debased the many, Luther wrote, the American revolution to secure liberty would not be complete. "We shall soon . . . be enabled to form a *front*," he concluded, "which will show all *monopolists*, and all TYRANTS, that we are not only determined to have the name of freemen, but that we will LIVE FREEMEN and DIE FREEMEN."[2]

As these two selections suggest, the development and use of new water- and steam-powered machinery in the first half of the nineteenth century fostered intense debate and disagreement among American men and women. This is perhaps not surprising, given that the several decades before the Civil

War saw an uneven movement from familiar craft and household forms of production to new, mechanized forms of production. Those witnessing and undertaking this disorienting transition raised a host of questions. What could machinery accomplish? Was there no end to the "progress of the arts"? What was the work of machine-tending like? Would machinery promote equality, or would it widen the distance between the rich and the poor? Among the most contentious questions were those focusing on the social consequences of mechanization. If machine enthusiasts highlighted the extent to which machines relieved "mankind" from toil, critics like Seth Luther pointed out that people were required to tend the machines, and that such work was fundamentally degrading and exploitative, belying any vision of "progress." By the early 1830s, Luther and others were inclined to use an explicit and oppositional language of class to describe society in the age of machinery. In his address to the working men of New England, for instance, Luther clearly believed that the most salient divide in the world of mechanized work was between the "producing classes" and those who possessed "monopolized wealth." The latter, for Luther, constituted the "rich," which included "owners, agents, and overseers," not the people who actually did the work of tending machinery. Elsewhere in his address, he pointed to this distinct class divide when he noted that "the *wives* and *daughters* of the *rich* manufacturers would no more associate with a '*factory girl*,' than they would with a *negro slave.* So much for equality in a *republican* country."[3]

Indeed, historians over the last thirty years have argued that what we see in the words of Seth Luther—and in the actions of those wage-workers who supported workers' political parties, struck for higher wages or the ten-hour day, and collectively resisted the authority of their employers—is the making of an American working class. Luther first delivered his remarks in March 1832 before a group of Boston workers striking for a ten-hour workday. By the time he spoke, wage-earning journeymen from across the trades and in cities and towns around the country had launched a variety of movements opposing what they saw as the inequities of an emerging industrial order, including Working-Men's parties, general trades' unions, and radicalized craft unions. It is now clear that an oppositional understanding of class came into focus in these acts of collective resistance. But at the same time that activists such as Luther helped to promote this oppositional understanding of class, others such as the *North American Review* author helped to promote a very different understanding of social relations in an industrial society. For them, mechanization was disruptive for sure, but in ways that were much more about creating new possibilities than about destroying something that had been ideal. Rather than inscribing inequality, mechanization tended to undo hierarchies of old and make it possible for everyone to improve themselves and their lot. If Seth Luther gave voice to an emerging working class, this was the voice of an emerging middle class.

This book is about the making of a class society in America during the early decades of the nineteenth century. Like other studies of class formation in America, it considers industrialization—in essence the creation and spread of mechanized and closely labor-divided forms of production—to be central to the formation of distinct class positions among antebellum Americans. The focus here is on a particular question: how did members of a nascent middle class manage to promote and defend their social authority in the face of troubling and divisive questions about work and mechanization? In addressing this question, this book locates class formation not so much in the material conditions of the workplace, but in a broad, popular discourse on mechanization, one that occurred in movements and activities that were for the most part on the periphery of more traditional notions of industrialization. These included educational movements such as the mechanics' institute movement and the manual labor school movement, health reform activities, and efforts to solve the seemingly intractable problem of steam boiler explosions. My principal argument is that American men and women who were coming to perceive themselves (and be perceived by others) as middle class in the decades before 1860 consolidated their authority and minimized the potential for class conflict in part by representing the social relations of the industrial workplace as necessarily cooperative rather than oppositional. They did this by participating in a popular discourse on mechanization in which they defined the relation between proprietors (and the overseers, foremen, or managers they employed) and wageworkers as analogous to three other sets of relations: between head and hand, mind and body, and human and machine. By mapping a vexed social relation onto a series of less contested relations understood to fall outside the social realm, middle-class Americans offered a conception of class that authorized the relative power of owners and managers without seeming to undermine the autonomy and dignity of workers. At the same time, workers lost ground in their effort to mount an effective challenge to the emerging industrial order, in part by participating in this popular discourse on mechanization without challenging its fundamental terms. One conclusion is that class is as much about the comprehension of social relations as it is about the making of social relations. Class formation in America, then, needs to be understood not only as a social struggle, but as a conceptual struggle, one in which men and women elaborated and defended competing visions of class relations.

This emphasis on concepts of class should not minimize, however, the importance of work to the making of class. Over the last several decades, social historians have shown that the reorganization of work in the first half of the nineteenth century fostered profound social transformations that extended far beyond the workplace. By 1860, water- and steam-powered machines had been introduced to a host of productive pursuits, from the spinning of thread and the weaving of cloth, to the making of pins and rope, to printing. At the same time, sharp divisions of labor and new systems of "outwork" degraded traditional craft work in a number of trades. Together, mechanization and the division of labor marked a fundamental transformation in the social relations of production. Traditional productive arrangements outside the home, as depicted in the prescriptive literature of the day, had a master craftsman working closely with his journeyman and apprentice, imparting craft knowledge and supervising the acquisition of skill. The apprentice would in time become a master himself, amply prepared for the duties of life. The mechanized shop was quite different. There the productive capacity inhered less in the skilled craftsman than in the ingeniously wrought machine. Rather than contracting an apprentice, owners of machinery hired men, women, and children as machine-tenders, placing them under the supervision of a new coterie of overseers and managers who made many of the decisions about the work to be done and enforced new patterns of discipline deemed necessary for the mechanized setting. As managers and workers took their places on the shop floor, conception separated from execution, "head" from "hand." Historians have shown that, by the 1830s, many Americans viewed this division between wage-workers and proprietors or managers, between people who did manual work and people who did mental work, as marking a class division. By 1860, and especially in cities and industrial centers, American men and women had forged distinct working-class and middle-class identities through a variety of social and cultural practices, identities that frequently brought them into conflict with one another.[4]

This book tries to show that the cultural arena provided opportunities for antebellum Americans to make sense of and give order to the profound social changes that were underway. In what I am calling a popular discourse on mechanization, labor leaders and ministers, college professors and journal editors, indeed writers and lecturers of all sorts gave voice to vastly different ideas about mechanization and work, and about the world that was being made in the "age of machinery." Historians of culture have explored how men and women articulated these ideas, not only in sermons, books, speeches, articles, and essays but in a variety of cultural forms, including poems, works of fiction, paintings, sculpture, exhibitions of machinery, and parades. This study seeks to contribute to this inquiry by considering how cultural activities that expressed explicit ideas about machinery and work expressed as well, often in much more implicit ways, ideas about class. What is striking about the texts that are assembled here is that, although they derive from an array of activities and speak to quite diverse problems, they share one assumption. Whether dwelling on the benefits of mechanics' institutes, or describing the manual labor system, or deploring the problem of steam boiler explosions, they imagine that a critical relationship had been either undone or unsuitably formed, and that the specific problem at hand could be solved by constituting that relationship in its proper state. Here I have tried to show how these disparate and seemingly unrelated activities and discussions circulated a rather coherent set of ideas about class—about a relationship that seemed dangerously undone to some, and to others seemed unsuitably formed—and that in doing so, they helped to settle in some people's minds thorny questions about the social relations of industrial work. In this way, cultural expressions that seemed to have little to say about some of the most contentious questions of their day served in fact as crucial arenas not only for formulating and diffusing ideas about class, but also for creating a class society.[5]

As anyone who has considered the subject knows, the term "class" has had and continues to have different and sometimes competing meanings. At its root a term that simply denotes difference, "class" becomes freighted with economic, political, and moral meanings when it is used to mark real and perceived social difference and to conceptually organize that difference. Historians, sociologists, and others have used the term to make sense of historical change and social conditions, finding variously the rise of a working class, the elaboration of middle-class conventions, the shifting class composition of neighborhoods, and so on. A category of analysis for some, a social reality for others, the meaning and usefulness of the term "class" have evaded anything like consensus. My intention is to engage this very contemporary discussion by considering how men and women in the first half of the nineteenth century came to view American society as a class society, and how doing so was crucial to the making of a class society. Clearly, the people whose words are the subject of this study understood by the late 1820s that certain seeming truths (both assuring and dispiriting) about their work, and about the possibility of moving up or making a living, were coming undone. Some of them used an explicit language of class to describe the new social world, in which occupation and income joined with a variety of social and cultural practices to mark what they perceived to be a clear (although, for some, breachable) divide between a new working class and a new middle class. It is on this *perception* of class, and on the sometimes oblique efforts to conceive and promote certain ideas about the nature of class relations, that this study focuses.[6]

The designation "middle class" is also problematic. If people have, at least since the 1840s, used the phrase to describe their own social position, or the social position of others, what, historically, has it meant to be middle class? Historians and others have for some time noted the difficulty of this question, pointing out that the designation "middle class" has at times been so all-encompassing as to be virtually meaningless as a category of distinction. Nonetheless, textbooks, articles, and monographs routinely refer to middle-class Americans—to middle-class readers, middle-class households, middle-class consumers, and middle-class values—often with the sense that there is little need to explain who, precisely, these people were, or what it was that made them middle class. At the same time, a growing body of scholarship has sought to define the specific characteristics of the American middle class. These studies generally point to the making of a distinctively middle-class experience or middle-class culture beginning in the early decades of the nineteenth century. Some have focused on how men and women who were coming to see themselves as middle-class employed various means to refine themselves and their surroundings, cultivating new habits of "gentility" or "respectability" in their dress, their manner of speaking, and their social interactions more generally. Others have pointed to the importance of home and family life to middle-class identity, arguing that the home was not only a place for displaying these refined habits, but also a crucial arena for cultivating respectability. Here, the ideology of domesticity figures prominently, whereby women were to work in the home in order to raise virtuous children and provide for their husbands a refuge from a heartless world. While it is clear that the work women did in the home was crucial to middle-class self-understanding through most of the nineteenth century, other studies have examined how the work that men did outside the home was equally crucial. Here the focus has been on occupation, and on the increased income and prestige that generally went with occupations defined as nonmanual, or that were understood to require some measure of formal education and could be included among the "professions." This latter set of class distinctions is what most informs this book. My focus, then, is on the largely male realm outside the home, and on ideas about work and about certain occupations, particularly those ideas that distinguished between manual labor and nonmanual labor. The middle-class individual here could be a master cabinetmaker in 1847, who had worked for years with his hands but had recently acquired enough capital to purchase a small steam engine and several woodworking machines and was now devoting most or all of his time to expanding his business, leaving the work of making things to his growing number of wage-workers. Or it could be a minister in 1835 whose duties had recently come to include editing a

monthly periodical, so that much of his time was spent reading articles, meeting with his printer, and cultivating authors and readers. How was it that
these men came to be conceived as sharing a common class position, and
how did members of that class position define their social authority?[7]

If this book turns to cultural activities to answer these questions, it needs
to be noted that there is nothing new to the insight that class formation
can be located in activities far removed from the material conditions of the
workplace. Nonetheless, my hope has been to illuminate the historical vagaries
of class formation in ways that other studies have not. First, I have tried to
consider class formation more in terms of how power is wielded than in terms
of how power is resisted. Although historians have studied the middle class
as a social group in America, most have focused on the elaboration of a distinctive culture or experience in an already-present middle class rather than
on the formation of the middle class at its point of nascent instability. In general, the history of class formation in America has largely remained the
province of labor historians, who have tended to locate class formation in
the emergence of class "awareness" or class "consciousness" among manual
laboring men and women. In this scheme, "class" is defined primarily as
"working class" and is most evident in the ways that wage-workers collectively resisted the authority of their employers, both on and off the shop
floor. Inspired by E. P. Thompson's magisterial *The Making of the English
Working Class,* published in the mid 1960s, labor historians working within
this framework have given close scrutiny to the shared and often resistant
work, family, and leisure activities of wage-working men and women,
seeking to recover oppositional working-class ideologies and cultures. But
although they have revealed much about working-class formation and real
social contestation in America, these studies have given too little attention
to the idea that class, like race and gender, is necessarily a relational category, and that the history of class formation needs to examine as well the
making of a middle class. In returning the middle class to the story of industrialization and class formation in the nineteenth century, I have moved away
from scenes of workers' control and workers' resistance. Instead, I have examined some of the means by which, and the venues in which, members of an
ascendant middle class worked in often subtle ways to define and assert their
social authority. My focus, therefore, is on the proprietors and the managers,
and their middle-class allies who helped to conceptualize the relation between
owners and wage-workers in terms that were difficult to resist and favorable
to their class interests.[8]

Second, I have tried to account for the relative success of the middle class
in consolidating its social and cultural authority by considering how classes

formed discursively at the same time that they formed socially. Labor historians typically chart how the interplay between ideology and social "experience" gives rise to expressions of class consciousness. Most imply a one-way causality, in which the materiality of social experience (or social being) leads to—or in some cases, fails to lead to—class consciousness. Some historians, such as Gareth Stedman Jones, have challenged this interpretive model, arguing for a different set of causal relations. In his book *Languages of Class,* Stedman Jones argues that class derives not from the materiality of experience, but from the "linguistic ordering" of experience. Language, in other words, stands prior to class, giving structure and meaning to those experiences that come to constitute the experience of class. The task of the historian seeking to understand class formation, then, is to explore the "complex rhetoric of metaphorical association, causal inference and imaginative construction" by which class is made. Following this lead, I have examined how the terms, images, and metaphors used in popular discussions of machinery, mechanics' institutes, manual labor schools, human physiology, and the problem of steam boiler explosions helped ultimately to authorize the relative power of the middle class. "Words," Daniel Rodgers reminds us in his discussion of political language in America, "create those pictures in our heads which make the structures of authority tolerable and understandable."[9]

Some historians have criticized the so-called "linguistic turn" in historical analysis, arguing that shifting from the study of historical actors to the study of texts or language deprives the historian's account of agency. They suggest that eschewing historical materialism for the analysis of language amounts to a "descent into discourse." They challenge the notion that language structures reality, taking the position that being stands prior to saying, that "language is not life." Many of their arguments address interesting theoretical questions. But rather than dwell on what ultimately are metaphysical debates about whether language has a meaningful extradiscursive referent, or on the question of whether language structures or is structured by "social reality," I have taken as my starting point the notion that the social experience of class has both a material element and a discursive element, and that one is always giving shape to the other. Class cannot be meaningful outside of the concepts used to define it, but those concepts gain the currency and power they have in part because they are understood to delimit something that is "real." In taking this approach, I have said relatively little about the lives or politics of the editors, reformers, and others who entered the popular discourse on mechanization. Nor have I examined in depth the individuals who read newspapers and periodicals, gathered to listen to lectures, attended mechanics' fairs, or enlisted in health reform movements. Instead,

I have focused on the languages people used to describe their experiences, articulate their opinions, express their hopes, voice their fears, and in so doing, subtly but surely constitute a class society.[10]

Finally, my hope is that by shifting from particular sites of class contestation and appeasement to a broad popular discourse on mechanization, I have been able to illuminate how classes formed nationally rather than locally. Studies in labor history have usually focused on single communities or regions. This fact derives largely from the imperatives of the social historical method—charting workforce populations, income levels, and so forth—which necessarily limit the scope of inquiry to the manageable size of the community study. But local studies invite efforts at synthesis. Participants in the popular discourse on mechanization lived and worked in New Orleans and New York, in Boston, Cincinnati, St. Louis, and Charleston. Local differences certainly prevailed, but so too did a certain sameness: men and women from these and other communities used a common language to express their ideas, hopes, and concerns about the social dislocations attendant on mechanization. In taking this approach, I have been more interested in making generalizations, finding what was similar about the language people used and the meaning that language was likely to convey, than in making distinctions among local meanings or experiences.

My argument, then, is that antebellum Americans constructed a class society in a broad popular discourse on mechanization that flourished in the newspapers, periodicals, and pamphlets of the day. As participants in the popular discourse on mechanization struggled to reconcile the emerging industrial order with threatened moral and political ideals, they articulated a conception of class that authorized the relative power of managers without seeming to undermine the claims of workers. They did so by mapping the vexed relation between managers and workers onto a series of less contested relations, each of which helped to answer difficult questions about what that peculiar social relation would look like. The mechanics' institute movement turned to traditional ideas about the head governing the hand in order to codify the notion that the hierarchical relation between manager and worker should be cooperative rather than oppositional. In similar fashion, manual labor schools worked to bring head and hand together into harmonious and fruitful relation. At the same time, popular physiology tracts appealed to personal experience in urging that physical health depended on the mind properly governing the body, a body that writers and lecturers frequently depicted as a machine. In this way, all men and women were in a figurative sense machine tenders, and because the work they did as such was perfectly natural and an important species of mental labor, the work of machine-tending could not be said to be fundamentally degrading. Finally, discussions of the problem of steam boiler explosions—in the midst of concepts of a metaphoric relation between machines and humans, and between explosive steam engines and an explosive society—suggested that managers needed to maintain control over their workers in the same way that engineers needed to maintain control over their engines. Given the terrible destruction resulting from boiler explosions, all members of society had an interest in seeing both sets of relations properly constituted. Each of these discussions appeared neutral on the questions dividing workers from members of the middle class. Together, they established a series of analogous structures—manager was to worker as head was to hand, as mind was to body, as human was to machine—that enabled members of the middle class to defuse class tension and to further their class interests, without appearing to do so.[11]

In making this argument, it is not my intention to take a strong social control position, whereby those who participated in the popular discourse on mechanization in the terms that I discuss, and to the effects that I suggest, were necessarily clear in their intentions and collaborative in their efforts. Instead, I have found that these men and women, in facing the novelty and instability, the great promise and great danger, of the "age of machinery," often worked in unknowing and even paradoxical ways. Nonetheless, whether discussing machinery in general, or the benefits of mechanics' institutes or the manual labor system, or the need for physiological reform, or the problem of steam boiler explosions, antebellum Americans drew upon and expressed common languages, languages that helped to constitute a class society suited to the industrial age.

CHAPTER I

The Antebellum Popular Discourse on Mechanization

On a Thursday evening in April 1826, over one hundred people gathered at the National Hotel in New York City for the American debut of Johann Maelzel's exhibition of mechanical devices. Advertisements had been running in the newspapers for days, promising New Yorkers a viewing of the "celebrated and only Automaton Chess-player in the world," along with an "Automaton Trumpeter" and some "Automaton Slack Rope Dancers." While the opening night's attendance was relatively low, newspapers the next day proclaimed the evening's fare to be astonishing, especially the chess-player. "At the appointed hour," wrote the *New-York Evening Post,* "the curtain was withdrawn, and the figure of a Turk, seated at his chess board, was rolled forward on castors." Viewers saw before them a life-sized figure of a man seated behind a cabinet, its legs crossed and resting to one side, its hands placed on top of the cabinet. Dressed in a robe and wearing a blue turban, the chess-player faced the audience "with a long heavy black beard, and large grey eyes." After making much display of the machinery inside the device, Maelzel invited opponents to challenge it to a game of chess. Those who stepped forward did so to no avail. "Two accomplished chess players played jointly against him," noted one paper, "but were beaten with great ease." What was marvelous about the chess-player was that it could not only move in a life-like fashion—in the game, it was the automaton that picked up the chess pieces and moved them on the board—but it could play a game that was generally understood to require reasoning, and it could play it extraordinarily well. As the writer for the *Evening Post* observed, "Nothing of a similar nature has ever been seen in this city, that will bear the smallest comparison with it." To at least some observers, it seemed as if the impossible had been accomplished—a machine had been made that could think.[1]

Within days Maelzel found his audiences swelled by a storm of popular interest. Newspaper columns brimmed with descriptions of the chess-player, along with detailed accounts of how such a device—deemed by one paper "the greatest puzzle ever seen"—might work. Crowds gathered day after day, sometimes overwhelming the exhibition hall's capacity. Late in May, one paper reported that on the previous evening "it was found necessary to refuse admittance to nearly two hundred applicants, at the door."[2]

After several months of exhibiting his mechanical devices in New York, Maelzel packed up his show and took it on the road, first to Boston and then to Philadelphia. Maelzel eventually made Philadelphia his home, though he continued to travel up and down the eastern seaboard until his death in 1838. The popularity of his show seems to have waned little if at all over the years. In Boston during the summer of 1833, for instance, one newspaper speculated that nearly a third of those seeking admission could not get tickets. Though the other items in Maelzel's show—which came to include an elaborate panorama called the "Conflagration of Moscow"—were impressive, the chess-player remained in a league of its own and attracted much more attention. "We may appear to permit the automaton to occupy too much of our columns," confessed a New York editor in 1826, "but persons at a distance can form no idea how much the attention of our citizens is engrossed by it at this present writing."[3]

The exhibition of Maelzel's automaton chess-player was one venue in which antebellum men and women participated in the popular discourse on mechanization. A mechanical device that seemed almost magical in its operations, the chess-player was much like the new steam- and water-powered machines that were endlessly discussed by men and women in the first decades of the nineteenth century. The conceptual distance was short indeed between the chess-player and the kind of device imagined by a speaker at the Pittsburgh Mechanics' Institute in 1830 who suggested that "the day cannot be far distant when mechanical genius will invent some new mode of infusing mind into matter—some new application of power which will some day or other, in a great measure, supercede the employment of manual labor in many of its most complicated operations." In scrutinizing the chess-player, then, members of Maelzel's audiences had an opportunity to consider the possibilities of machinery more generally. As they marveled at and worried about the "progress of the arts" in these more general terms, antebellum observers engaged in often contentious debates about the effects of machinery on

individual men and women and on society as a whole. At the center of these
debates were questions about two sets of relations new to the age of mechanized production: the relations between humans and production machines,
and the relations between managers and mechanized workers. In tracing the
contours of the antebellum popular discourse on mechanization, this
chapter shows that these two sets of relations were at the center of an emerging understanding of class. Antebellum writers and lecturers saw that the
mechanization of production separated the manual labor of executing work
from the mental labor of planning and managing work. Many complained
that the men and women who were hired to operate powerful production
machinery had little time to use or cultivate their minds, leaving them simply "hands" in the workplace. As they began to equate "handwork" with
wage-earning employees, and "headwork" with managers and employers,
participants in the popular discourse on mechanization imagined the
social dislocations that would result when "head" separated from "hand,"
both in the individual worker and in society generally. The appeal of Maelzel's
chess-player rested in part in its ability to answer some of the difficult questions that arose in these discussions of mechanization. The exhibition of
the chess-player displayed a "thinking machine" supervised by a learned
and benevolent manager. Together, the chess-player and Maelzel modeled the
social relations of mechanized production in terms that both promoted the
emerging industrial order and ensured the relative power of the middle class.[4]

As historians of early industrial development in America point out, the majority of men and women engaged in productive activity during the first half of
the nineteenth century did not work with power machinery. That is to say,
while the machine was indeed becoming a reality in the workplace, it was by
no means the dominant reality, since most "producers" through 1860 still
made things using simple tools and the power of their muscles. The extent
of mechanization as figured in popular discussion, however, outstripped its
actual pace in the workplace. As men and women discussed new machinery in newspapers, periodicals, lectures, and sermons, they frequently wrote
and spoke as if the machine was present everywhere. The author of the "Effects
of Machinery" article, published in the *North American Review* in 1832,
could already assume of his readers that they "live in the midst of machinery," and that they "see machinery on every side, abridging the processes of
labor, and making the difficult easy." Whether optimistic or pessimistic about
such developments, observers frequently anticipated a day "not too far distant" when machines would be made to do just about anything. If the machine
was not yet a salient feature of the work life of most men and women engaged

in productive activity, participants in the popular discourse on mechanization expected that it would be one day soon.[5]

One site of mechanized production that was widely discussed during the antebellum decades was the textile mill. Mechanized textile manufacturing in the United States began in the early 1790s, when the Rhode Island firm of Almy, Brown, and Slater started a water-powered spinning operation in Pawtucket. In the years 1810–20, a group of Boston investors founded the Boston Manufacturing Company and launched mechanized spinning and weaving operations, first in Waltham, Massachusetts and then (as the Merrimack Manufacturing Company) in Lowell. With their integrated manufacturing from raw cotton to woven cloth, their largely female workforce of machine tenders, and their vast productivity, the Lowell mills received considerable attention in newspapers and periodicals. By 1855, fifty-two mills at Lowell produced over two million yards of cloth per week and employed more than thirteen thousand workers. The Philadelphia area was another significant scene of mechanized textile manufacturing, with cotton spinning and weaving operations centered in Manayunk to the north of the city, the Rockdale region to the west, and several other communities. Visitors to textile mills could find a variety of machinery inside, including the carding engine, used to prepare the cleaned cotton fibers for spinning, the throstle and the spinning mule, both of which were used to spin the cotton into yarn, and the power loom, which was used to weave yarn into fabric.[6]

For many antebellum Americans, the development of mechanized textile manufacturing was compelling evidence of the "progress of the arts," but perhaps even more so was the development of various "labor-saving machines" for use by carpenters, printers, metalworkers, and other craftsmen. Although the mechanization of the crafts varied from trade to trade—one study has shown that printing and several woodworking trades were among the first to be affected in New York City—the array of new steam- and water-powered devices receiving patents or on display at mechanics' fairs suggested to many observers that any work done by hand was being transformed by the use of machinery. A writer for the *Farmer and Mechanic,* for instance, observed in 1850 that "there is scarcely a department in mechanics, or a branch of the profession, which has not been greatly improved during the last few years, by the introduction and use of machinery." The following year, a reviewer of a two-volume dictionary of "machines, mechanics, engine-work, and engineering," upon glancing through the book's pages, noted simply that "it would seem as if almost everything was done by machinery." By the 1850s, readers of the popular press would have known that paper manufacturers were now using large, complex machines to make paper, that newspapers were being printed on steam-powered printing presses, and that sewing could be done by machine.[7]

The introduction of powered machines into the workplace spawned a broad, popular discourse on mechanization that was conducted in a number of venues. In lyceums and mechanics' institutes, Fourth of July celebrations, accounts of factory tours, mechanics' exhibitions, automata displays, and worker protests, antebellum American men and women gave voice both to shared assumptions and to vastly different outlooks on how mechanization would change society. Their words and descriptions of their activities appeared in print in books and pamphlets, but especially in periodicals and newspapers, which in addition to publishing the texts of speeches, excerpts from pamphlets, and so forth, regularly printed reports on new machinery or more general reflections on "the progress of the arts." Indeed, general periodicals of every stripe, from learned quarterlies such as the *North American Review,* to family-oriented compendia such as the *Family Magazine,* to literary gazettes such as *Graham's Magazine* and *Harper's Monthly Magazine,* to avowedly political publications such as the *Democratic Review,* devoted space to discussing the promises and perils of mechanization. Alongside these more popular publications, where such discussions for the most part appeared only occasionally and alongside a host of other subjects, was an array of specialized journals devoted to disseminating information on new machinery or modes of production, including commercial reviews such as the *Merchants' Magazine* and *DeBow's Review,* technology reviews such as *Scientific American* and the *Farmer and Mechanic,* and technical journals such as the *Journal of the Franklin Institute.* Here those interested in new machinery or in the effects of machinery on society could find an endless supply of information and ideas to contemplate. Daily and weekly newspapers also printed occasional reflections on machinery and the consequences of mechanization more generally. Much more common in the newspapers of the day, however, were articles on steam boiler explosions, mechanics' institute lectures, exhibitions of the arts, and other topics related to "the age of machinery," so that on any given week, virtually any newspaper in the nation contributed in some fashion to the popular discourse on mechanization.

These discussions of machines and mechanization flourished in a climate of eager anticipation of the new and marvelous. Editors looking for items of interest to their readers readily printed accounts of new machinery, even the sometimes dubious. "Every discovery in science or art, every improvement in husbandry or household economy, in medicine or cosmetics, real or supposed, is immediately proclaimed," noted an article in the *Merchants' Magazine* in 1843. The attention devoted to developments in the "useful arts"

and to other practical items moved one editor that same year to characterize the time as a "universal-diffusion-of-useful-knowledge-age" marked by
a "newspaper-paragraph and magazine-writing mania." Machines and mechanization provided ample material to feed this mania. The editor of a weekly
paper, the *Pearl and Literary Gazette,* wrote in 1834 that the topic of machinery offered an easy solution to the problem of producing copy when time
was short. "There is one blessing which has followed the application of steam
power," he wrote in an amused tone, "which has hitherto remained unsung
and unnoticed. We mean the immense advantage it has been to newspaper
editors in concocting paragraphs, and filling out their columns, when no better subject was at hand." The hurried editor, then, might pick up any paper
and find there an account of "some newly discovered engine" with which to
produce an "ingenious and erudite article on the wonderful power of steam."[8]

Conventional practices of reprinting helped make this popular discourse
on mechanization national in scope. Newspaper and periodical editors
regularly copied articles or portions of articles from one another or from
other printed sources. The practice of borrowing and adapting from other
publications would have been quite familiar to antebellum readers of the
popular press. An article written for one publication, then, might appear in
a somewhat different form, or with additional comment, in another publication some days or weeks later. Although not always the case, editors frequently made it a practice to credit their source. An article entitled "Statues
Made by Steam" that appeared in the *Troy Whig,* for example, explicitly
addressed itself to a piece on Thomas Blanchard's lathe that had been published in the *Boston Courier.* The *Troy Whig* article, in turn, appeared with
a credit line but without comment in the July 31, 1847 edition of the *Supplement to the Courant,* published in Hartford, Connecticut. The editor of the
Pearl and Literary Gazette made light of such practices, describing one editor borrowing or stealing from another on the subject of steam power until
"poor steam runs the gauntlet of the whole editorial community from Maine
to Georgia." The decision by editors to dwell on machines and mechanization fostered the popular discourse on mechanization, but so too did some
of the very machines that were the topic of discussion. The rapid communication afforded by the steamboat in the first decade of the century, the railroad by the 1830s, and the telegraph by the 1840s, along with the development of new printing technologies like the steam press, facilitated the
abundance and diffusion of textual references to machines. Together, these
mechanical devices made possible a discussion in which accounts of new
machines became, in the words of one enthusiast in 1846, "facts which mingle in the news of every day."[9]

The machine that seems to have elicited the most widespread comment in the popular discourse on mechanization was the steam engine. The rise of steam power in the first decades of the nineteenth century was perhaps the most vivid sign of the progress of the age. Indeed, in many cases the word "steam" came to stand for the triumph of human ingenuity. Boats powered by steam had the magical agency built into their name—steamboat—and many cities had, by the 1850s, at least one "Steam Press" listed among their printing establishments. When Samuel Slater tried his hand at steam-powered textile manufacturing in the late 1820s, he called his new enterprise the Steam Cotton Manufacturing Company. If the cloth produced by the mill met a certain standard of excellence it was stamped "Steam Loom" before being shipped for sale. Observers of mechanization often marveled at the manifold uses of steam power. "We spin, we weave, we even make boots and shoes, we pump, we excavate, we lift the greatest weights, we warm the house, we wash," wrote one enthusiast in 1833. "These are the advantages," he continued, "which we owe to improvements in steam machinery." Some observers suggested that the potential uses of steam power were almost without limit. A writer on "The Probable Application of Steam Power to Various Purposes," also in 1833, wrote of steam power that "every day brings to light some new form in which its irresistible energies may be employed." Nearly twenty years later, another writer would still marvel that "the steam engine . . . is being applied to almost every conceivable variety of manual labor." As one observer put it in 1858, "Steam is the wonder and glory of our age. It is destined to accomplish results of which we can as yet hardly dream."[10]

Participants in the popular discourse on mechanization frequently noted that the steam engine displayed a power and almost self-directing agency that were unlike any other kind of machine. Prior to the steam engine, the notion of "the machine" carried a sense of order, regularity, and wholesale determination. The clockwork mechanism dominated this conception of the machine, with its array of functionally integrated parts and its unwavering devotion to a determined task. The steam engine, however, was something altogether different. What was interesting about the steam engine was not the functional relation of parts, as with the clock, but the internal dynamism of the machine. The steam engine thus added to the notion of the machine a sense of power, vitality, and almost willful autonomy. Even textile machines, so captivating in their unwavering devotion to a set course, seemed small in comparison to the steam engine. "The little busy bee-winged machinery of the cotton factory dwindled into insignificance before it," wrote one observer of a steam locomotive in 1850. The array of goods that steam-powered machinery could be made to produce amply demonstrated the dynamism of the steam engine. In 1858, one observer noted that "steam weaves our cloth, man-ufactures our machinery, prepares the materials for our houses, and makes the carpets and furniture we put into them; grinds our grain, helps make our shoes, hats, and clothes, and prints our newspapers." A contributor to the *American Quarterly Review* nearly thirty years earlier marveled as well that "the steam-engine has, within our own recollection, become the most useful and extensive in its application, of all the prime movers of machinery. No resistance, however intense, appears to withstand its power; no work, how-ever delicate, is beyond its action." If clocks and other intricate mechanical devices were about structure and authority, steam engines were about agency— steam engines made things happen.[11]

The steam engine also conveyed a new sense of power by displaying the human triumph over the forces of nature. Antebellum writers and lectures frequently described advances in machinery—for production, for transporta-tion, and for communication—as akin to harnessing nature. "Man has impris-oned the very elements," declaimed a speaker on the "nature and objects of the modern philosophy" in 1830, "compelling them to toil for him, like giant slaves, propelling his vessels, or moving his mighty engines (as in the appli-cation of steam)." Many argued that the steam engine was perhaps the finest example of the human ability to direct the brute and disorganizing powers of nature. "Man, as it were, yokes the hostile elements of fire and water, and subjects them to his bidding" marveled the author of "Effects of Machin-ery" as he contemplated the steam engine. Another observer in 1845 simi-larly cheered the human triumph embodied in the steam engine. "Thus, not only the mechanical powers of the lever, wedge and wheel, are made to aid man in his industrial pursuits, but the very elements are subjected to his sway, and made to do his bidding."[12]

The steam engine, then, emblematized the human mastery that steam- and water-powered machinery in general displayed. For the "Effects of Machin-ery" author, modern production machines were "splendid triumphs of the intellect over matter." For Timothy Walker, who professed to "look with unmixed delight at the triumphant march of Mechanism," nature was less chaotic than it was intransigent. Modern machinery, he argued in an 1831 essay published in the *North American Review,* marked man's success at "forc-ing inert matter to toil for man," whereby "from a ministering servant to mat-ter, mind has become the powerful lord of matter." In this regard, new and powerful machines elevated humans to the status of creator and master, akin to the divine creator of the clockwork universe. One observer, referring to the manifold new powers of man in the age of steam, mused only partly in jest that "he is more than human, and little less than Divinity." The people who best displayed this almost divine creative ability, whose minds held such great sway over matter, were the inventors of machinery. Participants in the popular discourse on mechanization routinely exalted the "inventive genius" and "resolute perseverance," not only of such celebrated men as Eli Whitney, Robert Fulton, and Samuel Morse, but also of the clever improvers of machinery whose ingenuity could be seen and appreciated at the mechanics' fairs that became so popular by the early 1830s. "It is a common error to attribute mechanical invention to a happy chance," noted an article on Robert Fulton published in *Graham's Magazine* in 1851, "but no branch of human pursuit more directly originates in the calculating energy of the mind."[13]

Indeed, for many observers, it seemed that in steam-powered machinery man had approached divinity by creating all but life itself. Steam, noted numerous participants in the popular discourse on mechanization, gave life to machinery, rendering active what had been inert. The author of "Effects of Machinery" wrote in 1832, for instance, that it was "hardly a metaphor" to dub steam "the vital principle, the living soul of modern machinery." Machinery, he wrote, "substitutes bodies of iron, with souls of steam, to do the work of living men." Using virtually the same language, a speaker in Cincinnati in 1848 wondered "what *have* mechanics done?" in considering the progress of the arts, before answering, "They have created both god and armor—a Titan with body of iron and soul of steam." Two years earlier, a contributor to the *American Review* depicted the steam engine as if it were matter imbued with life. "The very constructors themselves stood aghast," he wrote of the earliest steam locomotive developers, "and like the artificer of Frankenstein, recoiled in affright from the work of their own hands." But if this artificial human seemed threatening, it could also be pressed into a level of productivity that far surpassed that of human workers. A poem appearing in the *Knickerbocker* in 1839 heralded both the speed and the stamina of the "Iron Horse" (a term which the author unconventionally used in reference to both steam locomotives and production machines). "He's the fastest workman that ever you saw; / He'll set more card-teeth, and braid more straw, / Than all the fair maids from New-York to Cape Cod." Here was a machine that displayed not only the functional relation of parts, but also a dynamism and almost self-directing power.[14]

For some observers, the manifold abilities of new steam- and water-powered machinery, along with the almost willful manner in which it pursued its tasks, suggested that machines could actually think. One admirer of a pin manufacturing machine, for instance, wrote in 1839 that "the whole process" of single-machine pin manufacturing was a marvelous sight, noting that "as one pair of forceps hands the pin along to its neighbor, it is difficult to believe the machine is not an intelligent being." Joseph Story, speaking before the Boston Mechanics' Institution in 1829, described the workings of a carding machine in similar fashion. "I must confess," he told his audience, "that when I first saw it, it seemed to me to be almost an intelligent being, and to do every thing but speak." Indeed, by the 1830s, the notion that machines could be made to think—or at least to display the self-directing qualities of thought—seemed less implausible than it would have two decades before. In the mid 1820s, Charles Babbage, a British inventor, became the subject of transatlantic discussion as writers expressed both fascination and doubt over his proposed calculating machine that would carry out complex mathematical calculations. In 1826, a writer for the *New-Harmony Gazette*, in a brief introduction to an article on Babbage's machine, marveled, "Who would have thought that even *mental* exercises may, in some instances, be executed, and with unexampled precision too, by mechanism." Similarly, an article published in 1835 in the *American Magazine of Useful and Entertaining Knowledge* waxed sensational about Babbage's "proposition to reduce arithmetic to the dominion of mechanism—to substitute an *automaton* for a compositor,—in a word, to throw the powers of thought into wheel-work!" In addition, inventors and manufacturers developed machines that displayed remarkable irregularity in their function, as if their motions were not bound to the undeviating laws of nature. In 1819, for example, a New York inventor, Thomas Blanchard, patented a lathe that could turn out such irregular forms as gun stocks and shoe lasts. The 1847 *Supplement to the Courant* article entitled "Statues Made by Steam" described how Blanchard's "eccentric machine" had been applied to replicating statues and busts, whereby the machine had replaced the artist. "The finishing blow has been given to the poetry of Art," noted the author. "Only think of Phidias being rivalled by a steam engine—of a turning lathe being the competitor of Greenough and Clevenger and Powers." As accounts of Babbage's sophisticated machine and Blanchard's curious lathe entered into the popular discourse on mechanization, the province of the mechanical seemed to expand. Thus, a writer for the *Democratic Review* in 1848, in discussing the recently developed electric telegraph, imagined a future world where "the human race are [sic] to live by machinery" and "steam is to perform all the operations of thought." Indeed, participants in the popular discourse on mechanization sometimes expressed an unwillingness to discount any possibility when it came to mechanical development. "Where shall we expect to stop in this career of progress?" inquired one writer for the *American Review* in 1846. "Where does the possible end and the impossible begin? What is a miracle?"[15]

But however marvelous new machines appeared to be, most observers carefully avoided suggesting that machinery really possessed the capacity for thought. Instead, they appealed to the conventional formulation that machines were "almost intelligent." For many observers, the limitations of even the most marvelous machinery remained apparent. In his widely published essay "Why I Left the Anvil," Elihu Burritt regarded the intricate workings of production machines as ultimately deficient in comparison with humans. "They were wonderful things" he wrote of the textile machinery that so transfixed him when he was younger, "as they caught up a bale of cotton, and twirled it in the twinkling of an eye, into a whirlpool of whizzing shreds, and laid it at my feet in folds of snow-white cloth." But however remarkable their operations, however abundant their production, textile machines had no "attribute of Divinity in them"; they could not "spin thoughts." For Burritt, machines were not like humans because they replicated only a small portion of a human's being. "Thoughtless iron intellects" and "iron fingered, sober, supple automatons," textile machines embodied only the power of muscle. Burritt found the steam locomotive to be similarly lacking. "But for its furnace heart and iron sinews," he wrote, "it was nothing but a beast, an enormous aggregation of—horse power." J. D. B. DeBow similarly recognized the metaphysical distinction to be made between humans and machines. For DeBow, the notion that machinery might one day arrive at "such perfection as to discharge the whole mass of labor" was an "impossible hypothesis," impossible unless "we can make thinking matter, or, in short, a man." Thinking matter was by definition man, DeBow argued, and the prospect of a man-made man seemed so unlikely as to obviate the need for further discussion. According to both Burritt and DeBow, the new machines of the nineteenth century were merely powerful, and they would never take the place of humans.[16]

While machines were like humans in many ways, then, in at least one way the divide between them was unbreachable. For someone like Burritt, the machine bespoke confinement, and its destiny was far less than the destiny of man. Humans, unlike machines, possessed the attributes of mind. They had memory and judgment, which meant that they could accommodate themselves to uncertainty and recognize alternative courses of action. To the extent that machines evoked the language of order and regularity, they were seen to be bound by rigid mechanical laws to a determined set of motions. But irregularity was everywhere present in the mechanized workshop and needed to be accommodated. In textile mills, for instance, threads broke and needed to be repaired, bobbins filled and needed to be replaced, and looms jammed and needed to be stopped and untangled. While the machines pointed up by even the most avid enthusiast appeared quite remarkable, none could be seen to complete such tasks on their own.

Thus, in terms of their ability to take up the burden of labor, most observers understood that machines could not operate without human assistance. However many bodies of iron replaced bodies of flesh in the workplace, bodies of flesh remained a necessity, because machines needed tending. "To be sure he wont [sic] work alone," admitted the *Knickerbocker* poet who otherwise could not say enough about the abilities of the "Iron Horse." The speaker before the Pittsburgh Mechanics' Institute in 1830 who envisioned a future where mind had been infused into matter recognized that even these mindful machines would require human assistance for "setting in motion and feeding the machinery." Without men and women to supervise their operations, devices like the power loom or the pin-making machine would have strayed from the narrow course of efficient production. Steam power seemed especially in need of human attention in order to remain productive. One observer in 1846 regarded steam as an "illimitable force, requiring all the moral, intellectual, and physical energies of his [man's] nature, to direct it to the ends of which it is capable." Daniel Webster, in a lecture before the Boston Mechanics' Institution in 1828, similarly viewed steam as productive only under the guidance of human agency. "Bestow but your skill and reason to the directing of my power," he imagined steam saying to the artisan, "and I will bear the toil." The site of productivity in the antebellum mechanized workplace, then, necessarily entailed a physical union of humans and machines.[17]

The consequence of this material union between humans and machines proved to be a point of intense debate and contention among participants in the popular discourse on mechanization. At the center of these debates was the question of whether machinery degraded the men, women, and children charged with overseeing their operations. Daniel Webster spoke of the "skill and reason" required to direct the power of steam, but the skill and reason called for in a mechanized shop varied considerably, depending on the machine and the type of work performed by the machine tender. Some operatives viewed themselves as skilled workers who brought to their work considerable knowledge and expertise. Judith McGaw has shown that the elaborate paper-making machinery developed by mid century called for the constant attention of its tenders, many of whom considered themselves to be highly skilled. Workers had to ensure a constant speed in different parts of the machinery or the paper would tear. In addition, uniformity of paper weight called for regular adjustments to the machinery. "Only periodic human intervention," McGaw writes, "kept wires and felts taut and prevented them from slipping to one side of the machine or the other. When felts clogged with fiber, machine attendants had to remove and scrub them. They also had to detect and replace worn wires or felts before they left marks on the paper."[18]

But the common perception among those joining the popular discourse on mechanization was that machines demanded from their tenders relatively little skill or knowledge. "To be sure he won't work alone," remarked the *Knickerbocker* poet in detailing the qualities of the "Iron Horse," only to add that "but then / Not a fig would he give for his choice in men; / Only let him have one, howe'er loose his wits, / And he'll spin you a yarn, or knit you a stocking." The experience of many operatives seemed to affirm this perception. Workers frequently described machine-tending as monotonous, wearying, and mentally unstimulating. "Tasks were constantly being broken down into simple, discrete, repetitive motions to maximize efficiency and output and management's control over production," notes one study of mechanized production in antebellum New England, "while decreasing workers' knowledge of, and ability to control, the productive process." Seth Luther was only one of a number of observers who noted that the monotonous and repetitious work of machine-tending stupefied machine operatives who, under other circumstances, might develop their minds. "Hark! don't you hear the fact'ry bell?" queried a poem titled "Picture of a Factory Village" published in 1833. "Of wit and learning 'tis the knell." Similarly, although in a less troubled tone, a speaker before a group of Philadelphia mechanics six years earlier admitted that "in all extensive manufactories, we meet the veriest dolts, who become, as it were, a part of the operative machinery; performing, from habit, the business allotted to them, with a degree of dexterity and precision which appears almost miraculous." For this observer, who was the editor of the highly regarded *Journal of the Franklin Institute,* it seemed that slaves were particularly well suited to the work of machine-tending, "as only a small degree of intelligence is necessary to the acquisition of the utmost skill in the performance of an individual operation, however delicate it may be."[19]

In addition to its diminished mental content, the work of machine-tending was widely understood to be exhausting and physically degrading because of the unrelenting nature of machine production. As many observers noted, machines did not tire in the way that humans did. "He will toil all night, he will toil all day," wrote the *Knickerbocker* poet. In 1828, Daniel Webster argued that steam set into motion machines that were superior to humans in their ability to labor, in that they would "bear the toil—with no muscle to grow weary, no nerve to relax, no breast to feel faintness." Similarly, a speaker at a mechanics' fair in Washington, D.C. in 1857 depicted textile machinery as possessing "metallic fingers—more skillful and far more untiring than those of the human body." As writers frequently pointed out, human workers could not easily match the pace and duration of tireless machinery. Thomas Carlyle, in an 1829 essay titled "Signs of the Times," noted the hard conditions that the "Age of Machinery" presented to working men. "On every hand, the living artisan is driven from his workshop," he wrote, "to make room for a speedier, inanimate one. The shuttle drops from the fingers of the weaver, and falls into iron fingers that ply it faster." A speaker before a group of Boston mechanics that same year urged a similar point about the difficulty for humans to keep up with machines. "Mere manual skill and dexterity are nothing," he averred, "when put in competition with the regularity, rapidity, and economy of machinery, working under the guidance of science." Given the ability of the machine to labor rapidly and without tiring, some observers noted that mechanized labor was fatiguing in a way that traditional forms of labor were not. The editor of the *Commercial Review* in 1846 highlighted the argument that tireless machines placed difficult demands on human workers. "They toil on, it is said, in cruel competition with machinery," he wrote, "whose relentless speed strains their faculties to the utmost, admits no intermission, makes no allowances for human feebleness, but unnaturally taxes flesh and sinews to keep pace with wheels and arms of iron."[20]

Some participants in the popular discourse on mechanization argued that the mental and physical degradation resulting from the material relation between humans and machines in the workplace separated mind from body, thought from action, head from hand, in the individual worker. While the skilled craftsman laboring at his trade evoked images of head and hand working together in productive activity, the machine tender evoked images of degradation and an unremitting toil that called little upon the mind of the laborer. A speaker before a group of mechanics in New Orleans in 1854, for instance, in a speech titled "Influence of the Mechanic Arts on the Human Race," argued that production machinery denied the machine tender his or her uniquely human characteristics. In a broad indictment of conditions in Northern factories and the insidious labor practice "by which a man becomes the slave of another without becoming his property," the speaker evoked a grim scene of machine tenders slipping away from their fundamental humanity. "He who has not been thrown into contact with the operatives in manufacturing districts which are celebrated all over the world," he implored, "and who has not witnessed with a sickening heart the last spark of human intellect flickering dimly in the dull sockets of their brains," had no idea "of the curse entailed on the overgrowth of population and of the Mechanic Arts." An essay published in the *Dial* more than a decade earlier and reprinted in the *New-Yorker* similarly noted the diminishment of the machine tender.

Worried that the operative might be lulled into acquiescence to the new productive order by a consumerist desire for "red curtains to his windows, and
a showy mirror to hang on his wall," the author contended that the worker
in the mechanized setting might easily be made content "to grow up a body—
nothing but a body." Steam- and water-powered machinery thus embodied
a new form of productive power that seemed to separate the work of making things from the knowledge that guided the skilled artisan and household
producers. According to the apparent logic of mechanized production, if
knowledge was an important feature of the productive enterprise, it no longer
needed to be in the possession of the producer.[21]

But if machinery degraded the machine tender and undid the unity between
head and hand—leaving the worker to be "nothing but a body"—where was
the place for mind in the mechanized workplace? This question went directly
to the question of class. At the same time that it was seen to degrade wage-
earners into mere "hands," mechanization was also seen to lift some people out of the realm of manual labor and into the realm of mental labor.
As the author of "Effects of Machinery" noted in 1832, "machinery has
released some from hand-work, who have applied themselves to head-work."
In the mechanized workplace, "head" workers constituted a new coterie of
proprietors, managers, and overseers. In many cases separated physically
from the machines tended by operatives, these men engaged in important
work, but it was widely viewed as the work of the head rather than the work
of the hand, the work of writing, reading, calculating, speaking, and so forth,
all toward managing the operations of a business. This divide between manual and mental labor, between work done with the hands and work done
with the head, was crucial to antebellum Americans' understanding of work.
It was also crucial to an emerging understanding of class. In his study of the
rise of the middle class in nineteenth-century America, Stuart Blumin convincingly argues that the division between people who worked with their
heads and people who worked with their hands came during the antebellum
period to mark a divide between the middle class and an increasingly self-
aware working class. For Blumin, mechanization played a crucial role in
the separation of manual from nonmanual labor. As machines entered the
workplace, owners, managers, clerks, and other members of a growing "white
collar" workforce removed themselves physically from the place where products were made. While machine tenders continued to labor in the grime and
noise of the shop floor, nonmanual workers took their place behind desks in
separate office spaces. Mechanization also contributed to the rise in retail
establishments that employed large numbers of men in the nonmanual labor
of selling goods. According to Blumin, the divergence in the workplace between

people who worked with their hands and people who worked with their heads was accompanied by a divergence in income, wealth, opportunity, and attitudes. As they divided along these crucial indicators, manual and nonmanual workers came more and more to constitute different classes, and to recognize the significance of that difference.[22]

In the popular discourse on mechanization, "head" and "hand" were terms that were often used—sometimes critically—for manager and worker, respectively. The manager (or proprietor) was the head of the shop, the person who controlled the nature, pace, and duration of the work to be done. The wage-earning machine tender was the hand, employed by the owner, supervised by the manager, and given little freedom to make decisions about his or her work. Some observers noted that the common practice of calling manual workers "hands" diminished their claims as persons. "Malign Circumstance has grudged him a full development," said Horace Greeley of the unremitting manual laborer, "his class are significantly advertised for as '*Hands wanted*'—not men." Others sought to retain for manual workers their deserved dignity—and to defend the value of nonmanual labor—by pointing out that both forms of work were necessary in any productive enterprise. "There are many varieties of industry, and the common distinction is a just one between head-work and hand-work," wrote James Waddel Alexander in *The Working-Man* (1843). Adding that both were required in any establishment, Alexander noted that "neither party should look upon the other with jealousy" or ill feelings: "The skilful director of a cotton-mill, who contrives and manages, is just as necessary as the operatives." But if the nature of the relation between managers and workers was still being defined, the relation between head and hand was clear. A speaker before the Massachusetts Charitable Mechanic Association in 1856, in discussing the relation between head and hand in the laboring individual and in an increasingly mechanized society, figured the relation in hierarchical terms. "Up, then, from Hands to Head," he urged after a lengthy discussion of the functions and limitations of the hand. "The hands administer; the head legislates. The hands perform; the head organizes. The hands execute; but it is the head still that originates, or invents."[23]

As many observers noted, the implications of reducing workers to "mindless" implements were far-reaching. The presence of mind in the "human machine" had, at least since Descartes, been regarded as the defining characteristic of humans. As one writer for the *Hartford Pearl and Literary Gazette* averred in 1834, the "physical machinery" of the person did not indicate his greatness as much as did his mind. "The dwelling is worthless but for its inhabitant," he wrote. "It is the mind of man that imparts to him his high dignity—that shows his nearest affinity to the Maker of the universe."

Similarly, James Madison Porter remarked before a group of mechanics the following year that the mind signaled man's primacy over the rest of creation. "Whence then does the superiority of man arise? It is from *the mind,* the immaterial mind, which enables him to lord it over the rest of creation and make them subservient to his wants or caprices." Stripped of this divine appointment, the body was no greater than the rest of material creation. As one writer noted in 1831, without mind a person was "a mere animated machine—a living mass of corruption—a fettered slave—a moving sepulchre." If humans were to be characterized as thinking matter, labor-divided modes of production and relatively unskilled work like machine-tending appeared to some to undermine this status. Just as machines seemed increasingly human in their capacity to pursue complex tasks, humans assigned the job of "manning" machines seemed increasingly machine-like both in their restriction to closely regimented and narrowly defined tasks and in their denial of a mental content to their work.[24]

In fact, observers sometimes employed the epithet "mere machine" to describe the status of mechanized workers or workers performing strictly labor-divided tasks (which for most observers would have included machine-tending). "In modern times, the division of labour is carried to a vast extent; in some cases so far as to reduce the human body to a mere machine," wrote a contributor to the *American Quarterly Review* in 1829. "Such machines are useful to their employers, and add to the general wealth," he continued, "but they are not entitled to the rank or privileges of free agents, unless they be animated by an intelligence that will suffice for their own direction." A writer in 1835, in similarly assessing the social consequences of the close division of labor, wrote that society should give to laboring men and women the opportunity to secure a dignified livelihood "instead of converting them into *mere machines* for the acquisition of wealth." Whenever workers were described as mere machines, the meaning conveyed was that they had been denied a part of their fundamental humanity. "It is [the] possession of *only* the capacity to use the thews and sinews, the bones and muscles of his body," noted a speaker in Baltimore in 1849, "that makes what is sometimes called a human machine—a term indicative of the smallest amount of humanity which is required to exercise a certain quantity of brute mechanical force." As another writer noted in 1852, once workers had been systematically reduced to machines, their moral claims on the rest of society became tenuous. "Improvements in machinery," he observed in an essay published in the *North American Review,* "tend to make the operative less and less an intelligent agent, and more and more a machine, in which last capacity he will be fed and clothed at the cheapest rate at which he can be kept in working order."[25]

For participants in the popular discourse on mechanization, this figurative relation between human and machine precipitated not only a metaphysical crisis, but a political crisis. To the extent that they were like machines themselves, mechanized workers seemed to some observers to be like slaves rather than virtuous citizens, or wives, or mothers. Indeed, the language of servitude and enslavement permeated discussions of mechanization and the relation between humans and machines. By their very nature, machines were understood to be bound by the laws of nature and to lack the free will characteristic of humans. In this sense, the machine—in its circumscribed ability to perform complex tasks, or its heedfulness, or its docility—was like a slave, with metal and wood instead of flesh and blood. Robert Dale Owen employed this trope in an essay published in 1830, when he urged his readers to think of machines as akin to slave laborers. Referring to mechanization in Great Britain, Owen wrote that "modern scientific labor-saving power" put into place conditions that were the same as if each worker "*had forty slaves laboring for him day after day, from morning till night, without a moment's idleness;* yet requiring neither food nor clothing for their services." Daniel Webster employed a similar although much more mollifying image in a speech before the U.S. Senate later in that decade. For Webster, the machine was a "cooperative" to human workers, a "mute fellow-laborer" who served with no complaints and few needs. "The eating and drinking, the reading and writing, and clothes-wearing world, are benefitted by the labors of these cooperatives," he argued, "in the same way as if Providence had provided for their service millions of beings . . . able to labor and to toil, and yet requiring little or nothing for their own consumption or subsistence." In this context, some argued that machinery—when made to be almost human in its operations—would in fact spell an end to chattel slavery in America. A writer for the *Atlantic Monthly* in 1858, for instance, wrote that "with our prodigious development of mechanical inventions, iron and coal, our mighty steam-driven machinery for making machines, the time for chattelizing men . . . has passed by." Two years later, Thomas Ewbank, in a pamphlet titled *Inorganic Forces Ordained to Supercede Human Slavery,* argued the same point. "Living motors are the poorest; insensible ones, artificially excited, the last and the best," he wrote. "The former are delicate, easily deranged, require stated and oft recurring periods of rest, are limited in their powers of endurance, and the amount of work they can do, while the latter are in these several respects the reverse." "Nothing is wanting but a proper combination of mechanical skill," he concluded, "and, when that is realized, slavery dies, and dies amid the hosannas of both pro and anti-slavery men."[26]

But for Seth Luther and others, slavery did not die with mechanization; it was extended to the shops and factories throughout the country where mechanized and labor-divided modes of production were put into place. Robert Owen, the father of Robert Dale Owen, used a language of mutilation to describe what he saw occurring when workers were treated as "mere implements of production," whereby the individual working man or woman was turned into "a creature far inferior to an inanimate machine." For Owen, the strict division of labor that characterized modern production practices served to "mutilate (if we may so speak) the character of man," and "reduce him in fact to a small fraction of an intelligent human being." It was true that this mutilated worker could be counted on to "create abundantly whatever can be necessary to the highest degree of comfortable existence," Owen continued, but he or she lacked those characteristics that were definitively human, "the capacity to understand all human knowledge and to enjoy or make the best of all the advantages he possesses." Reduced, in the words of Seth Luther, to the status of "mere machinery of monied aristocracy," the mechanized worker was as much a slave as the machine itself. "These *white* slaves," Luther enjoined a group of Brooklyn mechanics during a July Fourth celebration in 1836, "will celebrate independence *to-day,* and *to-morrow,* will sink into mere tools in the hands of heartless overseers. They will have no more control over their own movements than the lifeless machinery has." Of course, not everybody agreed that mechanized labor reduced the worker to slavery. "There are some persons," wrote one observer in 1847, "who are accustomed to look upon factory life as a thing in some degree akin to slavery, and to speak of the men and women who work in the mills as degraded morally, mentally and physically." Such a view, he continued, revealed "an entire ignorance of the factory system." But images of the factory operative bending and turning to the unremitting beat of the machine were compelling. Herman Melville's intrepid visitor to a papermaking factory in his short story "The Paradise of Bachelors and the Tartarus of Maids," first published in *Harper's New Monthly Magazine* in 1855, recognized the fearful implication of machine-tending when he witnessed the female operatives moving, like the paper being produced, "in unvarying docility to the autocratic cunning of the machine." Far from freeing the operatives, the machine bound them to its every need. "Machinery— that vaunted slave of humanity—here stood menially served by human beings, who served mutely and cringingly as the slave serves the sultan," mused the narrator. "The girls did not so much seem accessory wheels to the general machinery as mere cogs to the wheels."[27]

Here Melville's language of enslavement carried a sense of passivity that was common in discussions of machines and mechanized workers. Writers frequently noted that machines were compliant and required little as they engaged in their productive activity. "A machine feels no partialities," wrote the author of "Effects of Machinery" in 1832. "It works for one just as vigorously and efficiently as for another." Robert Dale Owen, who was more troubled by the passive quality of machinery, saw a grim future when he argued in 1848 that "we shall see masters engaging, as the cheapest, most docile and least troublesome help, the machine instead of the man." Appealing to the language used by his father, Owen called machines "powerful and passive slaves," slaves that were forever "patient, submissive, obedient; from whom no rebellion need be feared; who cannot suffer cruelty nor experience pain." But as Melville explored in two other stories written in the 1850s, "Benito Cereno" and "The Bell-Tower," the passive-seeming slave (in the former story) or machine (in the latter) possessed as well the potential for revolt. The 1858 writer for the *Atlantic Monthly* explored this notion in an extended comparison between steam engines and chattel slaves. Insisting that the steam engine—the "iron-boned, coal eating slave"—would soon be cheaper and more efficient than the "human corn consuming machine," the author raised the question that the problem of steam boiler explosions had been pressing for decades: "But will not our artificial slave be more liable to insurrection?" For this writer, both the steam engine and the enslaved laborer stood at the precarious brink of explosive destruction. "Almost everybody looks upon him as a sleeping volcano," he noted, suggesting both the machine and the human, "which must sooner or later flare up into irresistible wrath and do frightful mischief." If the machine was a slave, then, its docility could be eclipsed at any moment by dramatic and even explosive destruction.[28]

In this way, the conception of the mechanized worker as being like a machine carried both a sense of wholesale determination and a sense of power loosed from the moorings of productive certainty. If labor leaders such as Seth Luther tended to focus on the first meaning, viewing the human/machine as an image of degradation and a basis for challenging the emerging industrial order, middle-class writers were more likely to focus on the second meaning. They noted with considerable unease that meeting the regulatory needs of machinery might put into place the very conditions that would undermine the self-regulatory capacity of workers. They feared, in other words, that workers who tended machinery would be less able to tend to themselves, to control their own activities both on and off the shop floor. For them, the images of corruption and enslavement that permeated the popular discourse on mechanization spoke not so much to the unjust conditions of mechanized work as to the dire moral and civic consequences that many observers thought were sure to follow when workers were unable to control themselves in a world of easy pleasures and scheming demagogues.

At the same time, there was an alternative meaning to the human/machine image for advocates of mechanization, one that drew on the order and regularity of the clockwork machine rather than the pent-up power of the steam engine. If the person could be understood as a machine, some argued that his or her conduct could be made to exhibit the qualities of order, regularity, and efficiency that were the hallmarks of production machinery. By attuning their work life to the even rhythms of the machine, then, operatives could develop steady habits that would serve them in all stations of life. One visitor to Lowell in 1845 thus noted that "the strictest watchfulness was kept" over the operatives, and that "there was an elevated tone of morality and virtuous feeling" among them. This effort to promote morality among machine operatives was often trumpeted as a sure sign of the benevolence of owners, but it had a practical basis. The British political economist Andrew Ure, in his widely read *The Philosophy of Manufactures,* published in 1835, was only one of a number of observers who argued that the connection between a disciplined and virtuous workforce and the success of a manufacturing establishment was direct. "The neglect of moral discipline," Ure wrote, "may be readily detected, in any establishment." According to Ure, the moral shortcomings of the operatives would be manifest in the "irregularities of the individual machines" and in wasted time and material, so that it became the interest of every mill owner to establish what he called a "moral machinery" that was as sure as the machines on the shop floor. "Otherwise," he wrote, "he will never command the steady hands, watchful eyes, and prompt cooperation, essential to excellence of product." As employers and moralists sought to promote what Paul Faler has called an "industrial morality" among manual laborers, they articulated the imperatives of what was coming to be understood as middle-class respectability, which stated that one should cultivate "habits of industry," avoid alcohol, respect authority, and above all, control one's passions or appetites.[29]

Indeed, by the 1850s, some observers argued that those who tended machinery were in a real sense "headworkers" rather than degraded and exploited "hands." Machine-tending, they noted, was principally a mental rather than a manual occupation. Machines did the physical work themselves, needing only mental proficiencies from their tenders. According to this view, the handworking operative and the head-working manager engaged in the same activity. A writer for *Scientific American* expressed just such an understanding in an article titled "Machinery and Hand Labor," published in 1855. Responding to recent opposition to the use of new street-sweeping machines by the city of New York, the writer noted that "we frequently hear of machinery being denounced because of its superceding hand labor." For this writer, machinery did not so much take the place of labor as shift the locus of work from hand to head. "Machinery has not decreased the demand for labor," he wrote, "it has only changed its direction; it has become the drudge, man its director." The machine tender, then, was essentially a mental laborer, standing in the same relation to his or her machine as the manager to the worker.[30]

The writer for the *Atlantic Monthly* in 1858 concurred on this point. As machines stood in for humans in all forms of manual labor, he wrote, humans who once toiled with their hands would step up to the work of managing and overseeing their machines. "We shall make the human millions all masters, from being nearly all slaves," he wrote, broadening his conception of slavery to include all those bound to drudge work. When put to agricultural work, then, machines would be the "iron horses, iron oxen, or iron men" that plowed the soil and harvested the crops, and that labored "under the free and intelligent supervision of people who know how to feed, drive, doctor, and make the most of them." The effect of such an arrangement—in which the mental labor of supervising and regulating was called upon more than the manual labor of lifting, turning, pulling, and so forth—would be to elevate working men and women. "The laborer, in either section of our country, will be transformed into an ingenious gentleman or lady," the author promised, "comfortably mounted on a migratory steam-cultivator to direct its gigantic energies." In similar fashion, a writer for *Graham's Magazine* six years earlier had noted the elevated condition of the machine operative. According to this writer, the work of machine-tending was principally a form of mental labor. Arguing that "the head, and not the hand, is to be the chief instrument" in the mechanized workplace, the *Graham's* writer avowed that, in the new world of work, "the intellectual and no longer the physical forces are to predominate, even in the merest labor." Given their increased reliance on mind in order to both regulate the power of the machine and comprehend its many intricate functions, mechanics would, he continued, henceforth need to apply more hours to study. In doing so, they would distance themselves from the mere handworker—from "the delver, the ditcher, the hewers of wood and drawers of water"—and join the ranks of the headworker—"the thinker, the inventor, the creator." The introduction of machinery to production, far from degrading the mechanic, ensured him a station equal to his non–manual-laboring counterparts. The use of complicated machines, the *Graham's* author wrote, "is compelling the mechanic and hand-laborer to educate his head as well as to harden his hands; to develop his soul as well as his sinews, and to become himself head-worker no less than handy-craftsman."[31]

By the 1820s, then, antebellum Americans had entered into a broad popular discourse on mechanization in which they discussed often contentious questions about the relation between humans and machines. Participants in discussions of mechanization represented this relation in both material and figurative terms. Humans and machines entered into a material relation on the shop floor, where workers joined powerful machines to regulate their motions. Both workers and members of the middle class recognized this combination of the powerful machine and the mindful machine tender as a site of unprecedented productivity. Humans and machines entered into a figurative relation in several ways. For some, the human body was similar to a machine in its orderly design and functional relation of parts. At the same time, the steam engine and the machinery it powered seemed to be as alive as the laboring worker. As humans and machines drew together materially in the workplace, their figurative relation became more complex. Some observed that the machine operative was like a machine in his or her regularity of motion and reliability of production. For others, the relation adhered in the perception that machine-tending resulted in the mental degradation of the operative who was reduced to virtual servitude, a "mere machine." Here the orderly machine was not so much a metaphor for discipline as for enslavement.

At the same time, antebellum Americans struggled to define the relation between managers and mechanized workers. As they attempted to reconcile the demands of industrial labor with ideals of liberty and independence, writers and lecturers cast about for models on which to conceptualize (and ultimately materialize) the social relations of mechanized production. The next four chapters explore some of the cultural activities and popular discussions in which this work was carried out, but first I want to return to Maelzel's automaton chess-player. In raising many of the questions that circulated through the popular discourse on mechanization, the exhibition of the chess-player became a popular venue for antebellum Americans to address, in oblique ways, divisive questions about work and class.

Those who discussed and wrote about the chess-player entered into the popular discourse on mechanization by puzzling through the manner in which Maelzel's device addressed vexed questions about the relation between humans and machines. Many realized that, while automaton dancers and musicians had long been a staple of the itinerant show in America, Maelzel's device was like nothing that had been seen before. Able to play chess, it could display the uniquely human functions of thought and will as well as the more mechanical functions of bodily motion. As one observer wrote, the chess-player "not only imitates human actions, but seems capable of acting as external circumstances require, as if it were endowed with life and reason." The automaton chess-player, then, appeared to be a thinking machine, much like the water- and steam-powered production machinery so marveled at by observers of the industrial scene, such as the author of a book published in the mid 1840s who described the interior of a textile mill as "seeming to present a magic scene in which wood and iron are endowed with the dexterity of the human hand—and where complicated machinery seems to be gifted with intelligence." Although printed accounts of the chess-player did not draw explicit connections between Maelzel's device and other machinery, the similarity was implied every time the chess-player was described as "an extraordinary piece of mechanism," or as a "machine for thinking," or in some similar phrase. In 1848, an article published in the *Scientific American* that briefly discussed the chess-player did note that "the fine machinery in our cotton factories almost rival those of the finest automaton," and that "the same combination of mechanical powers that made the spider crawl, or the finger of the automaton move are now adapted to nobler and more useful purposes." And this was not the only observer to remark on the similarity between automata more generally and production and transportation machinery. When a mechanical diorama was displayed in New York in 1837, for instance, a contributor to the *Journal of the American Institute* suggested that inventors of more useful machinery might learn something from the astonishing device. "We think the makers of manufacturing automatons would derive useful hints from witnessing these movements," he wrote, "that might be applied in the formation of fabrics."[32]

Viewers drawn to the chess-player's puzzling display had first to decide for themselves whether the device was what it purported to be, an untended machine playing a game of chess. Edgar Allan Poe, who published an essay on the chess-player in the *Southern Literary Messenger* in 1836, insisted that Maelzel's careful display of the device's interior convinced many spectators that such was the case. "We find every where men of mechanical genius," he wrote, "who make no scruple in pronouncing the Automaton a *pure machine,* unconnected with human agency in its movements." But in spite of Poe's claim—made in part to draw the reader into his own "solution" to the puzzle—most observers writing about the chess-player agreed that human agency played a role in its movements. "That such agency is employed cannot be questioned," wrote one admirer of Poe's essay, "unless it may be satisfactorily demonstrated that man is capable to impart intellect to matter." Similarly, a Boston viewer wrote in 1826 that "it is not pretended, that a human figure, made of machinery and wood, although self-moved, can have volition or make mental combinations." Indeed, most people writing about the chess-player devoted themselves to arguing *how* the machine might be governed by Maelzel or some hidden agent, not *whether* it was governed as such. Those who insisted that the chess-player was not what it appeared to be, but that it was governed in some fashion by human agency, were in fact correct. Whenever Maelzel exhibited his device, a man was cleverly concealed in the cabinet behind which the "Turk" sat, following the progress of the game by means of metal discs hanging from the top of the cabinet interior that moved when the magnetized chess pieces moved, and operating the arm of the chess-player with a pantograph.[33]

This consensus about the chess-player's necessary relation to human agency derived from a clear understanding of what it meant to be a "pure machine." For Poe and others, machinery was by its very nature fixed in its motions. Bound by the narrow laws of nature, machinery plied an unwavering course to some determined end—wind up the clock, and it strikes every hour. "But," noted Poe, "the case is widely different with the Chess-Player." Wind up the automaton, viewers saw, and it monitors the room, engages in mental activity, and moves at irregular intervals. "With him," Poe continued, "there is no determinate progression." Because the movements of the chess-player were not predetermined and uniform—they could match the unpredictable movements of an opponent—they had to be directed by human agency. In a conceptual scheme dividing the human from the mechanical, the chess-player displayed the uniquely human characteristic of will: it could deliberate and act on its own "as external circumstances require" (in the words of one newspaper in 1826). For many viewers, this left little doubt as to the origins of the machine's movements. "It is quite certain, " wrote Poe, "that the operations of the Automaton are regulated by *mind,* and by nothing else."[34]

Antebellum Americans thus took the presentation of the automaton chess-player as an occasion to articulate the self-regulatory difference between humans and machines. Maelzel's device moved in a willful manner, so it had to be regulated by a person; humans could "mind" their own movements, but machines could not. It is no coincidence that so many viewers sought this opportunity at precisely the moment that new machines and new productive arrangements were thought by many to blur the self-regulatory difference between humans and machines. Launched into the scene of middle-class anxiety about worker self-control, the chess-player assumed the twin statuses of regulated machine and ideal mechanized worker. Viewers could locate in the chess-player the uniquely human traits of will and reason without having to remove these qualities too far from the mechanical traits of regularity and efficiency. Read as a regulated or "minded" machine, Maelzel's device showed the new productive order in place. Read as a self-controlled worker, the chess-player showed how autonomy and order might combine in the mechanized worker in the form of discipline. If workers and machines were going to look more alike, then, they were going to look more like the chess-player—at once closely regulated and unquestionably willful, capable of performing irregular actions, but always within the confines of a closely defined set of tasks. The chess-player enabled its viewers to imagine the approximation of humans and machines in terms that would allow the human side of the equation its definitive characteristics, thereby ensuring the machine side of the equation its vital regulatory principle.

In the same way that the chess-player assumed the status of the ideal mechanized worker, Maelzel represented the ideal middle-class manager. As the master and proprietor of the chess-player, Maelzel determined when and where it would work, supervised its activities, and accumulated whatever wealth resulted from its production. His actions on and off the stage, however, worked to allay any fear that such a man would wield his power without regard for others. Throughout his career, Maelzel fashioned himself as a respectable man of mechanical knowledge whose principal aim was to improve and supervise machinery. He was a consummate gentleman onstage, attentive to the needs of his audience and displaying a particular kindness toward children, for whom he often reserved the closest seats. But his interests were known to extend beyond the narrow purview of his daily occupation: one article published in 1837 touted him as an expert chess player, "alike distinguished for his skill in mechanics, his taste for the fine arts, and the extraordinary inventive faculties of his mind." Finally, Maelzel displayed an abiding benevolence for the "deserving" poor, making his good efforts known by periodically and quite publicly contributing door receipts to charitable organizations. Taken together, Maelzel's technical knowledge, pleasing cultivation, and selective benevolence assured him a position of respect and authority, while at the same time exemplifying some key characteristics of an emerging middle-class identity.[35]

Viewers of the automaton chess-player were watching a performance of how workers and managers might arrange themselves in the mechanized workplace. But Maelzel's exhibition not only modeled the social relations of mechanized production; it served as well to facilitate their realization. It did this by providing an opportunity for people to demonstrate their technical proficiency and mechanical reasoning skills. In so doing, they could distinguish themselves as well suited to the mental labor of managing machines and the people who tended them.

Maelzel's show effectively joined its viewers in a common state of ignorance about the machine on display. While it is difficult to say for certain, the social composition of a typical chess-player audience was likely mixed. Boston's *Columbian Centinel* noted that the desire to attend Maelzel's show was general "with all classes of citizens." Poe similarly observed of the chess-player that "numerous have been the attempts, by men of all classes, to fathom the mystery of its evolutions." Indeed, if published accounts made any effort to distinguish portions of the audience, it was to mention the presence of the more cultivated members of society. Thus the editor of Philadelphia's *American Sentinel* announced his delight in early 1827 at seeing a recent Maelzel audience "adorned by many of the fairest and most fashionable of our citizens." But whatever social and economic differences divided Maelzel's viewers outside the exhibition hall, inside they shared both ignorance and a desire to answer the question before them. "The learned and the unlearned, the ignorant and the scientific, continue to be sadly puzzled with this wonderful puzzler," noted one New York newspaper in 1826.[36]

The challenge posed by the automaton chess-player was to rise above this common ignorance by divining the governing principle of the machine. Toward that end, viewers elaborated countless theories as to how the movements of the chess-player were regulated. Some argued that Maelzel worked the machine himself, either by touching keys on the chest or depressing pedals in the floor. One contributor to the *New-York American* insisted that the device was moved by a dozen or so thin cables that ran from its arms and head to a person hidden behind the curtain. This account met with measured skepticism: "The invisible cords (for they must be nearly so)," remarked the paper's editor, "are about as difficult to imagine as the secret of the machine." Other viewers, including Poe, insisted that an operator was somehow hidden inside the cabinet, and that he or she governed the chess-player's movements. This too seemed implausible to many (even though it was in fact the correct explanation), both because the interior of the cabinet appeared to be filled with mechanism, and because it was difficult to see how such a person could remain unnoticed. "Could any human being have played so often and so long," wondered one respondent to Poe's essay, "without once betraying himself by a sneeze and a cough?" Although the essence of the correct solution—that a person inside the chest operated the chess-player—had been arrived at by more than one observer (in the spring of 1827, someone actually saw this hidden operator climbing out of the chess-player backstage, and his account made it into a number of newspapers), viewers were undeterred in their desire to see the device and puzzle through its mystery for themselves. The author of a pamphlet published in Boston in 1826 that closely argued that a person had to be hidden in the cabinet acknowledged that, even with a solution at hand, viewers remained captivated by Maelzel's chess-player. "Instead of satisfying, it seems continually to excite curiosity," he wrote, "and the more one goes to see it, the more desirous he becomes, to visit it again."[37]

As viewers scrutinized the chess-player and labored to solve its puzzle— to "master" the machine—they sought to join Maelzel in a position of knowledge and power. If ignorance marked the common lot, then knowledge would mark the lot of the privileged few. The mystery of the chess-player's motions, then, was a primary draw. "If his secret were known," said the *New-York American,* "he would cease to interest." But this would be true only if the secret were known by all. A writer in Philadelphia made this point while comparing Maelzel's show with another automata exhibition that was in town early in 1827. Noting the pleasures of discovering the governing principles of some of the simpler automata figures, the writer remarked that "the mind always derives satisfaction from a discovery of this nature, provided it be [a] discovery not *too* easily made, and which cannot be made by *too many* persons." As the greatest puzzle of them all, the chess-player demanded the highest levels of mechanical reasoning and technical acuity. By puzzling through the chess-player's display, Maelzel's viewers undertook a self-activated sorting process in which they strove to distinguish themselves as particularly well suited to the demands of technically oriented mental labor.[38]

Maelzel's American successes won him fame and modest fortune, and in time he became a welcome member of Philadelphia's scientific community. In 1837, he took his exhibition to Havana after having found strong interest there a year earlier. The trip was ill-fated, however. Maelzel's assistant and constant companion, William Schlumberger, died of yellow fever sometime during the spring of 1838. The loss devastated Maelzel, not only because Schlumberger was his friend, but because he was also the expert chess player who operated the automaton while it was on display. Already facing debt and unable to continue his show alone, Maelzel stayed in Cuba only a short time longer. When he boarded ship to return to Philadelphia, the captain, who had known him before, noted Maelzel's altered appearance. "It was evident that he was 'breaking up,'" wrote a chronicler of the chess-player in 1859, "that all the powers of body and mind were rapidly sinking, as though the source from which they had derived their strength had been suddenly withdrawn." On ship Maelzel kept mostly to himself, playing an occasional game of chess with the captain and drinking constantly from his ample supply of red wine. Maelzel's decline was steady, and on the morning of July 21, 1838, he was found dead. The captain ordered him buried at sea off the coast of Charleston, South Carolina.[39]

Packed in crates and stored with Maelzel's other effects in a warehouse in Philadelphia, the chess-player might have languished unnoticed for years after its exhibitor's death. But Maelzel owed money to the warehouse owner, who decided to sell whatever items he could in order to recoup his loss. John K.

Mitchell, a prominent physician and leading man of science in Philadelphia, enlisted a group of business and professional men to purchase the chess-player at shares of $5 or $10 each. Mitchell and his partners reassembled the device, determined how it worked, and exhibited it for a time among themselves. In 1840, the shareholders deposited the chess-player in Philadelphia's Chinese Museum, home of Charles Willson Peale's collection of curiosities. There it remained, unheralded and little remembered, until it was destroyed by fire when the museum burned to the ground in the summer of 1854.[40]

Ten years after Maelzel's death, *Scientific American* published an article cataloguing famous automata through the ages. Noting a relatively recent decline in the "passion for automaton machinery," the article insisted that machines made for entertainment had little role to play in the modern utilitarian age. "Instead of producing inventions to amuse," it argued, "the present age invents only to benefit man and increase the product of the earth." The history of Maelzel's automaton chess-player suggests that the line between amusing machines and producing machines is not so clear. The automaton chess-player was no less a site of production than a machine that made pins or cloth. Maelzel's machine simply turned out an effect rather than a product. This effect helped members of the middle class to conceptualize the social relations of mechanized production in terms that would ensure their relative power. At the same time, the chess-player offered its audience a view of what lay ahead for industrial society. Maelzel grew in wealth and status as the owner and manager of the machine, while his "operator" labored uncelebrated in a dark and solitary cell, the sound of machinery drowning out any indication of his presence. Despite the belief among some that such was the case, and despite the common understanding that the consequences of such an arrangement—on stage or in the workplace—would be dire for the hidden operator, the vision seems not to have caused alarm. Fixed on the wonderful effect, viewers did not mind what occurred out of sight.[41]

For the men and women undertaking the uneven movement from craft to industrial production, the nature of the novel relation between humans and production machines remained unclear. To what extent would machinery take up the work that previously had been done by people? Did industrial modes of production necessarily degrade the men and women who operated machinery? Could the machine provide a desirable model for human behavior? How would mechanization affect society more generally? Equally unclear was the relation between manufacturer and wage-worker. In this period of dramatic change and conceptual uncertainty, labor leaders offered an oppositional understanding of class that pitted exploited "producers" against heartless owners and managers who would gladly grow rich by the sweat of another man's brow. At the same time, those more sanguine about the "age of machinery" offered alternative conceptions of class, sometimes in subtle ways and in places that were not so obviously about contentious questions of the day. The exhibition of Maelzel's automaton chess-player, then, suggested to antebellum audiences one way in which questions about the relation between humans and machines, and between managers and workers, could be answered in terms that enforced the authority of the former without denying the autonomy of the latter. But there were other arenas in which arguments for the proper relation between head and hand, between mind and body, or between human and machine, promoted a harmonious conception of class. Chief among them was the mechanics' institute.

CHAPTER 2

Head and Hand

The Mechanics' Institute Movement and the
Conception of Class Authority

On the evening of November 27, 1833, Gulian C. Verplanck rose before an audience in New York City's Clinton Hall to deliver the introductory address for a course of scientific lectures organized by the Mechanics' Institute of the City of New-York. Verplanck was a well-known New York man of letters who had recently served in the U.S. Congress. His address, which the *Knickerbocker* later published under the title "The Influence of Mechanical Invention on the Improvement of Mankind," sought to highlight the role of the mechanic in the progress of civilization. Verplanck opened his remarks with an arresting image. "Suppose . . . that the human arm had terminated in a hoof or a claw, instead of a hand," he wondered, quoting a friend. "What would have been the present state of society, and how far would mere intellect have carried us?" For Verplanck, the answer was quite clear: without the hand to execute what the mind had conceived, the mind would be ineffectual, left to "barren speculation." Indeed, he noted, "we may thus trace back the comfort, the happiness, the safety, the splendor, nay the very affections and virtues of social and civilized life to the industry of the hand." But, he continued, the hand—which was by nature "bloody and dangerous" and "quick to injury"—required the guidance of the mind if it were going to be productive. Head and hand needed to join "in intelligent unison," he concluded, "and then the whole man and the whole frame of society will move together in cheerful activity, right onwards to their highest possible perfection and happiness." Verplanck devoted much of the rest of his address to cataloging those American artisans—including Benjamin Franklin, Eli Whitney, and Robert Fulton—who had combined head and hand to contribute so mightily to the improvements of the age. Several days later, a committee appointed by the Mechanics' Institute wrote to thank Verplanck for "the rich and splendid intellectual feast" he had provided, and to request a copy of his address so that it could be published "for the use and instruction of the members of the Institute, of mechanics in general, and society at large."[1]

For the members of the fledgling Mechanics' Institute of the City of New-York, Verplanck's speech surely marked a milestone. Established two years earlier for the express purpose of diffusing scientific knowledge among the city's mechanics, the Mechanics' Institute of the City of New-York had recently received its state charter, and its Board of Directors had just released its second annual report, outlining the steady progress of the last two years and the ambitious plans for the future. Verplanck's inaugural address, then, signaled that the Mechanics' Institute of the City of New-York was now poised to become a permanent fixture in the social and cultural life of the city.

Mechanics' institutes such as the one Verplanck addressed were common in American towns and cities from the 1820s, when the first institutes were founded in New York, Pennsylvania, and Massachusetts, through the 1850s. These institutes took their place alongside an array of other educational institutions—including lyceums, mercantile libraries, apprentice libraries, and young men's institutes—that were founded during these decades to provide educational opportunities to what many viewed as a woefully undereducated populace. What distinguished mechanics' institutes was their emphasis on scientific and technical subjects, their explicit appeal to artisans, and their particular activities, which included sponsoring public lectures, collecting and displaying models of machinery, forming libraries and reading rooms, holding exhibitions of the arts, and awarding premiums to inventions and products of particular merit. Some institutes, like the Franklin Institute in Philadelphia, the Ohio Mechanics' Institute in Cincinnati, and the Chicago Mechanics' Institute, remained active for decades and were major cultural institutions in their communities. Among their advocates, the principal appeal of mechanics' institutes was that they would help ensure the steady progress of the arts at the same time that they helped master, journeyman, and apprentice mechanics weather the uncertainties of mechanization. In this way, mechanics' institutes drew on two eighteenth-century institutional traditions: the societies for the promotion of the useful arts that were founded out of insecurity about domestic manufacture, and the mechanic mutual aid societies, formed primarily as benevolent organizations. But unlike societies for the promotion of useful arts, mechanics' institutes did not pursue overtly political aims (like advocating import tariffs), claiming instead an objective interest in the pursuit and dissemination of scientific and technical knowledge. Unlike mechanic charitable associations, mechanics' institutes usually refrained from avowedly benevolent activities, like collecting funds to support widows of deceased members. The rhetoric of the mechanics' institute was more one of self-improvement than mutual assistance. Sounding the ubiquitous call that "knowledge is power," proponents believed that the production and transmission of scientific knowledge would be the means by which their dual aim of promoting industry and elevating working men would be achieved.[2]

Despite their relative prominence in antebellum American cultural life, mechanics' institutes have received relatively little attention from historians. Labor historians of the nineteenth century have tended to focus on the emergence of an oppositional working class and have therefore virtually ignored mechanics' institutes, understanding them to be unimportant to their subject because they were generally dominated by employers. Historians of education have given greater attention to the mechanics' institute movement, although they have tended to view it as simply one of a number of similar antebellum educational reform movements that culminated in universal public schooling.[3]

The significance of the mechanics' institute movement becomes clearer in the context of early industrial development in America. It was during this period of tumultuous change that men in cities and towns across the country established mechanics' institutes to pursue the seemingly discordant aims of promoting industrial development and ensuring the social well-being of mechanics, those people whose work was most likely to be disrupted by the new productive arrangements. In the paradox of their purpose, mechanics' institutes became crucial venues in which participants in the popular discourse on mechanization struggled to define the complex and increasingly social (and contentious) relation between mental labor and manual labor. Proponents argued that the educational programs sponsored by mechanics' institutes would heal the rift between mental and manual labor, between head and hand, by helping manual workers bring a mental content to their work. By studying the scientific principles that stood behind the trades, mechanics would appreciate the beauty of their work and would be better equipped to improve their art. But in calling for the union of head and hand in this fashion, proponents of mechanics' institutes subtly and surely articulated a specific vision of industrial society. They did so by figuring the relatively unproblematic relation between head and hand as analogous to the much more contested relation between manager and worker. The work of the hand should be guided by the work of the head, they urged, whether hand and head were united in the individual working man or in the social relations between "hands" and "heads" in the mechanized workplace. Gulian Verplanck's call for head and hand to work together in intelligent unison, then, spoke as much to a conception of a social order as it did to a conception of a personal order. At the same time, proponents of mechanics' institutes hoped to provide a forum where men could demonstrate their suitability for technically oriented mental work, thereby making the mechanics' institute a place for differentiating between headworkers and handworkers. Thus, despite their egalitarian rhetoric of popular education, proponents of mechanics' institutes helped to formulate a harmonious language of class that was difficult to challenge and that worked to codify the social authority of a new middle class of manufacturers and managers.

When a group of craftsmen in Easton, Pennsylvania gathered in July 1835 to celebrate the nation's independence, they had as their guest speaker one of Easton's true luminaries, James Madison Porter, who had distinguished himself nationally as a lawyer and more locally as a founder of Easton's Lafayette College. In his speech, Porter discussed the rise of mechanized production and the challenges facing those who would keep up with the rapid changes in the workplace. Porter's address, which was later printed as a pamphlet, reiterated many of the terms of the popular discourse on mechanization. Pointing to the dramatic "improvements in the Mechanic Arts" in recent years, Porter noted that "steam and water by the aid of improved machinery are accomplishing wonders, and indeed it would seem that we know not where the perfection of machinery will end." Adding that "we must keep pace with the improvements of the times," Porter sought to correct the ill-conceived notion that mechanical improvements were "prejudicial to individuals, by depriving them of work." Like other advocates of mechanization, Porter insisted that any unemployment caused by new machines would be temporary and would be offset by the jobs created to meet an increased demand for inexpensive machine-made goods. For Porter, the best way for mechanics to ensure their stability in an ever-changing world was to gain instruction not only in the practice of a trade, but in the principles behind that trade. The mechanic in the age of the machine, he suggested, needed to unite science with art, theory with practice, in order to keep up with the pace of change. "Can you then better close the labors of this grand Jubilee of Freedom," he asked at the conclusion of his address, "than in associating yourselves permanently together, as a Mechanic's Institute, and by your united efforts obtain a library suited to mechanical pursuits, and make provisions for hearing during a part of the year, lectures from scientific men, on the various subjects connected with the sciences of Natural Philosophy and the Mechanical Arts." The craftsmen gathered that evening in 1835 agreed, greeting Porter's charge with enthusiasm. "His instructive address was not sown on barren ground," they cheered in a toast at the end of Porter's speech, "but will bring forth fruit beneficial to the mechanics and workingmen of our Borough."[4]

By the time Porter spoke in 1835, mechanics' institutes were still relatively new to the American scene but would have been quite familiar to the mechanics of Easton. The mechanics' institute movement as a whole traced its origins to a series of lectures given by George Birkbeck to a group of mechanics in Glasgow, Scotland in 1800. Birkbeck later moved to London, where he and Henry Brougham were instrumental in founding the famed London Mechanics' Institution in early 1824. That same year, institutes were formed in a handful of other cities in England and Scotland. The first mechanics' institute in the United States was the New-York Mechanic and Scientific Institution, organized in New York City in 1822 to "foster the Mechanic and Useful Arts, and to enlighten the minds and stimulate the genius of those who practise them." Though apprentice libraries were already in place in New York and other principal cities, the New-York Mechanic and Scientific Institution was the first organization in the United States to combine the several activities that would come to characterize the mechanics' institute. While its charter was granted for twenty years, the life of the institution was brief, and by the end of the 1820s it was no longer in existence. But word of the institute spread. In a speech before the Massachusetts Charitable Mechanic Association in Boston in 1824, Alpheus Cary favorably mentioned the New York group, adding that a similar organization (the Franklin Institute) was in the midst of its founding in Philadelphia. The following year, the Maryland Institute was founded in Baltimore. In 1828, a group of men formed the Ohio Mechanics' Institute in Cincinnati after John D. Craig, formerly a member of the Maryland Institute, delivered a course of scientific lectures in that city. By 1840, institutes had also been founded in Boston, Waltham, Newark, Wheeling, Pittsburgh, St. Louis, Norfolk, and other towns and cities.[5]

It is difficult to determine the number of mechanics' institutes that were founded in the United States. One historian writes that "scores" of institutes were formed during the initial spate of activity in the 1820s and 1830s. Although the movement did enter a decline in the mid 1840s, institutes continued to be founded through the 1850s and 1860s, especially in the South and West. Some institutes continued in existence for years and left considerable evidence of their activities, but others were short-lived, lasting only a season or two before drifting into disuse. When an editor of New York's *Mechanics' Magazine, and Register of Inventions and Improvements* called on his readers to "make a beginning" if an institute had not yet been founded in their community, he urged them not to worry about any lack of proper materials. "If you cannot procure a library," he advised, "borrow a pamphlet, or a tract, upon 'useful knowledge,' and meet and read and converse upon its contents." A laboratory could begin just as modestly with a few items from the kitchen, he continued, and the motions of the planets could be illustrated with an orange and an apple. A group meeting under such a plan might have called itself a mechanics' institute, but without additional means would likely have disappeared in short order, and in any case would have left little record. In addition, some groups that may have modeled themselves on mechanics' institutes did not call themselves that, instead taking the name of "mechanics' association," "mechanics' society," or "mechanics' lyceum." References to such organizations appear frequently in antebellum newspapers and periodicals, but it is difficult to say whether they took part in the rhetorical strategies of the mechanics' institutes. What is more, while members of mechanics' institutes tended to be quite clear about how their organizations differed from similar associations, other writers sometimes merged the various educational organizations. A writer for the *North American Review,* for example, noted in 1829 that the year-old Boston Mechanics' Institution was quickly being imitated in other parts of New England. "It is believed that as many as one hundred of these associations are now in operation in Massachusetts," he reported. The one example offered, however, was a lyceum in Northampton. But whatever the number of institutes that were organized, observers perceived them to be a common feature of antebellum city life. As early as 1826, one writer reported that "the number of Mechanics' Institutions is, at this moment, increasing so rapidly, that we doubt not that ere long, a similar society will be considered indispensable in all large cities." A speaker before the Lancaster Mechanics' Society in 1835 expressed similar confidence that the spread of mechanics' institutes would continue. "Mechanics' Institutes are now considered of such importance," he insisted, "that their establishment will become general, and not a town or city in the Union will be without so powerful an auxiliary in the promotion of knowledge and improvements in the arts." Assertions such as these, while exaggerated, were not simply the boosterist proclamations of a few interested parties. Indeed, by the time the movement reached its peak in the late 1830s, thousands of mechanics, manufacturers, and others "friendly to the Mechanic Arts" had become members of mechanics' institutes, seeking to promote or take advantage of their various measures for diffusing knowledge.[6]

Proponents of mechanics' institutes were quite clear about who they hoped would benefit from their activities. If colleges and other institutions of "liberal" education primarily served those with money and leisure, mechanics' institutes would serve those who worked for a living, especially those who worked with their hands. A speaker before the Kentucky Mechanics' Institute in 1853 urged that "it is our duty to see that all the young men of our city, whose lot it is to labor with the hands, have ample opportunity for self-culture and self-improvement." A spokesperson for the Boston Mechanics' Institution more than two decades earlier, stating a somewhat broader constituency, extended the purview of the institution to those "whose time is chiefly occupied with business or labour," seeking to give them "knowledge of a kind to be directly useful to them in their daily pursuits." The term "useful" was especially common among proponents of manual labor schools: the scientific knowledge that was to be imparted was to be made clearly relevant to the practice of the trades (or "useful arts"), so that those who acquired that knowledge would become leaders in their fields. As the spokesperson for the Boston Mechanics' Institution put it, "It is not our object to make deep philosophers, but intelligent and skilful mechanics." Thus, the constitution of the Mechanics' Institute of the City of New-York, ratified in 1831, indicated that the objective of the institute was "the instruction of Mechanics and others in popular and useful science, and its application to the Arts and Manufactures." Many institute leaders expressed a particular concern with educating apprentices, both to instruct them in the theoretical principles of their work and to guide them into productive citizenship.[7]

The most characteristic educational activity of the mechanics' institute was the lecture series. Usually given during the winter months, lectures were generally open to the public, though in most cases nonmembers had to pay a small fee at the door. Lectures were the principal means of instruction at mechanics' institutes and were believed by many to be particularly well suited to the purpose at hand. Given their focus on "useful knowledge," mechanics' institutes generally restricted their lectures and classes to scientific and technical subjects, including mechanics, chemistry, natural philosophy, and technical drawing. When the Boston Mechanics' Institution opened early in 1827, George B. Emerson outlined the subjects he believed would be of particular use to mechanics. At the top of his list were the "Theory of Mechanics," natural philosophy, and chemistry. That spring, lecturers at the institution delivered lectures on natural philosophy and chemistry, with the following seasons including lectures on physiology, the steam engine, and mechanics. At the Mechanics' Institute of the City of New-York, the lecture program in the first several years of the institute's existence remained fairly narrow in focus. In the spring of 1835, Leonard Gale, later president of the institute, described the lecture program in a letter to John K. Mitchell of the Franklin Institute. Gale wrote that lectures were on a two-year cycle, with natural philosophy the subject one year, chemistry the next. In 1836 or 1837, probably to draw a wider audience, the institute moved to a more open format in which lectures were given "on a variety of subjects connected with the mechanical professions." The 1836–37 series, then, included lectures by George Bruce on the history of printing, Thomas S. Cummings on "the advantages of the Arts of Design to the Useful Arts," and William Dunlap on the history of New York. Baltimore's Maryland Institute offered lectures on a wide range of topics from the very start. Its first season, for instance, saw lectures on history, music education, and elocution. In conjunction with their lecture programs, some institutes acquired collections of "philosophical apparatus" and models of machinery to be used for instructional purposes. Institute leaders viewed these collections as an important tool for the educational efforts of their institutes. At the same time, their value and durability served to add legitimacy to fledgling institutes and heft to established institutes. The Board of Directors of the Ohio Mechanics' Institute noted in 1843, for instance, that the institute's apparatus collection was "believed to be the best in the Western country" and that it "may justly be considered the pride of our institution."[8]

A second activity many mechanics' institutes engaged in was collecting books for the use of their members. Mechanics' institute libraries, at least at the outset, tended to focus their collections on works in science and the arts, though they added to their shelves books on other subjects thought to be important for self-improvement. A number of institutes had libraries of considerable size. Just two years after its founding, the Kentucky Mechanics' Institute possessed nearly five thousand volumes. By 1853, the library of the Ohio Mechanics' Institute contained over seven thousand volumes. As their collections expanded, so too did the types of works they contained. Books on steam engines, surveying, and chemistry were joined by biographies, histories, and even works of fiction. Institutes that had a library frequently also had a reading room housing current newspapers and periodicals. Reading rooms not only served the purpose of diffusing knowledge, but also provided members with a place where they could gather, catch up on news and the latest developments in the arts, and discuss topics of mutual interest. By early 1838, the reading room of the Mechanics' Institute of the City of New-York contained over fifty periodicals—including "the most important literary and scientific journals that are published in the English, and a few in other languages"—along with nine daily newspapers. Among the periodicals lining its shelves were the *North American Review,* the *Knicker-bocker,* the *Journal of the Franklin Institute,* and the *Family Magazine.* A report published that year stated that the reading room was "almost con-stantly occupied by numerous readers." Institutes either subscribed to news-papers and periodicals or received the publications as donations. The Franklin Institute in Philadelphia traded its own publication, the highly esteemed *Jour-nal of the Franklin Institute,* for subscriptions to other publications. Accord-ing to one observer in 1840, the institute was thereby able to keep its "crowded reading room" supplied with "the best periodical literature of the day, with newspapers from all parts of our own country, and with every valuable jour-nal published in Europe, devoted to the advancement of the sciences and use-ful arts." The question of which periodicals should be acquired by mechan-ics' institutes could be controversial. In 1844, one angry member of the Ohio Mechanics' Institute resigned after learning that members of the institute's library committee, in defiance of a committee vote, had placed a subscrip-tion for an "eastern journal celebrated for its peculiar relish for scandal." Such a journal was unsuited for the institute, the angry member wrote, as it was "corrupting and vitiating to the taste and morals of society."[9]

A third important activity among institutes was sponsoring exhibitions of the mechanic arts. Institutes would invite mechanics, manufacturers, and others to bring out their products and machinery for public display. Insti-tutes that sponsored fairs were numerous, including the Maryland Institute, the Franklin Institute, the Ohio Mechanics' Institute, the Kentucky Mechan-ics' Institute, the Chicago Mechanics' Institute, and the Mechanics' Institute of the City of San Francisco. Visitors to such fairs could see a variety of goods on display, including hats, boots, furniture, cutlery, engravings, stoves, and musical instruments. Machinery was also displayed, sometimes powered by steam engines brought in just for that purpose. At the first annual fair of the Mechanics' Institute of the City of New-York, held in 1835, the *New-York Transcript* moved its double Napier printing press to the exhibition hall so that its print runs could be witnessed by those in attendance. These exhi-bitions, many of which drew thousands of visitors and were among the most popular events of the year, served several express purposes. They were meant to edify the public as to the progress of the arts, which, in turn, might swell the civic, regional, and national pride of viewers. At the same time, mechan-ics' fairs fostered a competitive spirit among artisans and manufacturers engaged in the same trade, spurring them to improvement. In order to fur-ther encourage competition, many institutes awarded premiums to objects or inventions judged to be of particular merit. In addition, mechanics' exhi-bitions provided artisans and inventors with an opportunity to show their wares to a purchasing public. Purely economic purposes were usually depreciated, however, in favor of higher ends. "Your mechanism does not parade in Faneuil Hall to get itself admired, and flattered, and so to advertise the dealer's stock," said one speaker at the 1856 exhibition of the Massachusetts Charitable Mechanic Association. "It comes on a nobler errand; comes to quicken invention, to stimulate drudgery, to re-inspire routine, to put new illumination into old task-work, to raise the tone of life, to expand civilization, to finish and edify society."[10]

Some of the larger institutes published journals as an additional means of diffusing knowledge. In the 1840s, for instance, the Chicago Mechanics' Institute took on editorial responsibility for the "Mechanical Department" of the *Prairie Farmer,* a popular agricultural journal devoted to "Western Agriculture, Mechanics, and Education." In 1857, the institute began publishing its own journal, the *Chicago Magazine.* The best-known mechanics' institute periodical was the *Journal of the Franklin Institute.* Launched in 1826, the *Journal of the Franklin Institute* quickly took its place among the premier scientific and technical publications of its day. A leading member of the institute praised the journal in 1834, calling it "remarkably well calculated for the promotion of knowledge among mechanics, and the furtherance of the scientific reputation of the country." While the *Journal of the Franklin Institute* focused almost exclusively on science and technology, the *Mechanics' Magazine, and Register of Inventions and Improvements,* published between 1833 and 1837 in association with the Mechanics' Institute of the City of New-York, printed articles on a broad array of topics that fell under the rubric of "useful knowledge." There readers were as likely to find an article on bee hives or smoky chimneys as on railroads or a new safety valve.[11]

In addition to these principal activities, different institutes sponsored an array of other educational programs. Some institutes organized schools for the children and apprentices of members. The Mechanics' Institute of the City of New-York, for instance, established such a school in 1838, which remained a source of great pride for the institute through the early 1850s, even as many of the institute's other programs ended. Some held "conversational meetings" where members could gather to discuss topics of mutual interest and share their problem-solving experiences. Some had committees that investigated and made reports on topics of general interest to mechanics. Others formed committees to review and report on the merits of new inventions, techniques, and products. Some institutes, including the Ohio Mechanics' Institute and the Franklin Institute, managed to raise enough money to construct their own buildings. While every organization that called itself a mechanics' institute engaged in one or more of these activities, there were significant differences among institutes in the scope and emphases of their efforts. The Boston Mechanics' Institution, for instance, did little more than sponsor lectures, finding itself unable to step outside of the shadow of the larger and older Massachusetts Charitable Mechanic Association. Indeed, by the early 1830s, the Massachusetts Charitable Mechanic Association had essentially become a mechanics' institute, adding a popular lecture series and an annual exhibition to its other activities. Philadelphia's Franklin Institute reigned through the middle decades of the century as one of the premier technical schools in the country, its reputation bolstered by its journal and by the high regard placed on its scientific research, especially a study on steam boiler explosions completed in 1836. The Rock County (Wisconsin) Agricultural Society and Mechanics' Institute, on the other hand, remained much more local in its purview. Founded in 1851 by a group of farmers seeking to improve their methods of agriculture, the society placed all of its energies in sponsoring an annual fair, which was dominated by displays of animals, fruit, and farm implements.[12]

As institutes launched into their various activities, thousands of men across the country signed their names to institute membership lists. Eligibility for membership varied from institute to institute. The constitution of the Chicago Mechanics' Institute, which was incorporated in 1843, limited membership to "any Mechanic of good moral character." In the mid 1850s, members of the institute debated whether men working in certain occupations were considered mechanics—and hence, whether they could become members. "It was finally decided by vote," noted a report published in 1856, "that butchers, bakers, brewers, tallow chandlers, house-movers, wig-makers, and lard-oil manufacturers, *were mechanics,* and eligible to membership." The constitution of the Franklin Institute stipulated that members "shall consist of Manufacturers, Mechanics, Artisans, and persons friendly to the Mechanic Arts," the last designation opening membership to anyone, regardless of occupation. Other institutes were equally open. The constitution of the Pittsburgh Mechanics' Institute stated simply that "any person who shall sign this Constitution, and shall pay to the Treasurer, annually, three dollars in advance, may become a member of this Association." Membership requirements as broad as this meant that, for some institutes, a number of members were not engaged in any form of "productive" activity. A memoir of one of the first officers of the Boston Mechanics' Institution, for example, indicates that members included "numbers from the manufacturing and mechanical pursuits," but also "clergymen, professors in the college, lawyers, physicians, merchants and traders." In most cases, prospective members had first to be nominated by a current member. Proposed names would then be brought before a meeting of the members, and a vote would be taken. The minutes of the members' meetings of the Ohio Mechanics' Institute indicate that very few of the names brought to a vote were turned down. Prospective members of the Mechanics' Institute of St. Louis had to undergo the moral scrutiny of the institute's leadership. "No person of an immoral character shall be deemed eligible to membership in this Institute, under any pretext whatever," stated the institute's constitution, "and it shall be the duty of the Council to examine, without prejudice, critically, into the moral character and standing of all persons proposed, before taking the vote upon their admission."[13]

The membership of the Mechanics' Institute of the City of New-York in the years immediately after its founding is probably typical of the first decade of the movement. Members included some professionals but were mostly master and journeyman mechanics from a variety of trades, including stonecutters, printers, machinists, tailors, blacksmiths, painters, carpenters, shoemakers, hatters, and cabinetmakers. Some, like Alexander Masterson and George Bruce, were master mechanics who were at the top of their trades as large employers in the city. Others were small masters, operating tenuous businesses on the slender margin between success and ruin. When Horace Greeley's name appeared on a complete membership list published in 1835, for instance, Greeley was only two years beyond his journeymanship, editing the weekly *New-Yorker* and struggling desperately to keep the fledgling journal from losing more money than it already had. Still others were journeymen in their trades, working with their hands for wages and seeking to rise in the world. While the number of journeyman was almost certainly low, it was probably much higher in the mid 1830s than it was in the 1850s. Of one hundred randomly selected names from the 1835 membership list, the only such list published by the institute, only sixty-five could be located in the city directory published that year. Because wage-workers generally were among those who were not included in city directories, this suggests that a significant proportion of the membership—possibly as high as 35 percent, although the number was probably somewhat lower—were journeyman craftsmen or other men who worked for wages.[14]

At the Mechanics' Institute of the City of New-York, members of such a relatively diverse group were not always sure what to make of one another. In his 1835 letter to John K. Mitchell, Leonard Gale, a physician who was then the corresponding secretary of the institute, mentioned with some frustration members of the institute whom he recognized to be, as a group, different from himself in educational attainment. "The regular or monthly meetings of the Institute," he wrote, "have not generally been very interesting and

from the fact I judge that the mechanics as a body have not enough of science to render a scientific subject interesting: it may be more owing perhaps
to another cause namely the fact that they as a class have little leisure to
attend to subjects of a scientific nature." One of the less educated mechanics that Gale wrote of might have been Oliver White, who was elected to the
Board of Directors early in 1835. In a letter to the actuary of the Franklin
Institute in April of that year, White alluded to discord between the institute's leaders and its members. Asking several vague questions about the
"experiance [sic]" of the Franklin Institute in different forms of government,
White wanted to know what "class of citizens" constituted the majority of
the Franklin Institute's membership. "It now so happens," he wrote, "on a
question of what it is best for us to do, that I am in the minority in the Board
of Directors, and in the majority in the Institute."[15]

As White's letter suggests, the Mechanics' Institute of the City of New-
York also attracted men holding widely different political views. John Windt,
for instance, was a member of the institute's Board of Directors in 1836
alongside Richard Hoe, the proprietor of a firm that had dismissed Windt
two years earlier for his radical political activities. Working Men's Party
candidates William Leavens and George Bruce were leading members of the
institute during the 1830s, as was James McBeath, an officer of the General
Trades' Union which called on journeymen from across the trades to collectively address their common grievances against their employers. But so
too was Daniel K. Minor, the publisher of the *Mechanics' Magazine* who,
in an encounter with Gulian Verplanck in 1833, expressed what must have
been contempt for the recently formed General Trades' Union. In early
December, shortly after his address before the Mechanics' Institute, Verplanck stopped by Minor's print shop to deliver a copy of the address for
publication in the *Mechanics' Magazine*. Minor, who wrote to Verplanck
several days later to explain his remarks, apparently mistook the former
congressman for Ely Moore, the president of the General Trades' Union,
who had also recently delivered a talk. "If my memory serves me rightly,"
wrote Minor, "I made some remarks, which I intended to make to the gentleman who delivered the address before the '*Trades Union*,' at that time
mistaking you for him." Minor's remarks must have been unfavorable,
and he apparently sent Verplanck away without accepting his address. In
his letter, however, he promised that if Verplanck would forward a copy of
his address, Minor would gladly place it in the *Mechanics' Magazine* and
two other journals he published.[16]

If members of mechanics' institutes ran across a broad spectrum of occupations, income levels, and political leanings, they did have several things in

common. First, they were all men. While their constitutions were not specific on this point, mechanics' institutes appear to have denied membership to women. That is not to say that women were not welcome to participate in the activities of the institutes, however. Women attended lectures, enrolled in some classes, and entered items in the annual exhibitions. But those women who participated in these ways faced prevailing ideas that limited their role in the production and transmission of scientific and technical knowledge. John K. Mitchell, for instance, speaking at the Franklin Institute at the end of the 1833–34 lecture series and seeing women in his audience, welcomed their presence, not for what they might contribute in the workshop or the laboratory, but for what they might contribute in the home. According to Mitchell, because mothers were "intrusted with the discipline of thought, at that critical period of life, when, through the flexibility of the mind, a bent is easily given to character," women should learn the wonders of nature so as to "brighten in the bosom of her child" a taste for science and the arts. "She should not be found often unable to satisfy the curiosity of her child; nor should his eager thirst after knowledge be destroyed by the oft repeated declaration of impatient ignorance." In addition, it is likely that mechanics' institutes included few, if any, black members. This is due at least in part to the fact that, by the 1830s, white employers and workers in the north worked to exclude free black men from practicing many of the skilled trades. Again, few direct references to race appear in the records of mechanics' institutes, but it is almost certain that the desire among white craftsmen to deny black workers entry into the craft shop informed the membership rolls of mechanics' institutes. A vote at a meeting of the Ohio Mechanics' Institute in 1847 is perhaps revealing on this point. According to the membership meeting minute book, nine men—a pattern maker, a founder, a cabinetmaker, a tanner, a minister, a clerk, and three carpenters—were proposed for membership at the October 12 meeting. After some discussion, eight of the men were submitted to a vote and elected. The ninth man, a minister named A. E. Graham, was "laid over" and subsequently dropped from consideration. A note penciled into the minute book explained that Graham was "a negro."[17]

Mechanics' institutes provided a place where some men, both employers and the employed, could join in a common project of attaching their personal progress to the marvelous progress of the arts. In this way, mechanics' institutes helped to obfuscate the divide between wage-earning manual workers and mental workers. In considering how institutes sought to promote industrial development, elevate the working man, and attune productive labor to scientific principles, one can see how they addressed themselves to the problem of class in early industrial America.

For proponents of the mechanics' institutes, the power of scientific knowledge would be the basis of both individual and social prosperity. Science would, in the first place, spur the useful arts toward what one speaker before the Boston Mechanics' Institution in 1827 called "the point of attainable perfection." With their various educational activities, mechanics' institutes would be the place where mechanics could go to study the science of their art. For Joseph Story, speaking before the same organization, the benefit of such a program would be immense. "Ask yourselves," he implored his audience, "what would be the result of one hundred thousand minds engaged at the same moment in the study of mechanical science, and urged on . . . to acquire new skill, or invent new improvements. It seems to me," he continued, "utterly beyond the reach of human imagination." James Madison Porter, speaking before the mechanics of Easton, Pennsylvania several years later, concurred. Arguing that "every mechanic art is the reduction to practice of scientific principles," Porter insisted that "where a knowledge of principles is combined with practice, the advantage is apparent to all."[18]

Others were more specific about what those advantages would be. A speaker at the July Fourth laying of the cornerstone of the Ohio Mechanics' Institute in 1848 urged that artisans be instructed "in the scientific principles and natural laws" on which the arts rested. "In this manner alone, popular errors are eradicated, accidental discoveries improved, and the precious time and expense otherwise squandered in abortive undertakings saved." Similarly, a speaker before the Metropolitan Mechanics' Institute in Washington, D.C. five years later argued that "without a knowledge of science, the practice of art is mere empiricism—often involving operations which are not only unnecessary to the production of the desired result, but frequently detrimental."[19]

The advantages that Story, Porter, and others pointed to would accrue to society as a whole, which would be the ultimate beneficiary of improvements in the arts. But scientific knowledge would also promote the well-being of mechanics. This latter idea rested on the notions that knowledge is power, and that education is the key to social influence because it cultivates the discipline, stability, and wisdom characteristic of all rightly successful men. In an address at the commencement of a course of lectures on mechanics and natural philosophy at the Franklin Institute in 1828, the principal of the institute's high school, Walter R. Johnson, outlined the benefits that befell the mechanic who studied "the scientific principles of his employment." "By introducing ideas and habits of rational and orderly proceeding into the mind, and by pursuing a methodical course in the occupation of one's thoughts," he argued, "an impression of the value and advantage of order is soon transferred to the whole character; the moral nature is elevated and purified, while the intellectual man is pleasantly and profitably exercised." Proponents also hoped that the pleasures of knowledge would foster curiosity and contentment in even the most menial pursuits, thereby elevating the nature of the work and the quality of the workman. James R. Leib, in a lecture on "scientific education" given before the Franklin Institute in 1830, argued that scientific knowledge would ease the journey of improvement while protecting against intellectual and moral degradation. "It is scarcely possible for a mind, which has once sought and found pleasure in the lofty pursuits of science, ever to become utterly debased," he insisted. "It will revolt from the grosser species of depravity; if not from principle, at least from taste."[20]

Knowledge, then, both elevated those who possessed it and preserved social order. As a speaker before the Gloucester Mechanic Association put it in 1833, "Knowledge is not only power—knowledge is also safety. It is the stability of our times—our trust and stay amid the dangers that thicken around us." Similarly, a speaker before the Newark Mechanics' Association in 1830 urged that each citizen must "understand the nature of [the] government, and the interests of the people and of the nation." Otherwise, he will, "like the madman . . . scatter arrows, firebrands, and death through all our blessings, or will blindly follow the dictates of others, as a servile instrument in their hands." This specter of impending riot, and the concomitant belief that education would stave off ruin, were key terms in the rhetoric of the mechanics' institutes. The speaker before the Lancaster Mechanics' Society in 1835 argued that education promoted "the tranquility of society—the incitement to industry—exemption from riots" and "respect to persons in authority." He then assured the members of his audience that they were on the front line of the battle against social disarray. "A Mechanics' Institute," he insisted, "formed on the basis of popularity, must be productive of general good. . . . It is admirably calculated to promote among mechanics, a liberal spirit, which ought always to be cherished as the best supporter of our republican character; a spirit of lofty independence, resulting from an honest confidence in their native powers."[21]

Central to this understanding of the role of scientific knowledge in elevating both the arts and the artist was the notion that the work of the hand would be coordinated with the work of the head. Speaking before the Boston Mechanics' Institution in 1828, Daniel Webster urged that the aim of the institutes was "to bring the power of the human understanding in aid of the physical powers of the human frame; to facilitate the co-operation of the mind with the hand." Mechanics' institutes would imbue even the most menial pursuits with intellectual activity. John K. Mitchell, advocating the combination of theory with practice, described for the members of the Franklin Institute the "enviable condition" of the educated artisan. "The most advantageous position in which a mechanic can be placed," he argued, "is that which combines knowledge of principles, and familiarity with practical detail; intellectual comprehension, and manual dexterity; the power to conceive, and the ability to execute." Walter R. Johnson, speaking before the Maryland Institute in 1849, urged the advantage of education in terms of the difference between humans and machines. For Johnson, unquestioning repetition in the workplace was the province of the machine, while inquiry and understanding were the province of the human. "It is one of the purposes of the Mechanics' Institutes of our time," he implored, "to enable every mechanic, who is so disposed, while he retains the *human*, to put off the *machine*; while he works with the head and the hand conjoined, to gain all, and more than all, the success and profit of his calling, which could be expected while he wrought with the hand alone." By elevating both the ability and the character of the working man, mechanics' institutes hoped to make real the ideal mechanic that President John Quincy Adams evoked in an 1827 toast before the Massachusetts Charitable Mechanic Association. "The American Mechanic," he cheered, "invention in the head—skill in the hand—benevolence in the heart."[22]

But head, hand, and heart, in addition to being parts of the body, were metonyms for labor functions, each of which was increasingly being assigned to its own social group. If the head stood for mental work, the hand manual work, and the heart the work of moral instruction and benevolence, then calls for the coordination of head and hand imagined not only an orderly individual, but an orderly society as well. Here we see another aim of the mechanics' institutes—to bring head and hand together in a social sense, to articulate the cooperative relation between mental-laboring managers and manual-laboring workers. Daniel Read, a professor at Indiana University, expressed this hope in 1844 when he implored members of the Mechanics' Institute of Bloomington to recognize the harmony of interests among all those who worked for a living. "In this country we are all *operatives*, all *working men*. We obtain our livelihood by our respective toil," he argued. "Let there then be no invidious feeling among those who are fellow laborers, either of the head or the hand, in the common toils of life." A speaker before the Kentucky Mechanics' Institute in 1853 similarly imagined a social union of head and hand when he observed that journeymen and apprentices had joined "employers" in contributing to the success of the institute's first annual exhibition. "Our young lads and young men now working at wages, are to be the future exhibitors in this or some other hall," he implored, "and while we give due credit to the head that plans, we should never forget the strong arm and the skillful hand that executes." The exhibition, then, displayed the cooperation of employers and wage-workers—of heads and hands—both in the exhibited wares and in the mutual interest taken in the exhibition.[23]

A speaker before the Ohio Mechanics' Institute gave the name "social labor" to this coordination of divided labor functions. "What then, is *that* labor which is the demonstrated basis of the wealth and power for which the world contends?" he asked in 1838. "It is *social labor*—the labor of the *body* directed by the labor of the *intellect*—performing different duties, but mutually dependent, and indissolubly connected. The dominion of the earth is given to *mind*, not to *matter*." Heads that plan and hands that execute, bodies directed by intellect, mind holding sway over matter—these were not simply metaphysical imperatives; they were descriptions of how workers and managers would be organized in an industrial society. Members of the Massachusetts Charitable Mechanic Association would have been clear on this point after listening to the address "Hands: Brain: Heart," given at their eighth annual exhibition in 1856. The author of the address, a minister named Fredric Huntington, called the members of the association the "masters of industry and machinery," assuring them that they were "the men that are to manage the hands of the nation and the age." Appealing to the specter of social unrest that would accompany unregulated workers, the speaker urged that "these hands must be guided and poised by wise and seeing heads" in order that the power they wielded not be "reckless and demoniacal."[24]

Proponents of mechanics' institutes thus drew on notions of power and self-governance that had meaning in terms of machinery and in terms of politics and morality. They appealed to widely shared beliefs about the place of education in a republican society in order to bolster their efforts to subordinate manual labor to mental labor. They employed the simple language of head and hand to figure a complex set of social relations, using the same terms to imagine both the personal order of productive citizenship and the social order of mechanized production. Gulian Verplanck's 1833 speech before the Mechanics' Institute of the City of New-York fully expressed these social meanings of the terms "head" and "hand." When Verplanck asked where society would be if the human arm "terminated in a hoof or a claw, instead of a hand," the artisans in his audience would have understood that the real question was, "Where would the world be without them? His profession that the "very affections and virtues of social and civilized life" resulted from "the industry of the hand" sought to highlight the debt owed not simply to the human hand, but to those who worked with their hands. But Verplanck was quick to point out that "social and civilized life" depended on the subordination of hand to head—of worker to employer—noting that the progress of civilization was "the fruit of the labor of the hand guided by intelligence." His vivid claim that the hand "without the guiding mind" was "bloody and dangerous, quick to injury, and slow and awkward in any work of peace" spoke less to some abstract notion of mindless hands, and more to the present unrest among wage-earning "hands" seeking to challenge the authority of their employers. Likewise, his call for the cooperation of head and hand—"let them act together in intelligent unison, and then the whole man and the whole frame of society will move together in cheerful activity"—imagined both an individual and a social order.

In stressing the importance of scientific knowledge to the arts, then, and in relying on the common-sense understanding that the head should guide the hand, proponents of mechanics' institutes offered a conceptual framework that subordinated hand to head, and thereby ensured and naturalized the relative power of mental-laboring employers and managers over their manual-laboring workers. John K. Mitchell, the Philadelphia physician and member of the Franklin Institute, wove many of these strands together in an address he delivered at the close of the institute's lecture season early in 1834. Mitchell, who several years later would lead the effort to purchase the automaton chess-player from Maelzel's creditor, entitled his address "On Some of the Means of Elevating the Character of the Working Classes." Claiming for himself the "appelation of a workman" ("I have laboured long enough, too, among the dust, and smoke of a laboratory"), Mitchell began by asserting that his experience as a workman convinced him there was no "essential disjunction of the work of the hands from that of the head." If the American mechanic suffered degradation and low social esteem, it was partly because he labored under the prejudices and "artificial arrangements" of old-world feudalism. But it was also because mechanics often failed to cultivate the habits and interests—what Mitchell called the "companionable qualities"—that gave "zest and grace to society." To elevate themselves, members of the working classes should in their leisure moments eschew the theater and grog shop in favor of the library and classroom. A liberal or "classical" education for manual laborers, argued Mitchell, would be the best means of breaking down the "artificial barrier" that stood between "various classes of society," entitling mechanics *in the very best sense of the word, to the name of gentlemen.*"[25]

Even more than classical knowledge, Mitchell argued that scientific knowledge would raise the mechanic to his proper station in society. Maintaining that science entered "even the humblest and simplest mechanical occupation," Mitchell insisted that knowledge of scientific principles would be the hallmark of the elevated mechanic. "Henceforth," he argued, "a mechanic,

ignorant of the principles on which his art is founded, will scarcely be better tolerated than would a physician who should dare to practice his art,
when convicted of ignorance of the philosophy of the circulation of blood."
Those unwilling to embrace the science of their art had only themselves to
blame for their exclusion from the higher ranks of society. For those unable
to apprehend the science of their art—for lack of ability—it would be a natural rather than artificial barrier that settled their station. "In our country,"
Mitchell assured his listeners, "it is impossible to support long any other distinctions than those of talent and learning."[26]

Mitchell then applauded the mechanics gathered before him. They had
persevered through the long winter course of lectures, and their efforts would
not go unrewarded. At the same time, he warned that those who had monopolized scientific knowledge in the past would try to preserve their superior
standing. But this would only spur healthy competition that would be to the
benefit of all. "This is the only warfare," Mitchell averred, "which should be
conducted by various classes of society." Dwelling for a moment on the specter
of social discord, Mitchell assured his listeners that "it is vain for one section of society, in our country at least, to envy another its superiority or its
influence." Rather than begrudge the power and influence held by others,
one should seek to make oneself suitable to "direct the destinies of society."
For Mitchell, mechanics should seek to redress their wrongs, not in clashes
on the shop floor or in the streets, but in the halls of learning. "Buckling
on the armour of learning, and seizing the sword of science," they should
"advance to the combat for an equal station, with that ardour which must
conquer, and that knowledge which will make the victory honourable to
themselves and glorious to the country."[27]

But of course Mitchell and others had no expectation that every working man would gain an equal station with his non–manual-laboring coun-
terpart, only those with the proficiency and character to elevate themselves.
And as even the most avid proponents of the mechanics' institutes recognized, not everyone was drawn to or suited for the rigors of scientific study.
A speaker before the Metropolitan Mechanics' Institute in 1853 deemed one
of the "laws of industry" that "those are first released [from manual labor]
whose gifts or talents give to them the strongest acensive power." "Man,
laboring man," he added, "is elevated in proportion to his mental powers."
In America, social distinction would be based on talent and character in
combination with education rather than on unearned privilege. As a speaker
before the Maine Charitable Mechanic Association put it in 1829, "With us
it is not noble blood, nor is it wealth that marks the lines of distinction
between the different classes of society." The difference, he continued,

was caused "as it should be, by different degrees of intelligence, of integrity and education." This purpose of making knowledge, and particularly technical and scientific knowledge, a basis for social distinction—and ultimately for class difference—was implicit through much of the rhetoric around the mechanics' institutes. Occasionally, it became explicit. A speaker before the Portland Mechanic Association, for instance, used these class-specific words to spur his audience to find time for study: "Are not the *master workmen*, the *owners* and the *employers* of other men—are they not those who have made the best use, not of their *fingers,* but of their *thinkers?*" Similarly, a piece from the *London Mechanics' Magazine* reprinted in a Hartford newspaper in 1835 outlined the various benefits enjoyed by those manual workers whose thirst for knowledge sent them to mechanics' institutes. Their minds stimulated and their knowledge deepened by their studies, these men "are scattered over the earth in the shape of managers, superintendants [sic], and foremen, of flourishing works . . . [and are] doing the intellectual work of large mechanical establishments."[28]

By the 1840s, the mechanics' institute movement had entered a decline. Many institutes that survived into the 1840s had to struggle to continue their programs and to appeal to what was a dramatically changing population of craftsmen and wage-workers. The challenges faced by the Mechanics' Institute of the City of New-York from the late 1830s to its closing in 1860 are illuminating. The national economic crisis that began early in 1837 significantly affected the activities of the institute. In June, the struggling *Mechanics' Magazine* ceased publication, although its editor did later announce in his *American Railroad Journal* that paid subscribers would receive copies of the railroad journal instead, which would now be called the *American Railroad Journal, and Mechanics' Magazine.* Shortly thereafter, institute leaders decided to cancel the lecture series that was to begin in the fall because of its expense. The decline continued into 1839, when the institute held its final exhibition. In fact, during the several difficult years after 1837 the institute's only successful program was a day school for children—located on Chambers Street a short distance from City Hall—which opened in 1838 and soon sustained an enrollment of between two hundred and three hundred students.[29]

The institute did enjoy a resurgence in membership and activity when the country emerged from its economic depression in the mid 1840s. In 1844, the institute printed a new catalog of its library, which by then contained nearly three thousand volumes. That same year, probably to raise money, the institute published and made available for sale the *American Mechanics' and Manufacturers' Almanac, for 1845,* which combined standard almanac fare with long passages on the progress of the arts. The following year, members ratified a much more detailed constitution. The renewed vitality could not be sustained, however, and membership numbers declined as the decade drew to a close. In early 1849, the institute was forced to move out of its quarters in the basement of City Hall—where it had been since its founding—when the city's Board of Aldermen, in a period of extensive renovation and reassignment of rooms at City Hall, passed a resolution calling for the institute's rooms to be altered and put to other uses. The work was to be done "as soon as practicable." The rooms in City Hall had been far from ideal. An 1847 guidebook to the city, in describing City Hall, noted that the Mechanics' Institute—"one of the most estimable associations in the city"—had its rooms in the basement of the building. The description of the basement, however, betrayed a setting that members of the institute must have found unsuited to such an estimable association. Running along the sides of the hallway were "numerous cells, formerly used, when the criminal courts were held here, as cells for prisoners." These rooms were "dark, damp, and gloomy apartments," the guidebook noted, "better adapted to the use to which they are now applied—coal-holes, and wood-bins—than to the confinement of transgressors of the law." But at least it was a home, one that carried with it the tacit support of municipal authorities.[30]

By the time the institute was forced out of City Hall, the acknowledged character of its membership had changed. When James J. Mapes addressed the institute in 1845 as its new president, he clearly understood that most all of the men in his audience were master mechanics, with few wage-earning journeymen. He noted at one point that the annual income and expenses of the institute were "not greater in amount, than some of you pay your journeymen every Saturday night." Later, in highlighting the potential influence of the institute on the "rising generation," Mapes averred that the institute's educational programs could "render a hundred boys—your apprentices—who now wear red shirts and run after engines—*gentlemen* in a single winter." The institute, he continued, would "suffice to turn their tastes, to lead them to apply their leisure to better pursuits, and thus enable them to do honor to the craft to which they belong." As wage-earning New Yorkers continued to prefer alternative (and less edifying) leisure activities, writers and lecturers increasingly took a chastising tone toward mechanics who failed to support the institute. In late 1850, when the membership numbers hovered around six hundred, Horace Greeley noted in some remarks before the institute that few mechanics in the city belonged to any mechanics' association, adding that too many squandered more money in one month than what it would cost for a year's membership in the Mechanics' Institute. In early 1853, a writer for *Scientific American* rebuked the city's mechanics for their "apathy and want of taste" in failing to attend a recent lecture at the institute. "We are afraid," he continued, "that too many of our young mechanics go to hear songs and see mountebank exhibitions in preference to attending scientific lectures." According to this observer, the Mechanics' Institute suffered because of the unfortunate divisions within the very group it sought to serve. "The mechanics in New York City are not united, their efforts are conflicting, separate, and therefore feeble," he wrote in the same journal the previous week. "If they were united in one thing, they could support one of the finest Institutes in the world."[31]

One difficulty was that the word "mechanic" could no longer effectively unite masters and manufacturers with their journeymen and wage-earning employees. When Zadock Pratt became president of the institute in 1849, he delivered an inaugural address in which he referred to himself several times as a "plain mechanic," a designation he had earned as a tanner. But by the time he spoke, he was the wealthy owner of a leather manufacturing establishment in the town of Prattsville, New York, and a former U.S. congressman. For those who still worked with their hands, especially those who worked for wages, Pratt's claim to be a "*working-man*" must have seemed strained. A writer for the *Farmer and Mechanic* pointed to the distinction between a manufacturer like Pratt and a wage-earning worker when he urged that the institute be supported "not only by men of wealth who have realized fortunes from the genius and industry of our mechanics" but by "the mechanics themselves." As the term "mechanic" lost its capacity to describe both mental-laboring proprietors and managers as well as manual-laboring workers, observers began to use other terms to describe the members of the institute. In 1850, for instance, one writer noted that the institute counted among its members "some of the best scholars, and most scientific and practical men." The following year, a writer for *Scientific American* remarked that many of New York's "most able engineers" belonged to the Mechanics' Institute. Scholars, scientific and practical men, engineers—in 1851, these designations all signaled mental attainment and some measure of removal from manual toil. In a similar fashion, a list of newly elected officers published in 1854 identified the officers using both traditional craft designations such as "Sailmaker," "Picture Framer," and "Pianoforte Maker" and modern designations such as "Fur Manufacturer," "Iron Manufacturer," and the especially modern "Manufacturer of Telegraph Apparatus." Even Zadock Pratt's son, George W. Pratt, eschewed the term "Tanner" for the more accurate "Leather Manufacturer."[32]

Struggling to define both its constituency and its purpose in a city that was very different than it had been in the 1830s, the Mechanics' Institute of the City of New-York launched several dramatically new programs in 1853. The institute had by then moved to a spacious five-story building at the corner of Bowery and Division, after a brief stay at another location on Bowery. The new building, which had the words "Mechanics' Institute" emblazoned on the side, was a point of great pride for members of the institute and seemed to confer a sense of permanence. Chief among the new programs were a Mechanics' Institute Legion of Merit, which rewarded virtuous boys and girls with privileges at the institute, and a Ladies' Reading Room. Several more new programs were in the early stages of development, including day classes for women in drawing, painting, and music and an "Educational Depository" where teachers from throughout the city could consult textbooks, maps, globes, and other educational items. The institute's actuary, James Henry, Jr., outlined these new programs in early December 1853, in a lecture before the institute on "The Mechanics' Institute: Past, Present, and Future." Henry also proposed the establishment of diplomas and medals to be awarded to "good mothers" for "the highest excellence on their part in the physical, moral, intellectual, and social training of their children." The members of the institute also ratified a new constitution in 1853, one that incorporated the broader vision expressed by the new programs. The new constitution, for instance, reiterated that the purpose of the institute was to provide for the "thorough practical education of mechanics and others," but an earlier clause requiring at least two-thirds of the officers to be mechanics was dropped. It also granted "special and qualified membership" to women and minors for the first time, although it stated that these members could not hold office or vote "upon any question before the Institute."[33]

By the early 1850s, then, the priorities of the institute seemed to shift from technical to moral instruction. As Henry outlined the new educational programs, for instance, he said virtually nothing about the importance of instructing mechanics in the scientific principles behind their art. Instead, he emphasized the institute's role in cultivating morality among the "young and vigorous citizens" of New York. He argued that the institute's program of evening classes had "established throughout its departments, silence, attention, order, diligence, perseverance, and efficiency, unsurpassed by any institution in the city." Similarly, the Legion of Merit would reward "*Truth, Punctuality, Integrity, Industry,* and *Perseverance*" among apprentices, clerks, and pupils, thereby working to improve the "character of the youth of the entire city." Henry's proposal to award mothers with medals and diplomas, which he called "the most important of all the labors upon which the Institute may ever enter," also aimed to promote virtue among the city's youth. At the same time, Henry suggested a way that the institute might continue to pursue its older purpose of providing scientific and technical instruction to mechanics. He urged members to consider transforming the institute into a "Grand Polytechnic School," which would instruct its students in "every department of science and practical knowledge." Henry gave few details about his proposal, but an account in the *New-York Tribune,* which was reprinted among the appendices of Henry's address, described the proposed polytechnic school as a "Central High School of the Mechanics" in which "young men of rare promise" would gather to receive "that higher instruction and exercise which alone can impart to them the perfection and ability of masters in their respective occupations." The new institute as imagined by Henry, then, would make explicit a cleavage among its members that had been implicit in the 1830s. The Legion of Merit and other programs aimed at improving the morals of the young would foster those virtues believed to be necessary for success in any occupation, mental or manual. But the polytechnic school would select and instruct an elite corps of future proprietors and managers whose scientific training would ensure their social status as "heads."[34]

The changes made and proposed in 1853 appear to have done little to sustain support for the institute, however, and the polytechnic school appears never to have happened. From 1854 onward, the activities of the institute barely surfaced in print. In 1856, the institute left its building at the corner of Bowery and Division—which had been leased for five years—and moved into smaller quarters a few blocks away on Fourth Avenue. The Mechanics' Institute School must have closed about the same time, as it no longer appeared in the city directories after 1856. In late 1858, the institute was still announcing its regular monthly meetings in the newspapers, but the listing in the 1859–60 city directory was to be its last. Several years later, when Charles P. Daly delivered an address before the American Institute in New York titled "Origin and History of Institutions for the Promotion of the Useful Arts," he reported that the Mechanics' Institute of the City of New-York was "no longer in existence."[35]

When the Mechanics' Institute closed its doors for good, probably in early 1860, it had little property to disperse. It did possess a valuable library, however, which in 1854 contained five thousand volumes. The final disposition of this library is telling. In his two-volume *History of New York City,* Benson J. Lossing—who served as an officer of the Mechanics' Institute in the 1840s—wrote that "at its dissolution" the institute's library "formed the nucleus of that of the Cooper Union." Circumstantial evidence supports Lossing's account. The Cooper Union for the Advancement of Science and Art first opened its doors in November 1859, about the time the Mechanics'

Institute closed. Its founder, Peter Cooper (a man who had himself success-
fully moved up from hand to head), intended to establish an institution that
would, much like the Mechanics' Institute, "instruct, elevate, and improve
the working classes" of New York by providing a reading room and classes
in chemistry, mechanical drawing, mechanical philosophy, and related subjects. In their first annual report, published in January 1860, the trustees
expressed a wish to open a library; that same report listed the Mechanics'
Institute as a member of the "Society of the Associates," a designation that
granted members of the institute privileges at the Cooper Union. One year
later, in their second annual report, the trustees announced that a library
containing four thousand volumes had been established. Although they make
no mention of a donation from the Mechanics' Institute, it does appear that
the institute had arranged to move its holdings to the Cooper Union. In January 1860, Senator Preston King wrote to the Cooper Union transmitting
two volumes of a four-volume set of books. The other two volumes had previously been sent to the Mechanics' Institute, King explained, adding that "I
now send you the 2nd and 4th volumes of the same to complete the set of
four volumes." Perhaps the institute's decision to pass its sole material legacy
on to the Cooper Union signaled that a moment of uncertainty had passed.
If the institute had worked to conceal class divisions by insisting on a language of the "mechanic" even as it promoted those developments that undid
the meaning of the term, the Cooper Union unapologetically used the language of the "working classes" to describe its intended constituency. The
institute's professed aim of intellectually and morally improving mechanics would thus be taken up by an institution whose leaders felt more free to
acknowledge the class divisions of the industrial age.[36]

Beginning in the mid 1820s, mechanics' institutes sought to expose craftsmen and others to the scientific and technical knowledge that was so evi-
dently behind the mechanical progress of the day. In providing such educational opportunities to those who would otherwise have little access to formal
study, mechanics' institutes participated in an egalitarianism that suffused
popular educational movements in the antebellum decades. But at the
same time, mechanics' institutes served as important venues for class formation. Seeing both the enormous promise of industrial production and the disruptions it caused to traditional workplace relations, proponents of mechanics' institutes sought to define the new social relations of production as
harmonious rather than oppositional. They did so by representing the contested relation between manufacturer and wage-worker as analogous to the
relatively unproblematic relation between head and hand. In stressing the
importance of scientific knowledge to the manual arts, and in appealing to

the common-sense understanding that the head should guide the hand, proponents of mechanics' institutes worked to subordinate manual-laboring workers to mental-laboring employers and managers. The language they employed in seeking to elevate mechanics as a group, then, served as well to codify a particular conception of class that would be both ardently embraced and tenaciously resisted for decades to come.

THE BROOME STREET MANUFACTORIES.

FIGURE 1. An illustration of the New York City factory of R. Hoe & Company, published in *Graham's Magazine* in 1852. By the 1830s, the Hoe Company was a leading manufacturer of powered printing presses. Indeed, Hoe presses were instrumental in the antebellum print revolution that helped spread the popular discourse on mechanization. They were also objects of interest in their own right. When the Mechanics' Institute of the City of New-York held its first annual exhibition in 1835, the New York *Transcript* moved its steam-powered Hoe press to the exhibition hall, where visitors crowded in to watch the paper's daily print runs. According to the *Graham's* article, the Hoe works depicted here employed three hundred men, "literally of every nation, as nearly as may be, under the sun."

From "New York Printing Machine, Press, and Saw Works, R. Hoe & Co.,"
Graham's Magazine 40 (June 1852), p. [564]. Courtesy of the Beinecke Rare Book and Manuscript Library, Yale University.

SAW SHOP.

FIGURE 2. An interior view of the R. Hoe & Company factory buildings, published in the same issue of *Graham's Magazine*. Here Hoe's workers manufactured saw blades, which were a significant part of the company's business. Note the uneven mechanization, typical of the industrializing craft shop. On one side of the room are more than a dozen men, most of whom are working with their hands using traditional craft tools, while on the other side are just two men, tending machines powered in this case by a steam engine.

From "New York Printing Machine, Press, and Saw Works, R. Hoe & Co.," *Graham's Magazine* 40 (June 1852), p. 574. Courtesy of the Beinecke Rare Book and Manuscript Library, Yale University.

FIGURE 3. By the 1830s, it seemed to many people that just about anything could be done by machine. Here is a humorous view of the seemingly endless possibilities, published in a Virginia "comic almanack" for the year 1837. This is one of a series of fanciful illustrations appearing in the almanac. Others show a steam-powered machine for shaving, a steam-powered fishing machine, and a machine for pulling teeth by steam. "This is a great convenience for business men," blustered the text accompanying this particular illustration. "We hardly know what will be done with the Rail Roads."

From *Uncle Sam's Comic Almanack for 1837* (Wheeling, Virginia, [1837]), p. 18. Courtesy of the American Antiquarian Society.

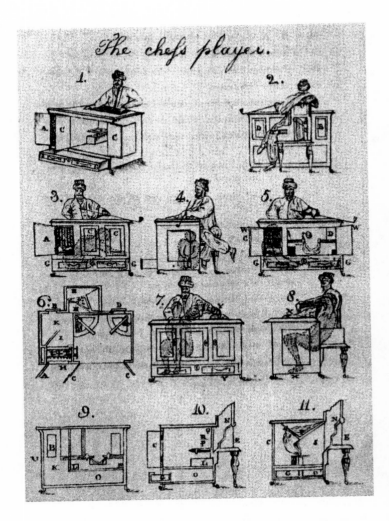

FIGURE 4. Surely it was in part the enthusiasm for machinery that was mocked by the "comic almanack" that spurred people in the 1820s and 1830s to go see the automaton chess-player. This illustration purporting to reveal the secret of the chess-player's operation appeared in a pamphlet by Gamaliel Bradford titled *The History and Analysis of the Supposed Automaton Chess-Player of M. De Kempelen,* published in Boston, when Maelzel first exhibited the chess-player in 1826. Here the ghostly figure of a person crouched inside the cabinet is a machine operative of a different sort, "minding" the chess-player so that it produces its intended effect.

From [Gamaliel Bradford], *The History and Analysis of the Supposed Automaton Chess-Player of M. De Kempelen* (Boston, 1826), p. [25]. Courtesy of the Massachusetts Historical Society.

VIEW OF THE INTERIOR

of the Eastern Wing of the Pavilion during the GREAT FAIR AT WASHINGTON, with the Machinery in full operation.

FIGURE 5. Lithograph accompanying a *New York Farmer and Mechanic* article on the "National Exhibition of Manufactures" held in Washington, D.C. in late May and early June of 1846. Organizers of the "National Fair" (as it was generally called) modeled the fair on the annual exhibitions that had already become the most popular events at mechanics' institutes around the country. But this fair—with exhibitors from Boston, New York, Philadelphia, Baltimore, and elsewhere—would boost the nation, not just a city or a region. The illustration shows the machinery exhibit, where visitors could gather to scrutinize a variety of machines, including a tanning machine, a carpet loom, and a spinning jenny, all powered by a steam engine. One newspaper reported shortly after the closing of the fair that as many as fifty thousand people had attended.

From "National Fair," *New York Farmer and Mechanic* 4 (July 1846), plate facing p. [223]. Courtesy of the Library Company of Philadelphia.

FIGURE 6. The silver medal diploma awarded by the Mechanics' Institute of the City of New-York at its second annual fair, held in 1836. The engraving shows a standing lady liberty gesturing down to an assortment of tools with one hand and up to the phrase "Knowledge Is Power"—ubiquitous in the halls of mechanics' institutes—with the other. Carved into the pillar are the names of some of the great contributors to scientific inquiry and mechanical knowledge, including Archimedes, Galileo, Watt, Bacon, and America's own Whitney. Note the smoke in the distance, from a steamboat on the left and possibly a factory barely visible on the right, joining a horizon still dominated in 1836 by sails.

"The Mechanics' Institute of the City of New York, at Their Fair of 1836, Awarded This Diploma to the Atlantic Silk Manufacturing Company at Nantucket," Manuscripts Large, Massachusetts Historical Society. Courtesy of the Massachusetts Historical Society.

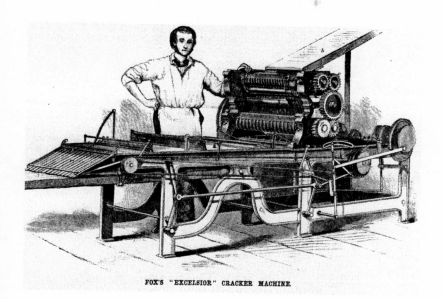

FOX'S "EXCELSIOR" CRACKER MACHINE.

FIGURE 7. A detailed illustration of a cracker-making machine, published in *Scientific American* in 1860. From the time it first appeared in the mid 1840s, *Scientific American* was a popular source of information on newly patented machines. Illustrations such as this one were crucial to conveying precisely how things worked. The man standing here could be the machine's inventor, Joseph Fox, or it could be the machine's operative, in which case the work appears to be unstrenuous and barely even manual in nature (notice that only one hand is placed on the machine). The accompanying text stated that this machine could be seen "in full operation" at Fox's "extensive bakery" in upstate New York, "doing the work of 90 men, with only 10 operatives."

From "The 'Excelsior' Cracker Machine," *Scientific American,* n.s., 2 (June 9, 1860), p. [369]. Courtesy of the Library Company of Philadelphia.

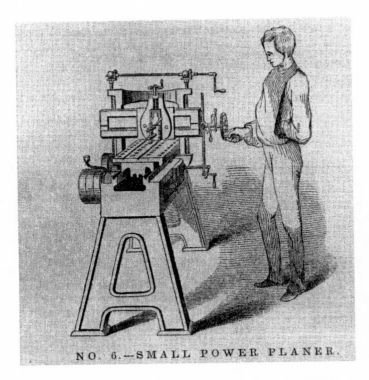

NO. 6.—SMALL POWER PLANER.

FIGURE 8. Here is a visual assertion that the work of machine-tending would be a form of mental labor rather than a form of manual labor. This illustration accompanied an article on new powered machine tools titled "Machinery, for Machine Making," which appeared in *Graham's Magazine* in 1852. Notice the one hand tucked in the operative's pocket—as if unnecessary for the requisite work—and the exaggerated brow. Clearly, this man is not simply a "hand"; he is more like a head, "minding" this machine in the same way that an overseer would be minding him. In this way, the illustration reiterated the text of the article, which claimed that in the age of machinery "the head, and not the hand, is to be the chief instrument," and that "the intellectual and no longer the physical forces are to predominate, even in the merest labor."

From "Machinery, for Machine Making," *Graham's Magazine* 41 (November 1852), p. 475. Courtesy of the American Antiquarian Society.

EXPLOSION OF THE STEAMER REINDEER, ON THE HUDSON RIVER.

FIGURE 9. The illustration accompanying the *Gleason's Pictorial Drawing Room Companion* article detailing the explosion aboard the steamboat *Reindeer* in early September 1852. Here is what could happen when the machine was not properly minded—peaceful progress (in this case up the Hudson River) could be violently arrested, sometimes to devastating effect. In what had become a convention by 1852, the illustrator (John R. Chapin) drew shapes in the cloud of steam and smoke that suggest fragments of bodies as well as of the engine and boat. According to the text of the article, two recent boiler explosions had left the public "keenly sensitive to everything relating to events of this character." Nonetheless, the article left little to the imagination of the *Gleason's* reader as it described the gruesome injuries caused by the explosion and the "heart-rending" scenes of despair among those searching for missing loved ones.

From "Explosion of the Reindeer," *Gleason's Pictorial Drawing Room Companion* 3 (September 25, 1852), p. 196. Courtesy of the Yale University Library.

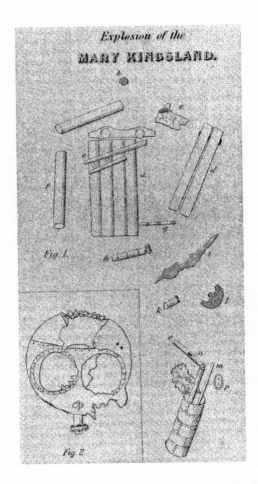

FIGURE 10. Early one morning in February 1852, a boiler aboard the steam tow boat *Mary Kingsland* exploded, killing eight people, as the boat passed about thirty miles south of New Orleans. Four months later, the *Journal of the Franklin Institute,* published by Philadelphia's premier mechanics' institute and at the time in print for more than twenty-five years, printed an account of the explosion, along with this illustration, showing pieces of the destroyed boiler collected after the explosion. The conventions of mechanical drawing are in place here—note the careful lettering of the pieces, all of which are explained in the accompanying text—but the disorganizing effects of the explosion are evident and even heightened by the odd and angled array of fragments. The author of the article, identified as an engineer, suggested that inferior iron and low water in the boiler contributed to the explosion. Later that year, Congress would pass a new set of steamboat regulations that by most accounts significantly reduced the number of boiler explosions in the United States.

From A. C. Jones, "Explosion of the Steamboat 'Mary Kingsland,'" *Journal of the Franklin Institute* 53 (June 1852), plate facing p. 416. Courtesy of the Yale University Library.

CHAPTER 3

Hand and Head

The Manual Labor School Movement

Several months before Gulian Verplanck stood before the Mechanics' Institute of the City of New-York to contemplate the limits of the hand without the head, the *American Annals of Education* published an article that took up a similar theme. The article, published in June 1833, was a review of a report just published by the Society for Promoting Manual Labor in Literary Institutions, a recently organized reform society seeking to combine physical exercise with study in the nation's schools of higher education. The author of the review—almost certainly William A. Alcott, the journal's editor—began by noting the indissoluble interdependence of mind and body. "We belong to that class of persons," he wrote of himself, "who possess, like their fellow men, a material and an immaterial part, mutually and intimately dependent on each other." But these two parts, he continued, were "yet so unfortunately trained"—at least in his own case—that "each is incessantly suffering by the neglect of the other, and each in its turn, retards the progress and impairs the comforts of its companion." The author then turned to the world of work, noting that if mechanics and other physical laborers were more likely to cultivate the body at the expense of the mind, men like himself, whose occupations required them simply to "open a book, or to hold a pen," cultivated only "the most delicate and frail portion" of the human apparatus—the mind—with unfortunate consequences to physical health. But like Verplanck, this observer found in the design of the human body guidance for right living. "We do not believe that any man, born with a perfect frame, was designed to live without bodily labor," he wrote. "If it were so, why were not his limbs originally formed of some material more delicate than bones, and muscles, and tendons, whose strength is sufficient, when they are not neglected or abused, to tear asunder wood, and even iron?" Like the "levers and cogs of a steam engine," he continued, the bodily systems were designed to do physical work, so that those who employed those systems were fulfilling nature's law. "We feel our inferiority," he wrote in comparing himself to "those in whom the material man has received something like the proper attention." Although he romanticized his vision of the working man—"we witness with astonishment the pleasure they derive from every sense, and every organ, the freedom with which they do and enjoy all that they desire, and the sweet repose that waits at their call, when they are temperate in all things"—his plea was genuine: "We lament that labor,—daily, vigorous labor, did not form a part of our education at every stage of its progress; and we long to see the rising generation exempted from this painful inferiority, and its more painful consequences." If Verplanck decried the social ills of hands unguided by heads, this observer decried the personal ills of heads unjoined from hands.[1]

In fact, during the late 1820s, just as the first mechanics' institutes were being organized in the United States, education reformers around the country founded schools of higher learning designed to address these personal ills by combining manual labor with a classical education. Usually called manual labor schools, these institutions sought to provide their students with workshops, gardens, and farm fields as venues for physical exercise. The novelty of the manual labor school was that its students engaged in agricultural or mechanical labor—in some cases, for up to four hours each day—as an integral part of their curriculum. In this way, their physical exercise was directed to productive ends. Proponents argued that the manual labor system offered a host of benefits: it would not only preserve the health of students, it would provide them with good habits, improve their studies, offer them a means for paying for their schooling, give them a trade to fall back on should difficult times demand it, and undo the tension between people who worked in the professions and people who worked in the trades. The manual labor program traced its roots to a school founded by Philip Emanuel von Fellenberg near Bern, Switzerland at the very end of the eighteenth century. Among the earliest manual labor schools in the United States were the Maine Wesleyan Seminary, founded in 1825, and the Oneida Institute of Science and Industry, which originated in a course of labor and study conducted in the spring of 1826. In the ten years between 1825 and 1835, scores of manual labor schools were founded throughout the United States, from Andover, Massachusetts, to Cincinnati, Ohio, to Maysville, Tennessee, to Macon, Georgia. At the same time, schools that already existed added or considered adding manual labor to their curricula. As early as 1829, one proponent averred that the manual labor system "is not an ephemeral novelty, but a lasting improvement in the system of modern education."[2]

The manual labor school—in seeking to join hand labor to the labor of the mind—was in many ways the obverse of the mechanics' institute. If the mechanics' institute aimed to provide manual laborers with a venue for pursuing mental activity, manual labor schools aimed to provide mental laborers with a venue for pursuing manual activity. In this way, both institutions sought to repair the rift between mental and manual labor, between head and hand. Although proponents of manual labor schools were less likely to use the language of "head" and "hand" than proponents of mechanics' institutes were, they clearly operated in the same conceptual universe. They saw that the work of the head and the work of the hand had been pulled apart, to deleterious effect. They argued that theirs was an institution that would do the crucial work of bringing head and hand together again, promoting the interests of the individual "worker" and of society as a whole. In Easton, Pennsylvania, the two educational movements converged in James Madison Porter, the lawyer who stood before the mechanics of Easton on Independence Day in 1835 calling for the founding of a mechanics' institute, but who three years earlier was instrumental in the opening of Lafayette College as a manual labor school. Several months after Lafayette first admitted students, Porter delivered an address at the college in which he briefly indulged his particular interest in mechanics' institutes, noting the importance of "the subject of natural philosophy as connected with the mechanic arts" and praising the elevating influence of the Franklin Institute.[3]

Education activists found in the manual labor system possibilities for very different popular education programs. Many of the early and most prominent manual labor schools—including the Oneida Institute—aimed principally to instruct worthy young men into a vigorous ministry. But this was by no means the sole purpose envisioned by proponents of the system. In an undated pamphlet, Peter Gallaudet appealed to Fellenberg's plan in proposing a school for "idle boys" who were likely to become "pests and burdens instead of useful members of society" because their parents—"in indigent circumstances, or intemperate habits"—were "disqualified to give that attention to their education which they require." In 1831, leaders of the First Annual Convention of the People of Colour, meeting in Philadelphia, announced a plan for a manual labor college—to be located in New Haven, Connecticut—that would provide for "the education of Young Men of Colour." The plan was never realized, however, in no small part because of the resistance of New Haven residents and city officials. The following year, the House of Representatives of the Pennsylvania General Assembly launched a study to determine the feasibility of establishing a state manual labor academy for the instruction of public school teachers. Thomas Dyott, a leading glass bottle manufacturer who would soon run into legal trouble over a paper money scheme, published a lengthy pamphlet in 1833 describing the educational programs he offered at his factory outside Philadelphia. According to Dyott, this system for "combining mental and moral with manual labor" would provide "to every worthy and honest son of Industry, all the pleasures that a prince can enjoy, all the independence that a freeman need desire, and all the education that can be useful to his condition." Robert Dale Owen turned to a similar system to pursue a more egalitarian agenda when he announced in 1835 his intention to found the "New Harmony Manual Labor College" at his father's utopian settlement in Indiana. "Thus only can be trained cultivated republicans," he wrote of the manual labor program, "men not too rude for any station, however elevated, nor too proud for any occupation, however humble: able to direct, willing to obey; capable of producing with industry and of enjoying with moderation." [4]

What proponents of the manual labor system shared was a prevailing sense that students who worked with their bodies as well as their minds would invariably benefit from the additional and very different labor. In a typical statement, one observer wrote in 1835 that *"the hand, the head, the heart* are so to be exercised" under the manual labor system "as not only to preserve each in health, but . . . to secure the advancement of each towards perfection." But if the explicit subject of statements such as this was the proper education of the individual, the implied subject was something far different. At just the moment when traditional craft work seemed to be coming undone by mechanization and labor-divided modes of production that separated "headwork" from "handwork" both in the individual and in the workplace, proponents of manual labor schools sought to bring head and hand back together, individually and socially. It was in this vision of the fruitful union of mental labor and manual labor, of head and hand, that proponents of manual labor schools offered a harmonious language of class, one that effectively defused the potential for conflict by undermining those in other quarters who were promoting more oppositional concepts of class. Instead of serving as a "critical reaction to an unfolding bourgeois culture," as one recent study has argued, the manual labor school movement helped to codify the social authority of a new middle class in terms that were difficult to resist. [5]

The manual labor school movement arose in the context of a much wider interest in promoting the physical health of the American people, especially those who worked with the mind more than the body. Observers through the first half of the nineteenth century found that men who devoted their time to study or to mental pursuits more generally were liable to what one writer in 1834 called a "vortex" of diseases. Books on the "diseases of a literary life" reached back to the previous century with S. A. Tissot's *An Essay on Diseases Incidental to Literary and Sedentary Persons* (1768), and included Chandler Robbins's *Remarks on the Disorders of Literary Men* (1825) and George Hayward's *A Lecture on Some of the Diseases of a Literary Life* (1833). The notion that intense mental application frequently resulted in mental and physical debility was commonly held throughout the antebellum period. A commencement speaker at Middlebury College in 1829, for instance, in pointing up the "frequent instances of bodily and mental debility and disease occasioned by application to study," noted that "at least one-fourth of those who pass through a course of education for the learned professions, sink into a premature grave, or drag out a miserable and comparatively useless life, under a broken constitution." Robley Dunglison, a physician and professor of medicine in Philadelphia, professed some skepticism over the frequency with which excessive study resulted in disease but admitted in 1844 that "the idea of the morbific agency of great intellectual application prevails universally, and has been adopted by many writers on the physiology, and pathology of the nervous system." This association between mental labor and physical disease did not bode well for an age that saw a rising number of men entering nonmanual occupations. In addition, writers and lecturers observed that men who worked in nonmanual occupations tended to forgo physical exercise to an unhealthy extent. An Ohio physician writing in 1847 quoted at length a passage that prescribed four hours of "brisk labor" per day as ideal for the preservation of health. "In the light of this required amount of exercise," the passage continued, "what shall we say of those merchants, clerks, lawyers, students, and the sedentary classes generally, who confine themselves to their offices, desks, and books . . . scarcely going out of doors, except to and from their business, and then TAKING AN OMNIBUS!" Another writer six years earlier pointed out that some women, too, failed to give due regard to physical exercise, to deleterious effect. Lamenting the "withdrawal from manual labor, from earnest physical employment" that he saw prevailing "in the upper class, and in a large portion of the middle class of the women of cities," this writer reminded his reader that "the power of the mind is augmented by the exercise of the body" before settling on an aphorism that would have won applause at any manual labor school: "By the sweat of thy brow, thou shalt be able to *think*."[6]

For those who embraced the "diseases of a literary life" notion, the consequences of stimulating and cultivating the mind at the expense of the body were dire. Men and women who led sedentary lives, who worked little if at all or engaged in pursuits that made few demands on the body, were seen to suffer from a host of diseases. "In all parts of the world, and under all circumstances, highly studious and literary men have infirm health," noted a physician named Charles Caldwell in a lecture in Lexington, Kentucky in 1833. The reason, he continued, was clear: "They exercise their brains too much, and their muscles, hearts and lungs, too little." Chief among the complaints of sedentary individuals was dyspepsia, understood to be a digestive disorder which gave rise to an array of symptoms including flatulence, dizziness, diminished memory, inattention, poor judgment, melancholy, anxiety, and misanthropy. Caldwell urged that dyspepsia was common not only among literary men, but among every "brain-worn class of persons," including "officers of state, dealers in scrip, daring adventurers, and anxious and ambitious projectors of improvements." Those who labored with their minds to excess, he urged, suffered the same: "Dyspepsia is their torment; and they exhibit deep traces of it, in their lean frames, and haggard countenances." Many would have agreed with the writer who noted in 1834 that students—and, it would seem, anybody else—who failed to regularly exercise their bodies were destined to "pursue the broad, beaten track, through the regions of dyspepsia and disease, in its thousand forms and with its attendant miseries, to a premature grave."[7]

Beginning in the 1820s, about the same time as the onset of the manual labor school movement in America, health reformers launched efforts to introduce gymnastic and calisthenic exercise programs in schools as a means of promoting the health of students. In 1826, a public gymnasium was founded in Boston, where men of all ages could go to exercise under the guidance of instructors. By 1828, gymnasia had been established in a number of American communities, including Northampton, Massachusetts, Providence, Rhode Island, and New York City. Popular interest in calisthenic exercise programs increased in 1831 with the publication of a book titled *A Course of Calisthenics for Young Ladies*. Addressed to "Mothers and Instructresses," this book urged the importance of physical exercise for children, pointing out in particular the perils of inactivity for young women. After enumerating several causes of poor health among schoolgirls, the author describes a variety of indoor exercise programs—some of which required novel devices like the triangle or the "oscillator"—designed to restore and preserve health. A series of engravings and instructions informed the reader of how young women should swing, bend, twist, jump, and stride about, sometimes holding weighted objects, in order to arrive at a host of health benefits, including an expanded chest, an erect form, and increased muscular strength. The movement to implement gymnastic and calisthenic exercise programs in schools and communities quickly faded, however. In 1834, one observer reported a decline in gymnastic exercise programs at colleges such as Yale and Amherst, writing that the instruments used for such exercises were "returning to the dust, as they were with great rapidity." By the mid 1840s a Boston area physician, in recalling that "the establishment of gymnasia through the country, promised, at one period, the opening of a new era in physical education," lamented that gymnasium exercises "have gradually been neglected and forgotten, at least in our vicinity."[8]

One criticism of calisthenics and gymnastics often made by proponents of the manual labor system was that they simply wasted energy. For these observers, scenes of young men and women spending their energy on unproductive activity evoked a sense of luxury and excess. In 1835, for instance, a writer for the *American Magazine of Useful and Entertaining Knowledge* called gymnastic and similar exercise regimes "artificial and useless labor," arguing that such nonproductive activities were perhaps excusable only among the "sons of the very opulent." For worthy citizens of a republic, he suggested, physical labor was better applied to productive ends, to tilling a field or turning a lathe. Even those who acknowledged the health benefits of gymnastics programs argued that it was not enough to simply produce health. A proponent of the manual labor system writing in 1828, in considering the "artificial system of gymnastic exercises [that] has been introduced into many institutions of learning," admitted that such programs had been "productive of excellent effects on the health of students," but nonetheless he called for a better use of the students' efforts. "Why resort to laborious exercises which require considerable expense and are productive of no profit," he wondered, "when the same labor or exercise may be so directed as to accomplish several important ends, besides the promotion of health?" Another writer in 1833 made a similar point when he compared the motions of gymnastic exercises with using an axe to chop air rather than wood, or swinging a scythe "where there is nothing to cut but vacuity."[9]

Critics such as these saw in the manual labor system an ideal alternative to prevailing forms of physical education. The purpose of manual labor schools, however, was twofold. First, their proponents did argue that productive agricultural and mechanical labor would preserve the health of students during their course of study. In making this case, they routinely gave voice to the argument that study without physical exercise was ruinous to health. "It has been found, by melancholy experience," noted one writer in a typical fashion in 1835, "that intense study for several years in youth, or early manhood, where there has been little bodily exercise, destroys physical health, vigor, and often life itself, prematurely." Two years earlier, a committee of the trustees of Allegheny College, which was considering introducing the manual labor system to the school, similarly noted that "a constant application of the *mind*, without giving the *body* suitable exercise, enervates the system, stupifies the faculties, impairs the health, and of course prevents vigorous application to study, and eminence in the attainment of useful science." Dr. John Bell, editor of the *Journal of Health,* urged the same point when he wrote, in support of the manual labor system, that "full health and pleasurable feelings can only be enjoyed on the condition that every organ of the living body shall be duly exercised." According to Bell, students, persons "generally engaged in literary and scientific pursuits," and all others "whose minds are long and intently occupied" and who exercised little, were out of conformity with the healthful condition, and they "suffer[ed] accordingly." The employments prescribed by the manual labor schools, Bell continued, were well suited to placing such sufferers on the side of health.[10]

But the second purpose of manual labor schools, and one that was also explicitly stated, was to lessen the financial burden of attaining a higher education. If saving the health of classical scholars seemed to some to be a rather modest endeavor beneficial only to the privileged few, then this second purpose enabled proponents of manual labor schools to profess a more democratic vision. Manual labor schools, they pointed out, made it possible for men with little means to acquire a higher education. They did this in two ways. First, manual labor schools provided their students with a way to secure a modest income to help pay for the cost of school. Students who worked in the fields or in a workshop were compensated for their labor, either in the form of credit against room, board, and tuition or, in some cases, in the form of money, which they could then apply toward school expenses. Students at Cincinnati's Lane Seminary in 1832, for instance, were able to earn— working a minimum of three hours a day—the full $70 required for one year's tuition, room, and board in the school's literary department. This plan to make manual labor a way for students to help pay for school was a significant feature of the manual labor school program and was frequently highlighted by proponents of manual labor schools. A Philadelphia minister in 1830, in a sermon titled "The Importance of Uniting Manual Labour with Intellectual Attainments," applauded the opportunities opened up by the manual labor system. "Every youth in our land, of proper talents and proper habits," he wrote, "may procure by his own hands, by the avails of his own independent labour, the best mental education which this country can give." In addition, by relying on the labor of their students to supply buildings, furniture, board, and goods to be sold on the market, manual labor schools were able to charge less for tuition and board, making them less costly to attend than conventional colleges and seminaries. At the Oneida Institute, for instance, students worked with a carpenter in constructing a number of buildings for the school, and they built most of the furniture for their rooms. Aware of the successes at Oneida, one proponent of the manual labor system pointed to this benefit in early 1832. "The expenses of obtaining an education may be so much diminished," he wrote, "as to place its privileges within the reach of every youth of talents."[11]

A number of additional benefits were said to accrue as a result of the manual labor system. Proponents argued that the exercise undertaken in field and workshop not only preserved the physical health of students but propelled them to excel in their studies. A writer for the *American Annals of Education,* for instance, wondered in 1835 "if there be no other benefit of manual labor schools, is not this enough,—that they are stated *uniformly* by those who observe them to accelerate the progress of the students?" At the same time, students working as farmers, cabinetmakers, blacksmiths, and printers acquired some knowledge of a trade, knowledge that might prove beneficial later in life, or might at least encourage them to give due respect to those who toiled with their hands. In addition, students who applied their leisure hours to productive labor rather than to idleness or vice would develop an independent spirit and other personal qualities that would benefit not only themselves, but society as a whole. As one proponent put it in 1833, the manual labor student would "in many or most instances form a character for usefulness, and lay the foundation of future wealth and honorable affluence in life, in the habits of industry which he contracts." One writer, appearing in the *Quarterly Register* in 1834, suggested that students need not rely on others to enter into a manual labor program and enjoy its many benefits. "Let no student suppose, because he is not connected with a manual labor institution, he is therefore necessarily cut off from the benefits of the system," he wrote. "Let him have a manual labor school of his own; one of which he himself shall be the inventor, the supervisor, and the practical operator." The benefits of conducting one's own manual labor program— of securing venues for combining labor with study—were many, according to this writer. The student would learn to be inventive, resourceful, and self-reliant, and he would acquire skills and habits that would equip him for supervisory work in the world of business. "Men of enterprise, especially if they manage various kinds of business," he wrote, "often acquire a remarkable acuteness, activity, and shrewdness." By "casting about for exercise, and turning his hand to different kinds of employment," the student might acquire some of the same characteristics. "A business habit is promoted not only in doing a piece of work which is already laid out," he offered, "but in looking up the work and planning it."[12]

The manual labor school movement entered into its most active stage in 1831, when a group of prominent educators, clergymen, and philanthropists— including Jeremiah Day, who was president of Yale College; Lewis Tappan, the New York merchant and philanthropist; and Theodore Frelinghuysen, the U.S. senator from New Jersey—founded the Society for Promoting Manual Labor in Literary Institutions in New York City. Its constitution stated that the purpose of the new society was to "collect and diffuse information, calculated to promote the establishment and prosperity of Manual Labor Schools and Seminaries in the United States," and to encourage the implementation of the manual labor system in schools already established. The leaders of the society hired Theodore Weld, a minister who had studied at the Oneida Institute, to be their agent. Weld soon embarked on a tour through a number of western and southern states, during which he gave hundreds of lectures on the benefits of the manual labor system and on temperance (Weld's second great passion at the time). Weld also collected information on manual labor schools while looking for the best location for a school to be established by the society. Upon his return to New York in the fall of 1832, Weld remained busy lecturing, corresponding with educators, clergymen, and others about the manual labor system, and preparing his report for the society. This report, which Weld submitted in January 1833, did more than any other document to bring the manual labor system to national attention.[13]

Weld essentially divided his report into two main sections, each of which contained multiple titled chapters. In the first section, Weld offered an invective against "the present system of education," arguing that it was destructive in almost all ways imaginable because it neglected physical exercise. Weld used as support for his argument long passages from a host of writers, many of whose names would have been familiar as leaders in the fields of medicine and education. One such writer, a college president in Kentucky, surmised that nine out of ten students he had seen over the years suffered ill health as a result of intense study without physical exercise. "In short," he forcefully concluded, "I cannot but consider a literary institution, which makes no provision for the regular exercise of its students, no better than a *manufactory of invalids, and the slaughter-house of cultivated talent.*" According to Weld and the experts he cited, an unhealthy body "effeminate[d]" the mind, or weakened its capacity for labor, while at the same time endangering the morals by breeding lethargy and dissolution. Such systemic decline, Weld continued, produced an "indisposition to effort" and destroyed "habits of activity and industry," leaving its victims ill suited for work. Indeed, in his travels Weld found that those who had received a higher education without regular exercise were commonly viewed as the least active and least enterprising of the business and professional world. "No remark is more common among [businessmen] every where," he wrote, "than that the present system of education *unfits men for the practical business of life.*" Weld devoted the second section of his report to describing the manual labor system, explaining the fullness of its beneficence, and defusing potential criticism. Detailed in its argument, filled with passages from scores of sources, and running in small type for more than one hundred pages, it was a remarkable achievement. "We regard it," wrote one reviewer of Weld's report, "as ranking with the most important works of this age of active benevolence."[14]

One of the earliest manual labor schools in the United States, one that preceded Weld's tour, was the Manual Labor Academy of Pennsylvania, founded in 1828 when a group of prominent Philadelphia-area Presbyterians formed a joint-stock association "for the purpose of establishing near the city of Philadelphia, a school in which manual labour is to be connected with the elements of a liberal education." The articles of association stated that the primary purpose of the school was to train men for the clergy, but that it would not refuse men of good moral character who desired to pursue other vocations. By December, the group had appointed a Board of Trustees and had begun raising capital by selling stock at $20 per share. That same month, John Monteith, a manual laborite who had been hired by the association to put its plans into effect, prepared a report on "the subject of connecting manual labour with study." In his report, Monteith (who had previously been associated with the Oneida Institute) gave voice to the principal tenets of the manual labor school system. He wrote that the "great end" of combining physical labor with study was to "cultivate the mind . . . in the best manner and at the same time to preserve such a vigour of constitution as to enable the student to serve by his attainments, the most effective practical purposes." He noted that most students who excelled at school or in professional study either lost their health entirely or suffered such debility as to be "unfit for the duties of their profession and to be liable continually to sink under the slightest shock or indisposition." Monteith added that the separation of manual labor from study was a relatively recent phenomenon—traceable to the monasteries of a few centuries before—so that the union of labor with study was less a novelty than a return to a more natural course, one that was economical, healthful, and productive of good moral character and "an independent and enterprising spirit."[15]

By early 1829, the trustees had secured a farm in nearby Germantown—complete with forty-two acres, a main house, and several outbuildings—and taken the name of the Manual Labor Academy of Pennsylvania. In May, the school opened with four students, a number which climbed to twenty-five within six months. Under the tutelage of Monteith and one other instructor, students studied classical subjects such as geography and mathematics, as well as surveying, bookkeeping, and penmanship. They also engaged in "useful bodily labor" for three or four hours a day, either tending the small garden near the main house, working on the farm raising wheat, rye, hay, corn, and potatoes, or working in the carpenter's shop that had been established on the premises. In addition to repairing and improving buildings, students built most of the furniture for the school, and they manufactured "small wooden articles"—by the fall of 1830 the focus was on trunks and packing boxes—for sale on order in Philadelphia. The principal purpose of the school at its outset was to "educate pious indigent youth who aimed at the Gospel ministry," and as the trustees pointed out in their first annual report, the manual labor program served this purpose both by enabling students of modest means to pay for their education (several students that first year were able to defray nearly all their $40 tuition plus room and board from their labor), and by broadening their skills and fortifying their health, making them "fit for the vicissitudes of life, particularly so, if they be destined for our new settlements, as christian missionaries." Most of the students learned as they went along because only a few were skilled at woodworking, and none were skilled farmers, but Monteith and William Burroughs—the only two instructors at the school—wrote in November that "no serious difficulty has been experienced in conducting the several branches of business."[16]

Over the next several years, the Manual Labor Academy of Pennsylvania largely succeeded at what it set out to do. The second and third reports of the trustees reported on increasing enrollment and detailed both the rigor of the students' study and the productivity of their labor, measured in terms of the yield of the farm and garden, the output of the workshop, the amount of money students earned toward school expenses, and the health of the students. But in spite of its successes, the school remained in a constant state of financial crisis. A heavy debt, incurred in part by the purchase of the farm, could not be alleviated by the sale of additional shares of stock, and since students worked rather than paying the full cost of tuition, room, and board, income from enrollment was difficult to predict and in any case low. In addition, the school's proximity to Philadelphia meant that costs for necessary supplies, such as fuel, building materials, and lumber for the carpenter's shop, were high, while income from the sale of items produced by slow and inexperienced students remained low. These difficulties surely contributed to John Monteith's decision to resign from the school sometime before August 1830.[17]

Monteith's replacement was a Presbyterian minister from eastern Pennsylvania named George Junkin. Born in 1790 into a prominent land-owning family south of Harrisburg, George Junkin worked in several trades—including carpentry and textile manufacturing—before entering college and going on to study theology at what would become the Union Theological Seminary in New York City. He married Julia Rush Miller of Philadelphia in 1819 and soon thereafter became pastor of a small church in Milton, Pennsylvania. Junkin consistently showed himself to be socially and culturally conservative. Over the course of his professional life, he defended nativism, mocked labor radicalism and what he called "the contemptible philosophy of infidel agrarianism," and marveled at the beneficence of the industrial age, arguing often that machines simply released mankind from toil, and as late as 1845 that Lowell was "an illustrious demonstration of the truth, that large masses of human beings may be crowded into manufacturing cities, and yet freedom, intelligence, truth, peace, virtue and happiness not be crowded out." Junkin came to manual laborism after having been inspired by a carpenter's apprentice who led prayer one day at Junkin's house after Junkin had become seriously ill. Upon recovering, Junkin took in the apprentice and gave him religious instruction in preparation for the ministry in return for his labor. When Monteith resigned from the Manual Labor Academy of Pennsylvania, Junkin learned about the open position through a personal contact he had with one of the school's trustees.[18]

Junkin's leadership at the school was strongly felt. Within a year of his arrival, the school had an enrollment of forty-eight students and had completed an enlarged shop for the carpentry work. Financial problems that had plagued the school since the outset persisted, however, and were compounded by "a measure of apathy" that, according to Junkin's younger brother, had "invaded the Board of Trustees." Nonetheless, at the close of the trustees' third annual report, published late in 1831, the author promised that "though we have difficulties, they are not insurmountable."[19]

George Junkin concluded otherwise, and in early 1832 he resigned. His problems at the school extended beyond the financial strains on the institution. During his tenure as principal, Junkin had become vocal in a theological dispute that pitted his "Old School" ideas against the "New School" views shared by many members of the Board of Trustees. At odds with his board and disappointed in the school's failings, Junkin resolved to continue his efforts elsewhere. By the time he turned in his resignation, he already had in mind Lafayette College in Easton, Pennsylvania. From its inception in 1824, Lafayette College had professed a mission that was somewhat similar to that of the manual labor schools. In an 1825 memorial to the

Pennsylvania legislature petitioning for incorporation, the school's founders stated their hope of combining literary and scientific study with military instruction. The military instruction, they insisted, would serve the twin purposes of ensuring a well-trained militia and "promoting and preserving the health of the students," the latter as a result of students marching and training on a regular basis. The college received its charter in 1826, but for the next six years, lack of funds and other difficulties prevented it from getting off the ground. After some discussion and a visit to Easton, Junkin agreed to take the helm of Lafayette College, on the condition that the military studies be dropped in favor of manual labor, and that the school provide the facilities for such a program. The trustees, led by James Madison Porter, agreed and went about having its state charter changed to reflect the move away from military instruction. As these arrangements were being made, the Pennsylvania Manual Labor Academy closed its doors permanently. In November 1832, William Darrach, who was the secretary of the Board of Trustees, received the final report from the school's treasurer showing that, in closing out the school's accounts, shareholders would receive a scant $2 per share.[20]

Junkin, meanwhile, faced considerable work in launching Lafayette College on the manual labor system. The college had virtually no capital and none of the supplies needed for even the most modest educational institution. The trustees had managed to secure a two-year lease on some property with a large house and several smaller buildings, but Junkin quickly decided another building was needed for classrooms and workshops. In early March 1832, he and a group of Manual Labor Academy students made the fifty-mile trip north to Easton and threw themselves into their first manual labor project at the new school, that of constructing the new building. Most of the rest of the Germantown students, along with the faculty, joined them at the end of the month, and studies commenced with more than forty students in early May. But even with the new building, the leased property was clearly inadequate to the needs of the college. By October, the trustees had made arrangements to purchase nine acres on a hilltop at the outskirts of town. Six months later, in April 1833, the college published a circular describing the principles of the school and its successes in its first year, and seeking to raise funds for the construction of a building on the new site. Ground was broken in June, but funds remained short, and by the end of the year, the building was not yet completed. As debt continued to mount, the trustees decided in December to forward to Harrisburg a memorial drafted by Porter petitioning the state legislature for financial support. The bill that was introduced later in the month called for the state to grant the college $20,000, half to be paid immediately and the other half to be spread out in equal payments over the next five years. A pared-back bill finally passed in early March, whose $12,000 endowment provided some relief but not enough to place the school on secure financial ground. Nonetheless, the new building was complete enough to occupy by the spring, and on the first of May, 1834, the college moved to its new site, and Junkin was formally installed as the college's president.

The manual labor system thoroughly informed the life of the institution during its first several years. Not only did students work to clear land, quarry stone, and construct buildings, but they also raised vegetables, cultivated acres of corn, oat, hay, potatoes, and other crops, built furniture and farm implements for use at the school, and manufactured packing boxes and trunks for sale. By virtue of their labor, students could (although few did) earn more than half the total cost of attendance, which for the first several years hovered around $100 per year. But life at the school was stringent. Morning worship, which students were required to attend, began at 5:00 A.M., after which students performed their manual work until just before breakfast at 7:00. Study and recitations went from 7:30 until 5:00 P.M., with an hour meal break at midday. Students then returned to their manual labor and worked until 7:00 P.M. Junkin and his small faculty, which until 1834 included Samuel D. Gross, who would go on to fame as a surgeon in Philadelphia, had to teach without benefit of a library. Students were required to provide their own furnishings—including bed, lamp, and lighting fuel—and they kept the buildings clean themselves. Those who boarded ate together at two long tables, and the provisions were sparse. Alexander Ramsey, who arrived at Lafayette in early September 1834, wrote in one of his first letters home that "the fare is such that beggars all description," adding that breakfast consisted of "coffee (so-called), sometimes a mackerel of the herring species, appropriated to about eighteen persons, a little cold meat in the same proportion, and bread and rank butter." Meanwhile, relations with the community were sometimes tense. In early 1834, scores of area residents signed a petition opposing the state legislature's bill for financial assistance to the college, calling such an endowment a waste of money and charging that Lafayette College was a sectarian institution whose leaders and supporters "wish it established for the purpose of disseminating a certain class of religious doctrines and tenets." At the same time, students venturing off campus were sometimes accosted by groups of boys or young men from town in encounters that were certainly laced with class tension.[21]

Such encounters would have seemed particularly unfortunate to proponents of manual labor schools, who regularly argued that the manual labor system would in fact mitigate social distinctions of wealth and status by making a classical education available to all. As a committee in the Pennsylvania state legislature put it in 1833, manual labor schools "tend to break down the distinctions between rich and poor which exist in society, inasmuch as they give an almost equal opportunity of education to the poor by labor, as is afforded to the rich by the possession of wealth." Similarly, a writer for the *American Magazine of Useful and Entertaining Knowledge* argued two years later that "the sons of common farmers, and of mechanics, should have an opportunity of receiving an academical or High-school education," and that manual labor schools—"where manual labor is required, and its avails would meet the expenses of instruction"—would serve such republican ends. A committee of the trustees of Allegheny College, in considering implementing the manual labor system at the college, acknowledged in 1833 the manual labor schools might be offensive to "some of our farmers and mechanics" who "may object that they do not wish to make lawyers, doctors, or preachers of their sons." But they urged that such offense would be mistaken, because a chief purpose of the manual labor system was to extend education to those who had previously been denied it, so as to foster a nation of educated farmers and craftsmen who could well serve the republic as citizens and office holders. "The farmer and mechanic should be learned," they wrote. "Learning is power: for the learned man has a greater share of influence than he would have without learning."[22]

In fact, proponents of the manual system argued that manual labor schools, in requiring manual labor of all their students and extending the advantages of education, would become exemplary scenes of class harmony. They noted that students accustomed by their upbringing to mental labor would join in the toil of field and workshop those more accustomed to manual labor. In doing so, they would grow to respect manual labor. Peter Gallaudet, for instance, argued that combining mental with manual labor would "raise bodily labor from that too degraded state, in which it is now viewed, (especially by youth,) and place it on a more respectable footing." At the same time, the sons of farmers and mechanics who paid for school with their labor would come to appreciate the merits of a classical education, and respect those who possessed one. Combining manual and mental labor, then, fostered a "*similarity of habits*" between the "learned and the laboring classes," as Theodore Weld argued in his report, producing a "familiarity of intercourse" and a "bond of union," and exciting a "feeling of mutual interest," among men who might otherwise view one another with disdain. The trustees of Lafayette College concurred on this point, arguing in their second annual report that the manual labor system would "operate in cementing the extremes of society together." "The sons of the indigent and of the wealthy meet together in the duties of the field, the garden, and the shop, and also in the labors of the study and the recitation rooms," they wrote. "There is a perfect equality. All labour and all study. They learn to esteem and love each other." In particular, Weld noted, laboring men would be less likely to feel contempt toward those training for mental occupations. "Let our students put on a working dress and spend three hours a day in agricultural or mechanical employment," he wrote, "and they would disarm the laboring man of his prejudices, and beckon him toward them. That discontent, jealousy, envy, disgust, and those heart burnings, which keep in a ferment the laboring classes in the vicinity of our higher seminaries, would give place to kindlier feelings." The manual labor system, then, would ameliorate class tension, enjoining manual workers and middle-class headworkers to "approach each other with looks of kindness, and form a compact, based upon republican equality, and the interchange of mutual offices of courtesy and kindness."[23]

But if an express purpose of the manual labor program was to foster class harmony, it also had the potential to worsen class antagonism. In 1839, George Junkin wrote of the suspicion that the "laboring public" held with regard to manual labor schools. "I am constrained to believe," he wrote, "that all classes of men who live by manual labor are hostile to its introduction into a College. It operates, even with them, to make the Institution unpopular." The reasons for this were several. Even as they celebrated the salutary effects of physical toil, proponents of manual labor schools clearly believed that it was sure progress to leave a manual trade for one of the professions. When the trustees of the Manual Labor Academy of Pennsylvania decided to list the "former occupation" in a table showing the productivity of the fifty-one students enrolled during the year ending in October 1831, for instance, the sense conveyed was that the farmers, carpenters, wagon maker, cordwainer, hatter, tin-worker, machinist, glass-cutter, and smith who were listed were clearly moving on to better things. At the same time, in putting students from all backgrounds to work as carpenters, printers, cabinetmakers, and stonecutters, manual labor schools undermined a notion deeply cherished by traditional craftsmen (and one that was increasingly under siege) that these were skilled trades that required years of training to be properly pursued and that were degraded when performed by unskilled workers. This complaint among craftsmen who worked in proximity to manual labor schools would only have been compounded when the schools sold their inferior goods in local markets, particularly when their proponents argued that schools should be given some kind of preference to compensate for the deficiencies in the workmen and make the goods more competitive. James Madison Porter, for instance, wrote to his state representative in December 1832, noting that the boxes and trunks that Lafayette students were in the business of manufacturing for sale in Philadelphia had to be shipped by canal. Porter implored that "it would be of no small importance to us to be permitted to use a boat on the canal to Philadelphia toll free, if the legislature would grant it to us in addition to pecuniary aid."[24]

Indeed, amidst their professions of class solidarity, proponents of manual labor schools expressed ideas that worked against the prevailing rhetoric of labor leaders. In arguing, for instance, that manual labor was—in the words of the first annual report of the trustees of Lafayette College—"a prophylactic remedy against the diseases incident to the sedentary life," proponents of manual labor schools implicitly argued that manual workers were not the only ones to suffer from the new productive arrangements that divided head from hand. If artisans and factory workers had complaints about the fatiguing and degrading effects of their excessive manual labor, care-worn proprietors and overseers too had complaints about the sickening effects of their excessive mental labor. Readers of Theodore Weld's report might have paused, for example, at the case of Barber Badger, who had worked as a printer before becoming editor of the *Christian Advocate and Journal, and Zion's Herald* and the *New-York Weekly Messenger.* Badger wrote in a letter to the Society for Promoting Manual Labor in Literary Institutions (published in Weld's report) that his health had deteriorated markedly after he began devoting himself full-time to editing. "My occupation was that of a printer," he wrote, "and while I *labored* at the business, my health was good." Even after he became an editor, he continued, his health remained intact as long as he gave some time over to manual labor. "But after I became the editor of 'Zion's Herald,' that paper having obtained an extensive circulation, and the committee of publication having provided for me a liberal salary, I gave my time exclusively to the duty of editing it." His health soon started to decline, "gradually, and almost imperceptibly," until "the disease finally terminated in a confirmed nervous head-ache." Finally, Badger had to give up his editorship because of ill health, the success of his publication and his own career taking its heavy toll. George Junkin, in an 1843 address, similarly pointed out that the mental labor of teaching and running an educational institution was true and taxing labor, despite popular opinion to the contrary. "No my friends, you mistake the case quite, if you suppose that the leaders of the educational corps, gain their rewards without labor, their victories without battle. May you not be unacquainted with their health-impairing toils? Are you certainly familiar with that spirit-exhausting study which is a weariness to the flesh? Are you quite certain, that they are gentlemen of leisure, who have two or three hours of light labor, and all the other twenty-one for sleep and pleasure?" Junkin two years later explicitly refuted the argument that professionals and others who did not work with their hands were non-producers, noting in his expressly conservative vein that "it will never do for these men to talk of a ten hour rule." "No! you cannot dispense with professional men," he wrote. "No! the educated men of your country are not non-producers: they are the most effective class of laborers in the production of wealth."[25]

In this more conservative tenor of the manual labor school movement, if "head" workers suffered as well from the excesses of their toil, then "hand" work—the province all along of artisans and machine tenders—was in fact beneficial to the worker. Benjamin Badger's familiar story of a man who had moved from a manual to a mental laborer, who had divorced the work of the head from that of the hand and suffered greatly as a consequence, did not end with his resignation. Mindful that his downward trajectory had begun when he left the printing trade, Badger purchased a small press and began devoting a portion of each day to working as a pressman. "The result has been entirely successful," he reported. "In less than a month from the time I commenced, I was enabled to perform a full days [sic] work with ease. I have continued the practice daily . . . and my health is perfectly restored." Badger's association of physical health and the toil of a trade was not uncommon. Beriah Green, who would soon become president of the Oneida Institute, wrote in 1832 (also in a letter published in Weld's report) that his poor health—brought on by intense study and the pressures of his ministry—had forced him to give up his books and the labor of "continuous, close thinking." Suffering under this adversity for some time, Green one day went into a workshop, placed an open book on a bench, and began working with a lathe until he became "warm with the effort." "I turned from the lathe to my book, and read, perhaps, *six or seven lines;* then again to the lathe; thence to my book. At length, under the immediate impulse of muscular excitement, I became able to read a minute, then, after a while, two minutes." By juxtaposing manual and mental labor in this way, Green inched his way back to health and back into his work as a minister.[26]

If leading proponents of manual labor schools typically gave priority to the health-saving benefit of the manual labor system, for students, saving money seemed to have a greater appeal. A study of letters written by students seeking admittance to Oberlin College, for instance, found that few prospective students spoke of the heath benefits of the manual labor system. Similarly, the handful of letters in the Lafayette College archive written by students in the 1830s contain discussions of the manual labor program, but not once is the health-saving benefit of labor mentioned as a reason for attending the college. In fact, when William Riddle wrote to his pastor back home in 1836, he almost mocked the notion that manual labor was important to good health. "Work or no work makes no difference," he wrote, "or if any, I would rather have no work for the sake of study. These two months and more I have had no manual exercise whatever, and I feel as well as amid my finest summer work." More willing to ascribe some value to manual labor was nineteen-year-old Alexander Ramsey, who wrote to a friend in 1834 describing the arrangements he had made to work as a carpenter at the college. He typically worked five hours each day, Ramsey wrote, adding that "my time thus far has been anything else than learned leisure or literary ease, having I believe worked harder with jack plane and saw at Lafayette college than ever I did in Jacob Colestock's carpenter shop." Indeed he admitted that the amount of physical work was "rather too severe upon the system," and that it caused "a lassitude destructive of mental nerve." Still, after a discussion of the cost of attending the school and the amount he could expect to earn, Ramsey praised the arrangement, noting that "few institutions hold out the same advantages in the way of labour, which to me is everything." H. M. Borden, who wrote to the college in 1835 as a prospective student, similarly focused on the possibility of working to pay his way through school. "You will greatly oblige a young man . . . whose means are very limited by giving me what information you can respecting the duties a student would have to perform, and also what expense I would be at after deducting what I would earn at the time used for labour," he wrote, saying nothing about a desire to preserve his health.[27]

This emphasis on the financial benefit of manual laborism is not surprising, perhaps, but it was almost uniformly anathema to proponents of the system. "The only motive . . . in entering such a school," one observer characteristically noted in 1835, "should not be economy; but the conviction, that it is the surest way to health, sobriety, and usefulness, should have a strong influence." William A. Alcott urged a similar point in 1839. "Against the idea of *saving money* to the parent, the school, the college, or the State, *as a leading idea*," he wrote in discussing the manual labor system, "we enter our most earnest protest." For Alcott, the principal aim of the manual labor system should be to educate the whole person—hand, head, and heart. "Let the grand point in all our schools be to develope harmoniously . . . the bodily functions, intellectual faculties, and moral powers," he wrote, "and if in doing this in the best manner, the avails of the labor of the student are of any value, he is fully entitled to them, to assist in defraying his expenses." Even a spokesperson for Lafayette, perhaps after having spoken with Borden, or Ramsey, or other like-minded students, was unequivocal on this question:

"Let us then, once for all, be distinctly understood," he wrote in 1835, "not *money-saving* but *health-saving* is our grand peculiar object."[28]

Given the apparent appeal of the money-saving possibilities of the manual labor system, why should its proponents have so strenuously emphasized the health-saving "desideratum"? Perhaps because it was in the argument about the diseases of a sedentary life and the healthful effects of manual labor that the conservative strain of the movement could give expression to a harmonious vision of class. If it was unhealthful to pull head and hand apart in the individual, as proponents of the manual labor system so ardently argued, then it was unhealthful as well to pull "head" and "hand" apart in society more generally. A petitioner for Lafayette College writing in 1833, probably James Madison Porter, suggested this social understanding when he wrote in a memorial to the Pennsylvania state legislature that "this divorce of learning from the pursuits of working men" that was characteristic of most colleges "is unnecessary and in a certain sense unnatural. It is unhappy," he continued, "in its tendency to produce disturbances in the ranks of society," disturbances that he credited to the social inequality attendant on the elevation of the "learned professions" over other pursuits.[29]

Theodore Dwight Weld was even more explicit in his 1833 report of the Society for Promoting Manual Labor in Literary Institutions. In a section of the report arguing for the "anti-republican" effects of prevailing forms of education, Weld wrote that "as knowledge is power, the sons of the rich, by enjoying advantages for the acquisition of this power vastly superior to others, may secure to themselves a monopoly of those honors and emoluments which are conferred upon the well educated." Thus, "society is divided into *castes,*" whereby "the laboring classes become hewers of wood and drawers of water for the educated." These two distinct groups, he continued, "stand wide asunder, no bond of companionship uniting them, no mutual sympathies incorporating them into one mass, no equality of privileges striking a common level for both." The "chasm" between the laboring classes and the educated was already "deep and broad," argued Weld, and if it were not "speedily bridged, by bringing education within the reach of the poor," then it would "widen into an impassable gulf," bringing down into it "our free institutions, our national character, our bright visions of the future, our glory and our joy." But earlier in his report, Weld evoked the very same imagery in discussing how the individual suffered under a system of education that divides mental labor from physical labor. "Such a system," he wrote, "sunders what God has joined together, and impeaches the wisdom which pronounced that union good. It destroys the symetry [sic] of human proportion, and makes man a monster." For Weld, the results of this disunion were as dire to the individual as the social disunion was to society as a whole. "It reverses the order of the constitution; commits outrage upon its principles; breaks up its reciprocities," he wrote. Weld then turned to a very clear image of a sort of internal hostility that, for readers of the day, could not help but evoke what were—by 1833—very public hostilities between "heads" and "hands" in the social realm: the cleavage of mental from manual labor, he wrote, "makes war alike upon physical health and intellectual energy, dividing man against himself; arming body and mind in mutual hostility, and prolonging until each falls a prey to the other, and both surrender to ruin." The "diseases of a literary life," then, were akin to the social ills of a class-divided society, in that both resulted from head and hand, or mind and body, being pulled too far apart.[30]

If "head" and "hand" worked by analogy to signify both distinct labor functions within the individual and distinct classes within society, then the healthful union of head and hand would have expressed a social vision as well as a personal vision. As has already been noted, Weld was careful to point out in his report that the manual labor system brought together manual labor and mental labor, hand and head, not only at the level of the individual, but at the level of society. The "learned and the laboring classes," he wrote, would come to feel a "bond of union" at manual labor schools. And as Weld made clear, if personal health depended on bringing head and hand together at the individual level, so too did the health of society depend on bringing head and hand together at the social level. Similarly, the petitioner for Lafayette College (probably James Madison Porter), in noting that the manual labor system at the college would "blend the knowledge of principles with practical skills," added that this union would breach not only a divide within the individual student, but a social divide as well. "Generally speaking," he wrote, "our artisans are not sufficiently scientific and our men of science are not skillful artisans. As things are, the mind of one conceives and the hand of another executes." Lafayette College, then, would help breach this social divide. Two years later, another spokesperson for Lafayette, probably George Junkin, evoked fully the social language of head and hand when he wrote that, at Lafayette, the union of head and hand would extend beyond the individual student to society more generally. "We wish to walk hand in hand, and side by side, and head to head, with the substantial farmers and mechanics of the country" he wrote. But even less overt expressions of social harmony carried the same sense. Thus a July Fourth speaker in 1833, also at Lafayette College, expressed a cooperative language of class when he applauded the college for its effort to "unite the learning of the closet with the labours of the field."[31]

Although they were much less likely to codify a clear sense of hierarchy in their visions of union, proponents of manual labor schools made clear that the learning of the closet would still guide the labor of the field, both individually and socially. The leaders of the Society for Promoting Manual Labor in Literary Institutions suggested this hierarchy in their instructions to Weld when they noted that the manual labor system would aid in "giving to the intellect an ascendancy over the body." In an address to Lafayette students in 1832, James Madison Porter spoke much more directly to the hierarchical relations of what he called the "age of mechanics" when he urged the students to consider the authority they would assume once their education was complete. By becoming "masters" of the scientific principles that stand behind the arts, Porter implored, they would "be enabled to aid and assist and direct the operations of the less instructed mechanics" of their communities. "How many of our mechanics, worthy and good citizens as they are," he asked, turning to a language quite familiar from the popular discourse on mechanization, "are mere machines, and know nothing of the principles which they are every day putting into practice." Thomas Grimké, in responding to a question from Weld as to whether the labor performed at manual labor schools would "have a tendency to establish common bonds of sympathy between the learned and laboring classes," agreed that "agricultural and mechanical employments" would "multiply the associations and sympathies between the best and the least educated classes of our country." But these associations, as they grew tighter in Grimké's view, would remain hierarchical, so that one result of the mutual sympathies in society would be that the best educated would gain "a greater influence" over the least educated, while the latter would enjoy some improvement primarily by "elevating their pursuits in the social scale."[32]

By the late 1830s, the manual labor school movement had begun to lose its momentum. Beriah Green, who was at the time president of the Oneida Institute, wrote in a letter to Theodore Weld in late 1838 that the institute "has in a great measure lost its hold upon our fickle countrymen." Several factors contributed to the movement's decline. The close association between some prominent manual labor schools and radical abolitionism cast the movement in an unfavorable light to some people. The Oneida Institute and Oberlin College, for instance, were known to be centers of abolitionist activity, and both schools admitted black students. When Theodore Weld, who had been the most public advocate of the manual labor program, left his post as the agent of the Society for Promoting Manual Labor in Literary Institutions in early 1833, he turned with even more avidity to abolitionism: at Lane Seminary he was at the center of a series of debates on colonization and Garrisonian abolitionism that created a schism among students and faculty and resulted in a number of students leaving the school, and he went on to become one of the most prominent abolitionist lecturers and writers of the 1830s. The association between manual laborism and radical abolitionism should not be too tightly drawn, however. In the 1820s, a number of future trustees of the Manual Labor Academy of Pennsylvania and future officers of the Society for Promoting Manual Labor in Literary Institutions publicly supported colonization over what one called "immediate and universal emancipation." Even after the rise of radical abolitionism in the early 1830s, leaders of the manual labor school movement parted ways on the question of colonization versus abolitionism. William Jay, who had been a vice president of the Society for Promoting Manual Labor in Literary Institutions, wrote favorably of radical abolitionism in 1835 while taking to task another former vice president, Theodore Frelinghuysen, for having reportedly accused abolitionists of "*seeking to destroy* our happy union." George Junkin was a supporter of colonization through the 1850s and a public critic of radical abolitionism, arguing in a pamphlet published in 1843 (titled *The Integrity of Our National Union vs. Abolitionism*) that the abolitionist movement was "treasonable . . . against the Constitution of the United States," and suggesting that American abolitionists were conspiring with the British government to "divide and destroy the republic."[33]

Whatever difficulties some manual labor schools may have had as a result of their association with abolitionism, they were far outweighed by persistent financial problems. Even before the onset of the economic depression in 1837, manual labor schools struggled with the perception that the labor of students would provide virtually all that was necessary to feed, house, and furnish students, so that the financial support of benefactors or the state was unnecessary. After the onset of the depression, it was even more difficult for relatively new, financially struggling schools to survive. In an 1843 speech, for instance, Beriah Green—still president of the Oneida Institute—accounted for the disappointments suffered by his school in part by noting the unfavorable economic climate. "Some of our debtors and many of our patrons, the Times have pinched," he told his audience, "and what we expected from their hands may never reach us." Financial pressures faced by manual labor schools raised the fear among some observers that such schools would come to focus on the pecuniary benefit of their programs at the expense of their health benefits. A writer for the *American Annals of Education* (probably its editor, William A. Alcott) expressed such a fear late in 1838. In describing a manual labor school in Holliston, Massachusetts, the writer noted that some of the school's students had found employment as shoemakers. "We do not know whether there is opportunity for any other manual labor in connection with the seminary except shoe-making," he wrote, "but we hope there is. For though we have no doubt that energetic young men may pay their way by shoe-making, yet we do not believe it is safe for them to do so." Insisting that the shoe bench was no substitute for exercise in the open air, the writer argued that, under the program in Holliston, "suffering must follow, sooner or later." The following month's issue, in discussing a more ideal manual labor school, returned to the danger of placing financial considerations above all others. "We are pained—we are more than pained, we are disgusted—at the idea of having pupils ruin their health in obtain[ing] a *cheap education.*"[34]

Fears such as these would only have been fueled by a reading of Delazon Smith's sensational pamphlet *A History of Oberlin, or New Lights of the West* (also titled *Oberlin Unmasked*), published in 1837. Smith, who had been a student at Oberlin College (and had, according to a later report, been "excommunicated from the Oberlin Church for infidelity"), described the abuse of the manual labor system at Oberlin as among the lesser scandals in a school that seemed to offer scandal at every turn. According to Smith, the manual labor program at Oberlin served more the financial interests of the institution than the health interests of the students. The school's self-promotion, he wrote, lured students with promises that a portion of their time at Oberlin would be spent in manual labor, labor that would both reward students financially and provide them with useful knowledge. On arrival, however, they found fields ill-suited for farming, few opportunities for other forms of labor, and very little care as to whether they blended labor with study at all. The work that was available, Smith noted, was hardly suited to promoting health. "Nearly all the labor since this Institution was first established, has been chopping, logging and burning brush; and this too, a great portion of the year, *ankle deep in mud and water!*" he wrote. "How beneficial *such* labor must be to a Student, and how pleasurable the transition from log-heaps and burning brush to books, is better imagined than described." The manual labor program at Oberlin, concluded Smith, was a *"wolf in sheep's clothing,"* designed to provide the college with relatively inexpensive labor to clear the land and build the institution, with little regard for the health consequences to the students.[35]

It is difficult to say whether Smith's pamphlet had any influence on public sentiment toward Oberlin College or toward the manual labor program more generally. A report on Oberlin's history published in 1860, however, did express surprise that "leading ministers of the gospel" in the Oberlin area had believed Smith's account. In any case, the manual labor school movement had already entered a decline by the time Smith wrote. Indeed, few of the scores of manual labor schools founded during the flurry of activity in the late 1820s and early 1830s appear to have survived the 1840s. One writer in 1851, in pausing at the half-century point to note the changes of the last fifty years, wrote of manual labor schools that "they have not been very prosperous" and "most of them have been abandoned." The Oneida Institute, for instance, closed its doors for good in 1843. Lafayette College survived as an institution, but the manual labor system did not. Despite his commitment to the school's manual labor program, Junkin realized that it was a chief source of the financial hardship that continued to plague Lafayette. The school's agricultural and mechanical departments decreased the amount of money collected from students, and they increased operating costs, since the school had to raise the money necessary to supply the land, tools, and materials for laboring students to work with. As enrollment rose in the years immediately after the school's move to its new site, Junkin found it increasingly difficult to supply students with work, and by 1836, he had decided to allow them to choose whether they would participate in the manual labor program. In a circular printed late that year pleading for funds for the school, Junkin made clear how dire the circumstances were, and how he had already sunk thousands of dollars of his own money into the school. This would be his "*last appeal,*" he wrote, adding that, should he fail, the college would be "a vacant house" within the year. It is unclear if Junkin raised the $2,000 he sought, but the college did not close. Circumstances worsened, however. Enrollment declined in 1837, due in part to the financial panic but also to Junkin's controversial position in a continuing theological dispute. Those students who did enroll during the years immediately after 1837 were, in some cases, unable to pay their expenses. In 1838, the school acquired a printing press and began publishing a weekly newspaper, the *Educator,* in both English and German language editions, but this effort to renew the manual labor program was short-lived. A typhoid outbreak on campus in the spring of 1839 that sickened most of the students only added to the sense of crisis. When the trustees published their annual report later that year, the first since 1836, they opened with a letter from Junkin in which he concluded that the manual labor system should simply be abandoned. "The labor never has been worth what it cost me," Junkin wrote, "nor am I of opinion that it is practicable to make it so on a large scale." The trustees concurred, and the manual labor program at Lafayette closed for good. Junkin remained president for another year, resigning in December 1840 to become president of Miami University in Ohio. [36]

Proponents of the manual labor school movement addressed what they believed to be a mounting labor crisis. "The time has come when sedentary invalids of all professions are rising up by hundreds—nay, by thousands," wrote one proponent in 1835, "and demanding in a voice which cannot fail to be heard, and which must be obeyed, that systematic and regular manual labor be incorporated into the very frame work of our new institutions." Mental labor and manual labor had grown too distant from each other, they urged, and the consequences would be dire. While their express aim was to preserve the health of those who labored with their heads, the language used by proponents of the movement worked as well to preserve the social relations of mechanized production. In this way, the labor problem they addressed proved to be much larger than simply preventing the ill effects of mental overexertion. Although it appears to have done little to win sustained support for the short-lived movement, or to convince students that saving health was more important than saving money, proponents of the system gave overwhelming priority to the argument for the healthful effects of manual labor. But if the argument was not productive of its express end, it may have been productive of other ends. By repeating over and over again the idea that students and others suffered from the excess of their mental toil, manual laborites suggested—in a much broader context—that wage-workers were not the only ones to be adversely affected by recent changes in the workplace. Whatever grievances they may have had in being reduced to hands, then, were matched by their employers, who were being elevated to pure heads. At the same time, by repeating over and over the idea that health depended on joining mental labor with manual labor, proponents of the system offered a conception of the fruitful union of head and hand that helped—also in a much broader context—to codify and naturalize a harmonious conception of class. In spite of the general failure of the manual labor program, advocates remained hopeful that some version of the system would ultimately prevail. "I do not know how soon a union between manual labor and mental exercise will be effected," wrote William A. Alcott in 1857, long after the movement had ended. "But of one thing I am well assured," he continued in a subtle but sure language of class, "which is, that such a union must one day be secured as the only method of keeping together what God originally joined, and has never divorced—the 'sound mind' and the 'sound body.' "[37]

CHAPTER 4

Mind and Body

Popular Physiology and the Health of a Nation

The manual labor school movement was an early and important venue for a much broader discussion of health and human physiology that extended through the decades before 1860. Like proponents of manual labor schools, writers and lecturers on the more general subjects of health and physiology implored American men and women to improve their bodies as well as their minds. According to these health reformers, whose ranks included physicians, clergymen, and educators, the ill use people made of their bodies—in their dietary habits, their work practices, and their manner of dress, to name a few—was injurious to health and threatened the progress of the age. As has already been suggested, many of these antebellum writers and lecturers particularly feared an impending health crisis for the nation, one that derived in large part from changes in work that seemed to have more and more Americans performing mental rather than manual labor. They argued that a healthful state, which was necessary not only for personal happiness but for the important work of serving God and securing the nation, depended upon a balance among mental, moral, and bodily functions, upon an equilibrium of head, heart, and hand. As one writer noted in an article titled "Physical Development in America" that appeared in *Scientific American* in 1859, "Pure health in a normal man is more the natural balance of thought, feeling, and bodily vigor than the mere absence of disease." But for mid-century Americans, he continued, "this balance has been somewhat impaired," with "physical development" standing in poor stead in comparison to the "brain force and nervous skill" upon which, he argued, the new nation had been built. Articulating a need for balance in an age that seemed to give priority of place to mental education, writers and lecturers pointed up what they believed, in the words of one writer in 1832, to be "the necessity of giving more attention to the health and growth of the body, and less to the cultivation of the mind."[1]

Antebellum health reformers commonly used the phrase "physical education" to describe what they wished to promote. At a time when education practices were coming under close scrutiny and calls for education reform filled the pages of popular periodicals, the notion that the education or training of the body should be given as much attention as the education of the mind made sense to many people. Thus a contributor to the *American Monthly Magazine* found in 1829 that "among the favorite doctrines of the day, none has exerted so general an influence or gained so general and deserved a reputation, as that of Physical Education." For Americans living in the first half of the nineteenth century, physical education meant more than simply exercise. In 1835, William A. Alcott, one of the leading health reformers of the antebellum period, specified the "numerous topics which physical education embraces" to include questions and prescriptions concerning exercise, cleanliness, air, ventilation, dress, food, drink, amusements, and sleep. Arguing that ignorance of right practice regarding these areas of daily life was resulting in a decline in physical health among the American people, health activists such as Alcott stressed that every man, woman, and child should learn the physiological laws governing the human body. These laws would, in turn, dictate rules for how, when, and what to eat; how and when to sleep; how to dress; whether coffee was ever permissible; and so on for a host of other areas of activity. Health reformers thus found that the road to health required that each individual closely monitor and control his or her behavior. Only by adhering to what Alcott later called the "laws of health" could personal health, and the health of the nation, be achieved.[2]

While these discussions may seem rather remote from the popular discourse on mechanization, historians in recent years have convincingly argued that many of the leading antebellum popular physiologists and health reformers were responding in various ways to the social tensions accompanying the market and manufacturing transformations of the period. Stephen Nissenbaum has suggested that the reform agenda of Sylvester Graham, who was even better known than Alcott, offered antebellum Americans a way to stabilize an increasingly unstable world—rendered so by the encroachments of market capitalism—by asserting control over their bodies. In her study of health reform in nineteenth-century Boston, Martha Verbrugge argues that antebellum health reformers appealed especially to a nascent middle class anxious to create order out of a world in which the home, the workplace, and the city were all in transition. The reformer's call for self-governance, she argues, "made particular sense to a middle-class audience, who hoped to check the turmoil of the outside world by regulating the internal one." Joan Burbick has offered a sustained analysis of how antebellum ideas about the body spoke as well to middle-class concerns about social order and the well-being of the nation. According to Burbick, the "language of health" used by nineteenth-century physicians and health reformers helped to defuse the myriad social tensions of nascent industrial capitalism. The human body, she argues, became something of a neutral ground on which social conflict and contestation could be worked out in terms that were universal and grounded in nature. "Prescriptions about health often became a way to critique the society at large," writes Burbick, "and to offer specific remedies that on the surface appeared less threatening to the stability of the nation since they were veiled in the language of the flesh."[3]

Popular physiology writers and lecturers entered into the popular discourse on mechanization quite explicitly in two ways. First, many argued that the fast pace of mechanized society, along with the conditions of labor that mechanization helped put into place, threatened the physical health of American men and women. In exploring this notion, some writers focused on the vulnerability to disease among both craftsmen and factory workers, resulting from their exposure to harmful substances, long hours in awkward positions, and insufficient supply of fresh air. Many noted as well that those who no longer toiled with their bodies or hands—members of the rising class of headworkers who had been released from manual labor—also suffered disease as a result of mechanization. Like proponents of manual labor schools, they pointed out that the mental demands and concomitant lack of physical exertion that characterized nonmanual occupations resulted in many cases in weakened constitutions and an array of diseases. According to this view, manual workers were not the only ones to suffer as a result of head and hand dividing in the workplace. Antebellum writers on health and human physiology also entered into the popular discourse on mechanization in their description of the human body as a machine that needed to be properly tended. In their books, articles, and lectures, health reformers routinely turned to the centuries-old metaphor of the body as a marvelously designed machine. According to this view, the study of physiology, as part of a proper physical education, provided the laws under which the body/machine should be placed in order to be used safely and effectively.[4]

As they spoke and wrote of the human body in these terms, health reformers and popular physiologists offered a conception of industrial society that both minimized the potential for class conflict and confirmed the authority of the emerging middle class. In calling the body a machine, popular physiology writers and lecturers helped to naturalize the work of machine-tending, since all humans bodies were, by design, like machines that required operatives to work well. They also undermined claims that the work of machine-tending was particularly distinctive or necessarily degrading, both by noting that all people are tenders of their own bodily machines and by noting the extent to which the proper tending of the body/machine—based as it was in inviolable physiological laws that could be studied and understood—was mental rather than manual labor, the work of the head rather than the work of the hand. If the body was a machine, and the mind its tender, then the former needed always to be under the guidance of the latter. To contravene this order was to threaten not only the health of the individual, but the health of the nation. In the broader popular discourse on mechanization, the essential prescription here was familiar and clear: the mind should govern the body, just as the human should govern the machine, just as the head should govern the hand. Here was another language of class.

By the early 1830s, especially in New England, American men and women had created a number of venues for discussing and disseminating ideas about human physiology. A leading venue was the popular physiology textbook. As Charles Rosenberg has noted, the year 1834 saw the publication of three popular physiology textbooks—William A. Alcott's *The House I Live In* (1834), George Hayward's *Outlines of Human Physiology* (1834), and Jerome V. C. Smith's *The Class-Book of Anatomy, Designed for Schools* (1834)—which established the convention of combining lessons in anatomy and physiology with discussions of hygiene, or rules for healthful living. Aimed at students and nonspecialist readers, these books both described the various anatomical structures and physiological functions of the body and prescribed natural laws said to govern everything from the best time of day for bathing, to the kind of bread one should eat, to the optimal position for sleeping. These textbooks arrived just as a growing chorus of writers called for the introduction of physiology and hygiene into school curricula. "When Anatomy, Physiology, and Hygiene shall assume an importance at least equal to Arithmetic, Mensuration and Surveying in our schools," wrote one observer in 1835, "then . . . shall we properly value the education of the physiological functions. Then may we expect to see the efforts of the head, the heart and the hands united in the amelioration of the condition of man." A number of writers and lecturers also argued that physiological knowledge should be used and disseminated in the home as well as the classroom. "Parents—and mothers in particular, on whom so much of our physical, intellectual, and moral well-being depend," wrote

William A. Alcott in 1833, "must have a knowledge of physiology. Of the redemption of man's physical nature without this knowledge, there is very little hope." Twenty-five years later, another popular physiology writer echoed this sentiment when she urged that "every family should possess one or more works on physiology." Indeed, Alcott, Hayward, and Smith produced numerous variant editions of their books over the next twenty years, perhaps in response to the many competing texts published through the 1840s and 1850s.[5]

The scores of popular textbooks on human physiology published in the United States between 1830 and 1860 varied in scope and depth. At one end of the spectrum were technical, highly detailed books like Robley Dunglinson's two-volume *Human Physiology* (1832), a book which, while written primarily for medical students, was nevertheless reviewed and recommended in nonspecialist periodicals. In the middle were the many volumes written for academies, common schools, families, and the general reader, books like Edward Jarvis's *Primary Physiology, for Schools* (1848), Worthington Hooker's *First Book in Physiology* (1855), and several books written by Calvin Cutter. At the other end were books like Jane Taylor's *Wouldst Know Thyself, or the Outlines of Human Physiology* (1858), a brief compendium of twenty-four lessons—in the form of questions and answers—designed for "the youth of both sexes." Taking the form of the cheap, yellow-paper, bound newsstand books that had become popular earlier in the decade, Taylor's book retailed for just ten cents, its cover imploring would-be readers to "Take It Home," promising that "This is a Most Valuable Book for Children."[6]

In addition to textbooks on physiology, antebellum physicians and health reformers founded a handful of periodicals and newspapers aimed at promoting the health of the American people. In 1835, William A. Alcott launched a monthly periodical called the *Moral Reformer, and Teacher on the Human Construction,* devoted to the sort of physiology-based reform that Alcott advocated in his lectures and other publications. Each month, readers of the *Moral Reformer* could find illustrated anatomical descriptions, prescriptive articles with titles like "Sleeping with Open Windows," "Confessions of a Tobacco Chewer," and "Is Tea Poisonous?" and brief overviews of reform activities and organizations around the country. Other antebellum health and physiology journals included the *Journal of Health,* published in Philadelphia beginning in 1829, and the *Graham Journal of Health and Longevity,* which was published between 1837 and 1839. In addition, some journals devoted to related topics—journals like the *American Annals of Education* (which William A. Alcott edited for a period beginning in 1837)—gave considerable attention to the many topics that fell under the rubric of physical education, including diet, posture, and exercise.

At the same time, lecturers took up physiology as a more frequent topic in lyceums, mechanics' institutes, and other popular venues. Reynell Coates, a Philadelphia physician and man of letters, delivered courses of lectures on physiology to nonspecialist audiences in Philadelphia and a number of other cities on the eastern seaboard beginning in the late 1830s. Mary Gove Nichols, who would later become a leading advocate of the so-called "water cure," launched her career as a lecturer on female anatomy and physiology in Massachusetts in 1838. Lectures she delivered on a variety of subjects, including diet, the "solitary vice" of masturbation, and the danger of wearing tightly laced clothes, drew thousands. In the years after the publication of *The House I Live In* in 1834, William Alcott lectured frequently on the subject of physiology and health reform, finally publishing his lectures in 1853 under the title *Lectures on Life and Health; Or, the Laws and Means of Physical Culture* (1853).[7]

Perhaps the most popular antebellum public speaker on physiology and hygiene was Sylvester Graham. Born in Connecticut in 1794, Graham trained as a minister before launching a career as a temperance lecturer. In early 1831, Graham began lecturing more broadly on health and human physiology, and by the middle of the decade his fame as a health reformer was secure. As he toured the States exhorting his audiences on the importance of coarse bread, a vegetarian diet, sexual moderation, and temperance in all things, Graham met with some ridicule among those doubtful of his rules for right living. Samuel Kettel devoted two chapters of his popular *Yankee Notions* (1838) to deriding Graham, one in the form of a poem titled "Death and Doctor Sawdust," the other a satirical sketch titled "The Science of Starvation." In the latter piece, a writer to the editor of the *Sawdust Journal*—and a follower of Dr. Sawdust—excitedly reports on a lecture on water porridge by "Brother Sappy," which included a "flaming description" of carrots. "He means next week to take up the question on the moral qualities of baked beans," reports the writer, whose name is Simon Scarecrow. Displeasure with Graham did not always take such light form, however. In June 1834, for instance, while Graham was lecturing in Portland, Maine, an angry mob formed to greet the visiting reformer. But in spite of his detractors, Graham enjoyed widespread popularity. A series of lectures delivered by Graham in Boston in the winters of 1835–36 and 1836–37 spurred a group of Boston area men and women to form the American Physiological Society in 1837. The purpose of the society—which had William A. Alcott as its first president and reached a membership of close to five hundred by 1839—was to diffuse physiological knowledge and the laws of health among its members and throughout society as a whole, thereby promoting health and longevity.

While not expressly Grahamite in its objectives, the society nevertheless professed admiration for Graham in its publications. The female members of the society, who often met separately to discuss issues of particular interest to them, collected a small sum of money in the spring of 1837 to be given to Sylvester Graham as a token of admiration.[8]

By the middle of the 1830s, then, health and human physiology had become popular subjects in American print and popular culture. "Indeed," one lecturer before the American Physiological Society observed in 1838, "a person can hardly enter a stagecoach, or steamboat, or railroad car, or sit down at the dining table of our hotels, without hearing some sage remarks concerning diet, the relative qualities of different kinds of food, and of different methods of living." Writers and lecturers who sought to spread physiological knowledge among the general public offered several arguments to persuade their readers of the importance of their subject. Some argued simply that physiology was a branch of knowledge that should not be overlooked by those seeking to claim a broad education. As Calvin Cutter put it in 1846, "Education, to be complete, must be not only moral and intellectual, but physical." Others urged that contemplating the body's many intricate and integrated functions would lead inexorably to contemplating its Divine Creator. George Hayward, for instance, wrote that he hoped to acquaint the young with human physiology because he was confident that "they could not fail to see in the structure and functions of their own bodies, the clearest evidence of wonderful contrivance and beneficent wisdom." Similarly, William A. Alcott wrote in the preface to The House I Live In (1834) that "no branch of natural science is more apt to lead us to look 'through Nature up to Nature's God,' than physiology." Other popular writers on physiology argued that widespread knowledge of physiological principles would spell the end of medical "quackery," which they believed threatened not only the health of credulous patients, but public confidence in medical practitioners in general. "Is it at all to be wondered at," wrote the author of a physiology textbook in 1856, "that every kind of medical imposture prospers in communities where almost every one believes that a man has one rib less than a woman?" Knowledge of physiology among the public, they urged, would ensure that patients seek the care of properly trained physicians. As Reynell Coates put it in 1839, "Who that has seen, portrayed in simple language, the immense complexity of that machine which justly claims the title of the master-piece of nature, would dare to tamper with its slender cords and delicate springs, or trust it in the hands of bold pretenders?"[9]

But by far the most common reason given for studying physiology and hygiene was that the health of the American people was declining, and for many, precipitously. Among writers and lecturers urging the study of physiology and attention to hygiene, the prevailing sense was that Americans were facing a health crisis that had moral, social, and political implications. More and more, it seemed, American men and women were suffering from debilitating chronic diseases that led them to the invalid's bed and an early grave. Physical health, they urged, was crucial not only to individual happiness, but to the survival of the republic. Illness bred moral weakness, and it tapped the energies necessary for vigorous citizenship and the preservation of a hearty American race. As a writer for *Graham's Magazine* (a Philadelphia periodical that had nothing to do with Sylvester Graham) put it in 1848 in a favorable review of Edward Jarvis's *Practical Physiology* (1847), "The physical character of a nation moulds its intellectual nature, and shapes its destinies." Given the apparent decline in the health of what the *Graham's* writer called the "over-fed, over-worked, and over-anxious people of the United States," the new nation seemed to be heading for a crisis.[10]

As has already been suggested, many ascribed this decline in health to two features of early nineteenth-century American life: increased mental activity and an accompanying decrease in physical exertion. Many writers and lecturers argued that the pace of modern living was faster, and the days full of more mental stimulation, than at any other time in history. Not only were cities growing crowded, but news traveled quickly, it was easy to get from place to place, and markets were awash in inexpensive goods. What is more, children were pressed into study and intellectual achievement at an earlier age, so that time once spent in sporting about was now given over to the confines of the classroom. As some pointed out, modern machinery, such as the steamboat, the steam locomotive, the telegraph, and the steam press, made possible the fast pace and rush of information that characterized modern society. And while many antebellum Americans saw the modern instruments for diffusing knowledge—the common schools, periodical press, lyceums, mechanics' institutes, and so forth—to be harbingers of a peaceful and prosperous future, others found them to be causes of mental overstimulation, which could lead to disease and national decline.

Amariah Brigham, for instance, in his *Remarks on the Influence of Mental Cultivation upon Health* (1832), wrote that "it is fearful to contemplate the excited state of mind which every where prevails throughout this republic, and the vast amount of *machinery* . . . which is in operation, to increase and perpetuate it." Among this "machinery," Brigham included his city's nine churches, two lyceums, seven political newspapers, five religious newspapers, and handful of periodicals. Mindful of the "common and just observation" that the republic's survival depended on the intelligence of the people, Brigham nevertheless worried that too much mental stimulation among the people might be as harmful to the nation as too little. "There may be other causes besides ignorance and vice," he wrote, "slowly and silently operating upon the physical man, which will *as assuredly lead to the ruin of the country.*" In the same way, a writer for the *North American Review* five years later noted the pathology facing modern Americans. "The very freedom of our institutions," he wrote, "by creating universal strife, and increasing the mental activity of all classes, causes much insanity." Like Brigham, this writer ascribed the danger in part to the popular press. "Our thousands of newspapers," he continued, "circulating in all parts of the Union, and their exciting articles read by all classes, create and perpetuate mental agitation." Charles Caldwell, in a lecture in Lexington, Kentucky in 1833, similarly characterized the age as marked by a "deep and extensive mental commotion," one that took its toll on the health of the American people. For Caldwell, it was the political and religious freedom enjoyed by Americans that occasioned so much mental excitement. "The fervor and commotion of electioneering intrigue has no respite," he wrote of party politics; of modern religious practices, he noted the "wild and convulsive emotion" produced by evangelical preachers. In addition, Caldwell argued that the pursuit of wealth was a source of "deep disquietude" among the American people, especially those engaged in risky business ventures. "Dealers and speculators," he wrote, "besides being constantly disquieted while awake, are tossed between sudden wealth and ruin in their dreams. They are equally distracted by the uncertainty and the unexpected occurrence of events." For Caldwell, the political, religious, and business practices peculiar to early nineteenth-century America, by stimulating the mind to excess, produced insanity and a host of other ills.[11]

The decline in physical exertion and concomitant elevation of mental activity among so many Americans, and all the debilitating consequences of both, were seen by some as hallmarks of an advanced—even modern—society. Edward Hitchcock, for instance, wrote in *Dyspepsy Forestalled and Resisted* (1830) that "nervous maladies belong to an advanced, and more especially, to a luxurious state of society." Charles Caldwell noted in 1833 that just as the invention of gunpowder had brought the strong and the weak into parity on the battlefield, so improvements in mechanics had diminished the necessity for physical exertion in peacetime pursuits. "Hence," he continued, "as respects the general business of life, the moderns have much less necessity for personal strength, than the ancients had." According to Caldwell, once mind supplanted body as the source of power and influence, the pursuit of physical development diminished markedly. "Physical education, the

chief source of superior strength of person, has been greatly neglected, especially by the higher orders of society," he noted, adding that such had been
the case for the last "two or three centuries."[12]

Others attributed the rise in dyspepsia and related ills to even more contemporary developments. Amariah Brigham, for instance, credited the mental overstimulation of modern living in large part to the relatively recent explosion of popular newspapers and periodicals and the equally recent rise of
lyceums. Reynell Coates, in answering the question "why has dyspepsia become
so much more general of late years than it formerly was?" noted in 1838
that "the habits of the greater portion of the community have been totally
changed since the days of our grandfathers." According to Coates, the
modern practice of eating too fast was surely to blame for much ill health,
but other causes were equally accountable. The man of several generations
before, he argued, was healthier because he was more likely to exercise in the
open air. "Cities were small," Coates wrote by way of explanation, "the manufacturing population did not exist, and the merchant did not disdain to assist
in packing his own goods; for the division of labour was not then carried, as
now, to a high degree of perfection." Another writer, in an essay appearing in
the *Southern Review* in 1829, similarly argued that "only of late" had the
sedentary habits and luxurious tastes that were the source of dyspepsia affected
"the whole mass of society," scattering "the seeds of this pestilence" throughout the country. "We are less exposed to the open air, take less exercise, are
more intellectual in our pursuits, and fare more sumptuously every day than
formerly," he wrote, "when there were few carriages, few books, plain food
and little wine. Our new fashions have sapped our strength, made us effeminate, indolent, and luxurious in all things. . . . Is it any wonder we have lost
our health?" An essay in the *Journal of Health* published the following year
insisted that the physical debility faced by so many Americans was a distinctly
modern phenomenon, one that resulted especially from the reorganization of
work. "Though, doubtless rum, tobacco, tea, and other poisons of modern
invention, have had their part in weakening the stamina of the human constitution," the author wrote, "yet we must attribute much of the present inferiority of size, strength, and vigour, to the disuse of those active exercises to
which mankind in former ages were obliged to devote so large a portion of
their time." Modern man had, according to this writer, substituted in place
of productive physical exertion "diversions of a sedentary kind, which not
only throw the body in a state of muscular inactivity, but require almost as
intense an application of the mind as in study or business."[13]

Catharine Beecher argued a similar point in her *Letters to the People on
Health and Happiness,* published in 1855. "It is the universally-acknowledged

fact," she wrote, "that the present generation of men and women are inferior in health and in powers of endurance to their immediate ancestors." According to Beecher, the decline in health and vitality among the American people could be ascribed in large part to recent changes in work practices. "The labor appointed to man in cultivating the earth, in preparing its fruits, and in many mechanical pursuits," she averred, "will be found to be that which exercises all the muscles of the body appropriately and healthfully." So too with domestic labor for women. But, she continued, "every man who can do so, avoids these healthful pursuits as less honorable, and seeks in preference those that shut him up in study, office, or store, to overwork his brain and leave his muscular system to run down for want of vigorous exercise and fresh air." In the same way, more and more women hired domestic servants to perform the labor in the home, devoting their time instead to "sewing, reading, and other inactive pursuits." For Beecher, the results of separating bodily toil from mental toil were written on the weakened frames and degraded minds of American men and women. "By this method of dividing the labor of life," she wrote, "one portion of the world weaken their muscular system, either by entire inaction of both brain and muscle, or by the excess of brainwork and the neglect of muscular exercise. Another large portion," she continued, "having all the work that demands physical exercise turned off upon them, overwork their bodies and neglect their brains."[14]

Some observers recognized that the imbalance between mental and physical activity described by Beecher and others—as overstated as it was, given that so few men and women actually left the work of the hand behind—could be ascribed at least in part to the development of labor-saving machinery. Amariah Brigham, in deploring the extent to which modern men and women had forgotten the importance of "physical education," wrote in 1832 that this forgetfulness had "no doubt, been produced by modern discoveries, inventions and improvements in the mechanic arts, which have rendered the employment of the physical strength of man less necessary than it was in past ages, and produced a general conviction that 'knowledge *alone* is power.' " Six years later, Reynell Coates argued the same point in discussing the changing work habits of women. Inviting his readers to remember the time when many women spun their own thread and sewed their own clothing, Coates urged them to consider how much had changed in the age of labor-saving devices. "Now, the progress of machinery has banished the wheel not only from the chamber of the metropolitan lady," he wrote, "but even from the garret of the farmer's wife!" The results of such "changes in domestic habits," continued Coates, were all too predictable: "Dyspepsia has increased to an astonishing extent among the women of agricultural districts."[15]

For Coates, Beecher, and others, the virtual disaggregation of head from hand, of mind from body, was reason for alarm and a potential threat to the republic. "The national health is becoming deteriorated," noted a writer appearing in *Graham's Magazine* in 1858, "the result of which must be that the national vigor will be lessened, and the national prosperity seriously affected." A number of writers insisted that men who cultivated their minds without at the same time cultivating their bodies were in a real sense not whole men. A writer appearing in the *Supplement to the Connecticut Courant* in 1829, for instance, argued that "the highest refinement of the mind, without improvement of the body, can never present any thing more than half a human being." Three years earlier, a writer for the *New-Harmony Gazette* had similarly argued that an education that cultivated the mind but not the body (or the body but not the mind) was "but a partial, imperfect, one-sided education, calculated to form only a fraction of a human being." That same year, a writer for the *American Journal of Education* made the same point using the familiar language of head, heart, and hand as the necessary components of the whole individual. "What would an individual be worth to himself or others whose mind, whose disposition, or whose corporeal system—or any two of these only, were educated? His head might be furnished, and his heart well disposed, but he would still need a hand to execute." The physically weakened mental laborer who suffered from the debilitating effects of dyspepsia or some similar complaint was but a partial man, no more suited to the challenges of republican citizenship than the mentally degraded manual laborer who was "content to grow up a body,—nothing but a body" (in the words of a writer in the *New-Yorker* in 1841) and who was ruled by his passions and easily swayed by demagogues.[16]

Changes in domestic labor for women held equally dire consequences for the future of the nation. Writing in 1855, Catharine Beecher averred that "if all the female members of a family divided all the labors of the cook, the nurse, the laundress, and the seamstress . . . it would exercise every muscle in the body, and at the same time interest and exercise the mind." But no such division was made, she wrote, with the consequence that "one portion of the women have all the exercise of the *nerves of motion,* and another have all the *brain-work,* while they thus grow up deficient and deformed, either intellectually or physically, or both." Thus, she continued, "American women every year become more and more nervous, sickly, and miserable, while they are bringing into existence a feeble, delicate, or deformed offspring." Two years later, a physician in New York, Russell Trall, made a similar observation about the deformities of some American women—those who had been freed from physical labor—and about the dim prospects for their offspring. "No observing physiologist can promenade Broadway," he wrote in reference to the scene where middle-class and elite men and women strolled to display their respectability, "without noticing the artificial *deformity* of most of the females he passes." Where they should have been round and plump, he noted, these women were "caved in," a sure sign of feebleness and a tendency to disease. "If these unfortunate victims of disease, ignorance, folly, or fashion would be restored to renewed vigor of constitution, with a promise of . . . the capacity to propagate a healthy and virtuous, instead of a sickly and vicious race," Trall continued, "they must . . . recover symmetry and beauty of form and figure."[17]

It was in the face of such present and future perils that health activists called for increased attention to physical education. For Russell Trall and many others, the best means of restoring the health of the public—thereby ensuring the continued progress of the age—was exercise. But most health reformers of the day would have agreed that what American men and women needed more than anything else was information about human physiology. For reformers like Alcott and Graham, the study of human physiology was the study of the natural laws governing the functions of the human body. These laws in turn prescribed the rules for healthful living. As a speaker before the American Physiological Society noted in 1837, "The great object of physiological research . . . is to establish the principle that life and health are subject to laws. It will follow that man is constituted capable of ascertaining those laws, and that obedience to those laws will infallibly secure health." Reynell Coates argued the same point in a lecture two years later. "Within the limits of physiology are included all the laws that regulate the actions of our vital organs," he noted, "and from it are deduced whatever rules are applicable to the preservation of health, and the cure of disease." Advocates of physiological and hygienic reform argued that the laws of health were as inviolable as other laws of nature, like those governing the motion of objects and all other aspects of the natural world. Elisha Bartlett, for instance, a physician who was also at the time the mayor of Lowell, Massachusetts, implored in an address before the American Physiological Society in 1838 that "the facts of hygienic physiology . . . should be taught as *laws*,—as invariable and unbending in their operations as are the laws of natural philosophy." William A. Alcott, writing nearly twenty years later in a book titled *The Laws of Health* (1857), concurred, stressing the importance of obedience to the "physical laws" of the human frame. "We must not only know these laws," he wrote, "but obey them, and that, too, perseveringly. We must obey early and late, at home and abroad, in sickness and in health, in labor and at study, in business and amusement." The body, Alcott and others urged, needed to be unyieldingly directed by an informed mind.[18]

For these popular physiology writers, individual and social health began when both mind and body, head and hand, were cultivated to their fullest. To attend to one without attending to the other, to strengthen and cultivate the body without the mind, or the mind without the body, was to do a great disservice to the individual and, in the aggregate, to the nation as a whole. The "nature" of man, implored Elisha Bartlett in his lecture before the American Physiological Society, was twofold, a "union of flesh and spirit," of body and soul. "These two elements are the essential components of humanity,—the lower and the perishable,—just as much as the higher and immortal. Every attempt at their separation is a violence done to this nature." For Bartlett, the "spiritual transcendentalist" unjustly denied the importance of the body, and the "sensualist" was to be chastised for denying the higher realms of mind and spirit. But his criticism of both groups—that they "mutilate humanity,—they destroy its proportions,—they attempt, violently and unnaturally, to sunder what God has joined together"—would have resonated with criticisms of new labor-divided and mechanized forms of work that seemed to divide manual labor from mental labor, head from hand. Francis William Bird, addressing the same group several months earlier, likewise spoke in a language whose meaning extended beyond the subject explicitly at hand. Claiming that physiology was the one true basis for needed moral reform, Bird argued that "the separation of the interests of man's physical nature from those of his intellectual and spiritual natures is as impossible as it is unnatural." Mind and body were naturally and inextricably linked, he argued, so that inattention to the care of one was sure to lead to the degradation of the other. When each was given its due, when mind and body were raised side by side, then individual and social health would prevail; then "peace shall return to the earth. Social intercourse shall not always be made up of the jarring of discordant elements and the clashing of conflicting interests. Harmony shall again reign between man and his brother."[19]

But what precisely was it that the informed mind governed? In describing the functions of the human body and prescribing the rules governing those functions, antebellum popular physiologists frequently represented the relation between mind and body as analogous to the relation between mind and machine. A common metaphor for the body in popular anatomy and physiology texts was the machine metaphor, whereby the body was described as a machine "fearfully and wonderfully made" that needed to be properly tended. For many writers and lecturers, the body was like an intricate machine because it was comprised of functionally integrated parts. Thomas Lambert, for instance, suggested in the introduction to *Practical Anatomy, Physiology, and Pathology; Hygiene and Therapeutics* (1851) that the human body was like a clock in that it was a "piece of mechanism of exceeding beauty, and with most wonderful perfection intended to fulfil certain duties." Similarly, Oliver Wendell Holmes, in a review essay published in the *North American Review* in 1857, wrote that "levers, pulleys, and even the wheel and axle, play their usual part in the passive transfer of the forces that move the living machinery." If the entire body seemed like an intricate machine, so did many of its individual parts. For many writers, the hand—that moniker of the working man—was one of the most marvelous mechanisms to behold. John H. Griscom called the human hand "an *instrument* which, for *perfection of mechanism* and *variety of uses,* surpasses every other yet known to man." William A. Alcott, in a book titled *The Structure, Uses and Abuses of the Human Hand,* published in 1856, asked, "Is there in the wide world a factory containing a tenth part as much curious and complicated machinery as the hand?"[20]

Indeed, writers frequently noted that the body manifested an array of simple and complex machines. The bones formed levers, they noted, the heart was a pump, the lungs were like a blacksmith's bellows, and the digestive system was like a mill. John H. Griscom, in the preface to his *Animal Mechanism and Physiology* (1848), wrote that "for the purpose of making the study of anatomy more easy and agreeable," he would treat the human body as "a *machine,* composed of apparatus of various kinds." In the pages that followed, Griscom compared the body's "circulating apparatus" with the waterworks of a city, referred to the heart as a "powerful and complicated machine" for pumping blood, and described the structure and function of various body parts in terms of levers, bellows, and toggle joints. Similarly, Worthington Hooker, in his *First Book in Physiology, for the Use of Schools and Families* (1855), described the body as a collection of machinery even more complex than man-made machines. Machines made by man, he wrote, were invariably designed for a single purpose: "A nail-machine makes nails, and does nothing else; a paper-machine makes paper; a locomotive draws cars on a track; and so of other machines." But, he continued, "the human body is not a single machine for a single purpose. It is a complicated machine, and serves many purposes." Hooker then catalogued the variety of machinery in the body, which included the "digestive machinery," the "machinery of the circulation," the "breathing machinery," the "nervous machinery," and the "machinery . . . for the purpose of making other machinery."[21]

In the same way that a machine in the workplace required a tender to ensure its proper direction, so the body required a directing principle, or it could do nothing. Thomas Lambert made this point in 1851 when he wrote that man's physical system was "merely a machine," and that while its form might distinguish it from other animals, "without something to use it, it can do nothing." But, Lambert continued, "when the action of the body is properly directed, the feeblest man is able to entangle the strength of the king of the forest, to capture the leviathan, outstrip the fleetness of the swiftest beasts, and bend the elements themselves to his wishes." This directing principle, this superintendent of the body, was the mind. While the notion that mind governed body was neither new nor particularly startling, antebellum popular physiology writers took care to stress the point. And they did so by figuring the body as a machine that the mind operated. Charles Caldwell, for instance, suggested that physical education cultivated "a better piece of machinery, for mind to work with." The physical system of man, he later continued, "constitutes the machinery, with which alone his mind operates, during their connexion, as soul and body." "Improve the apparatus," he wrote, "and you facilitate and improve the work, which the mind performs with it, precisely as you facilitate steam-operation, and enhance its product, by improving the machinery, with which it is executed." Worthington Hooker, writing in 1855, similarly called the body a "collection of machinery for the mind to use," adding that "the purpose of those parts which the mind does not use is to build those which it does use." Some writers noted that the mind, in addition to guiding the machinery of the body—like the machine tender guided the machine—also gave motion to the body, like steam or water did to machinery. "Our bones and muscles are like the machinery of a steam-boat or railroad-car," remarked one writer in 1848; "they are always ready to serve us; but as the machinery of a boat will not move without steam, so the bones and muscles . . . will not move, when we wish to do anything, without the aid of the mind." But the more common analogy was that the mind was to the body what the machine tender was to the machine, in that the former directed the operations of the latter. "The material body is not left to its own guidance," wrote Edward Jarvis in 1848, "but to each one is given a mind that shall direct it. Every human being is thus made responsible for the care of his own health, and the preservation of his own life."[22]

The work of managing the body, then, was a form of mental labor that every person was bound to perform. No matter what occupation he or she pursued, no matter what his or her station in society, each person was charged with tending the machinery that comprised his or her body. "The necessity of superintending the operations of life within his own body," noted Edward Jarvis in an 1845 lecture, "inevitably falls upon every one, of every condition and every age. Whatever else he may be engaged in, whatever may be his tastes and means, this necessity comes upon him; it comes first, it takes precedence of all." What is more, this work of superintending the human body would be done according to laws that were as sure as the laws governing the operations of production machinery. Popular physiology writers and lecturers returned again and again to the point that the body, like the steam engine, weaving loom, and other machines of the industrial age, was subject to natural laws. "The body is but a machine," wrote one physician in 1856, "worked according to fixed physical laws." According to this writer, the laws governing the human machine would one day be fully understood, so that "every operation of the human body can be explained with as much certainty as the operations of a steam-engine."[23]

For Edward Jarvis, who consistently figured the human body as comprised of an array of machinery, the analogy between superintending the body and superintending other machines was evident. But if the two tasks were similar, it seemed clear to Jarvis that the manner in which most people prepared to undertake one was quite different from the manner in which they prepared to undertake the other. "Before a man assumes the care of a machine," Jarvis noted in 1845, "he examines its parts, he learns its uses, the means of its movement, and the purposes to which it is to be applied. With this knowledge he is ready for his responsibility." But, Jarvis continued, "for the management of his own vital machinery he makes no preparation. Hence he makes such mistakes in the conduct and use of his own body, as he would be ashamed to show in regard to his wagons, his water-wheels, or his spinning-jenny." Dwelling on the unwise practices common in the use of the body, Jarvis pressed further the analogy between bodies and machines, and between what tenders do with their machines and what men and women do with their bodies. "No engineer would pour upon the gudgeons and pistons of his engine acids instead of oil, just for a change, because this would be in opposition to his knowledge of the laws of mechanics." Yet that same engineer, unaware of the rules governing his body, might "pour wine and brandy, and tobacco juice into his stomach, and tobacco smoke into his lungs, which are infinitely more delicate organs than any thing of wood or iron." Francis William Bird urged a similar point in a lecture before the American Physiological Society nearly a decade earlier. "The manufacturer who should not see that every gudgeon and bearing were kept oiled, and every weak belt strengthened," he argued, "would be considered shiftless and unqualified for his business." But, he continued, "with a machine so fearfully and wonderfully made as the human system, every thing goes at hap-hazard, and the whole business is to break down and to 'patch up.'" For Bird and others, the standard by which manufacturers tended to their machinery should be the same for each person in tending his or her body.[24]

Some writers represented the body as akin to a factory in its array of functional machinery. William A. Alcott, for instance, in a discussion of the "mechanism of the skin" published in 1853, suggested that a square inch of skin examined under a microscope would reveal a "vast amount of curious machinery" comparable to that found in a factory. "Perhaps you have seen some huge factory," he wrote, "say the gingham factory, at Clinton, Massachusetts—where, at one view, you can behold about an acre of spinning and weaving machinery, with the hundreds of operatives required to work it." Such a view, he continued, would not equal the complex array of vessels, glands, and nerves contained in the patch of skin. "Is it too much to say that in this little spot—this square inch of human skin—there appears to be vastly more of living machinery than there is of dead machinery in a whole acre of spinning jennies and power looms?" Thomas Lambert, in his *Practical Anatomy, Physiology, and Pathology,* published in 1851, similarly compared the human body to a factory. Noting that the body was comprised of a number of organs beyond those he had already discussed, and that "a general idea of the use of them can be gained by noticing what is necessary in a common factory," Lambert launched into an extended discussion of the workshops, furnaces, pipes, and other apparatus needed in a factory for the repair of normal wear and tear, the removal of useless materials, and the maintenance of the proper temperature on the shop floor. "These things must be done by means of nutriment, fuel, air, water, and such apparatus and assistance as the case requires," he wrote, before turning to the analogous functions of the body.[25]

In this way, the work of supervising the body's operations was akin not only to tending a machine but to managing a shop floor. According to this view, the relation between mind and body was more like a supervisor overseeing the operations of a factory than like an operative tending to a single machine. Thus Lambert, in a book titled *Hygienic Physiology* (1852), compared the mind—located in the brain—with an "overseer in a factory or hotel," to which "reports from all parts of the body shall be made," and from which "commands shall be issued to all parts of the system." Worthington Hooker, writing several years later, similarly imagined the brain to be the "central workshop" from which the mind "operates by the nerves upon all the machinery of the body." At the same time, a few writers figured the task of managing one's body as one of managing humans, as if the parts of the body were working men and women. Alcott, for instance, included in his factory view the "hundreds of operatives" required to operate the body's complex machinery. Later in the same book, Alcott urged that the body's internal system for manufacturing heat (Alcott used the word "manufacture" in this context) should always be used to maximal efficiency. "All the work which the calorific powers of the system can perform without being overtasked . . . should be performed. All our organs and parts are made to be—so to speak—working men." Similarly, Oliver Wendell Holmes, in his essay in the *North American Review* in 1857, called the muscles in the human body "these five hundred mute slaves," slaves that were, presumably, under the control of an overseeing mind.[26]

For antebellum popular physiology writers and lecturers, all people stood in relation to their bodies as machine tenders stood in relation to their machines. Both were charged with the responsibility of operating their machinery properly, ensuring that it produced whatever product or effect it was designed to produce. At the same time, all men and women stood in relation to their bodies as machine *owners* stood in relation to their machines. The effects of such a formulation in the context of the popular discourse on mechanization were several. It suggested that the work of machine-tending was essentially a natural form of labor, one that every person engaged in at all times. At the same time, it represented machine-tending as primarily a form of mental labor, in that what the body/machine required in order to function properly and safely was the guidance of mind. In addition, it worked to deny the opposition between those who were seen to work with their heads and those who were seen to work with their hands. It did so by figuring all men and women in a "mechanized" setting—supervising their bodies, tending production machinery, or managing a mechanized shop—and as engaged in the same form of labor. And by codifying the notion that the mind instructed in the laws of physiology was the proper and even indispensable superintendent of the mechanical body, it argued for the necessity of placing human over machine, head over hand, and—by analogy—manager over worker. In this way, popular physiologists who argued that personal health and the vitality of the nation depended on the proper constitution of these critical relations wrote and spoke in a clear language of class.

CHAPTER 5

Human and Machine

Steam Boiler Explosions and the
Making of the Engineer

In an 1853 speech at the first annual fair of the Metropolitan Mechanics' Institute in Washington, D.C., Joseph Henry, director of the Smithsonian Institution, urged the members of his audience to consider the analogy between the human body and a machine. "The human body is itself an admirably contrived complex machine," Henry observed, "furnished with levers, pulleys, cords, valves, and other appliances for the application and modification of the power derived from the food." Comparing the body to a "locomotive engine," Henry noted that both bodies and engines are directed and controlled by a "thinking, willing principle," which he called the soul. "Let, for example, a locomotive engine be placed upon the track, with water in the boiler and fire in the grate—in short, with all the potentials of motion, and it will still remain quiescent." Then, Henry continued, "let the engineer enter the tender and touch the valve, the machine instantly becomes instinct with life and volition—it has now a soul to govern its power and direct its operations; and, indeed, as a whole, it may be considered as an enormous animal, of which the wheels and other parts are additions to the body of the engineer."[1]

While Henry viewed the untended machine—the soulless body—as quiescent, others envisioned a much more perilous affair. William Bross, speaking before the Chicago Mechanics' Institute late in 1853, evoked the same image—the steam locomotive—as a figure for the human body. Like Henry, Bross highlighted the machine's reliance on a tender for proper functioning. But for Bross, mind did not so much give life to the body as give it direction. "A vessel without a rudder is at the mercy of every wind that sweeps the Ocean," he maintained, "and in the first gale it must founder and go down." Turning from an older nautical metaphor to one specific to the age of steam, Bross asked his audience members to consider the grievous dangers of an ungoverned steam engine. "So the locomotive, the emblem of modern progress, alike ready to do the work of the world, and to sweep from point to point with lightening speed, without the controlling influence of the engineer, becomes at once an engine of death and destruction."[2]

In designating the uncontrolled steam engine as an "engine of death and destruction," Bross evoked the dangers posed by steam power, of which his audience would have been well aware. Chief among these dangers was the threat of steam boiler explosions. In the decades before 1860, hundreds of steam boiler explosions occurred aboard steamboats and steam locomotives, and in steam-powered manufacturing establishments, taking thousands of lives and destroying millions of dollars in property. The steam boiler—that part of the engine in which water was heated to produce the steam necessary for the engine to work—appeared to explode for a variety of reasons, often to devastating effect. An explosion near Cincinnati aboard the steamboat *Moselle* in 1838, for instance, killed more than one hundred passengers and crew members. Boiler explosions were more common aboard steamboats than in steam-powered factories, but when stationary steam engines did explode, they also could cause terrible destruction. In February 1850, a boiler exploded at a manufactory in New York City, leveling a six-story building and killing over sixty people. The symbolic power of the steam engine derived in part from the fact that it was the most public of machines, seen and heard by thousands of steamboat and locomotive passengers, and by many thousands more who regularly witnessed boats and trains pass by. When steam boilers exploded, then, the scenes of death and destruction were often public affairs; indeed, boilers aboard steamships frequently exploded just after the fanfare of taking and letting off passengers, when crowds of people were still on shore waving goodbye to their loved ones. Alarm over the problem of boiler explosions remained high through the 1850s, leaving in its wake countless inventions, investigations, and recommendations for how to prevent the servant steam from becoming the master.[3]

Damaging not only to lives and property, but to a vision of industrial society as orderly and productive, steam boiler explosions held a prominent place in antebellum American culture and were a topic of sustained interest in the popular discourse on mechanization. Printed accounts of boiler explosions appeared regularly in newspapers and periodicals, detailing often grim scenes of death and destruction. Publishers sometimes printed broadsides and pamphlets after particularly devastating explosions. One writer in 1839 noted that the subject "agitates the whole United States at the present day—from the Atlantic to the wild deserts of America, and from the Gulf of Mexico to the head branches of the father of waters." Nearly twenty years later, a poet writing in the *Democratic Review* went so far as to represent the exploding boiler as one of the defining characteristics of the modern age, one not to be found in earlier periods: "Had they patent pills for vermin, / Bursting boilers, daily papers?" Hundreds of scientists, engineers, and others published their views on the subject, in forms ranging from pamphlets, to letters to newspaper editors, to testimonials favoring new safety devices, to memorials addressed to Congress. Ministers sermonized on the lessons of boiler explosions, while popular lecturers took the bursting boiler as a subject for addresses before lyceums, mechanics' institutes, and other educational institutions.[4]

As a subject in the popular discourse on mechanization, steam boiler explosions offered another opportunity for members of the middle class to conceptualize the relation between mental and manual labor in terms that helped legitimate their social authority. This was so because antebellum Americans generally understood boiler explosions in both material and metaphorical terms. Materially, steam boiler explosions were the height of the machine-out-of-control, exacting an awful toll in lives and property. Few questioned the need to solve such a problem. But, as a metaphor, the exploding boiler represented the personal and social disruptions that many feared would accompany mechanization. Because the exploding boiler operated in both material and figurative terms, efforts to solve the technical problem of boiler explosions could work as well to solve the social problem of coordinating "heads" and "hands" in ways that would defuse the potential for class conflict. By the early 1850s, the consensus among those who wrote and lectured (and legislated) on the problem of boiler explosions was that the problem inhered less in the steam engine itself than in the relation between the engineer and the engine. Boilers exploded, they argued, because the men who operated them lacked either the knowledge or the care necessary to properly control such powerful agents. According to this view, steam engines—in order to be safely and productively employed—had to be placed under the "management" of engineers whose character and technical training would be controlled by professional standards and a board of examiners. To do otherwise was to invite calamity. For participants in the popular discourse on mechanization, this conception of the proper relation between human and machine extended by analogy to the proper relation between people who worked with their heads and those they employed, who worked with their hands. The authority of proprietors and managers, like the authority of engineers, could be challenged only at the peril of all.[5]

In early September 1852, the steamboat *Reindeer,* on its regular Hudson River route between New York City and Albany, exploded near the town of Malden, New York, killing several persons on board. *Gleason's Pictorial Drawing Room Companion,* one of the most popular illustrated periodicals of the day, published a detailed account of the disaster, including an engraving of the exploding boat. According to the *Gleason's* story, the *Reindeer* was en route to Albany when it stopped at Malden early in the afternoon of September 4. As the lunch hour was at hand, many of the passengers on board were gathered at the dining table in the steamer's "after cabin." The pilot, determining that the boat was ready to get underway, signaled the engine room to "go ahead," and the boiler suddenly exploded. "By the force of the steam," the account reported, "the iron sheathing was ripped up, and beams and timbers were torn from their places and driven through the kitchen into the after cabin, carrying all before them, instantly scalding and killing those at the dinner table." The scene rescuers found was horrifying. "Those of the passengers scalded were found in the after cabin in great agony, with the skin dropping from their bodies." Some of the survivors were near death from inhaling the superheated steam. As word of the disaster made its way back to New York City, friends and family members of *Reindeer* passengers crowded onto trains traveling north, desperate to learn the fate of their loved ones.[6]

Readers of *Gleason's* would have known that the *Reindeer* explosion was no isolated incident. Steam technology was still relatively new in the first half of the nineteenth century, and while progress was being made in designing safer and more reliable engines, explosions occurred with a frequency that most observers found shocking. High-pressure engines, like those used on most steamboats on the Mississippi River and its tributaries and in virtually all steam-powered manufacturing establishments, seemed more prone to explosion than the "low-pressure" condensing engines more common on eastern rivers, though they also exploded to devastating effect. The exact number of explosions that occurred during the period between 1816 (when the first reported steamboat explosion occurred) and 1860 is difficult to determine, since statistics gathered by the federal government during those years are incomplete. Even more difficult to determine is the number of lives lost, because in many cases, explosions aboard steamboats occurred before an accurate count could be made of those on board. But it is known that no fewer than thirty-five steamboat explosions claimed nearly 150 lives between 1825 and 1830. The five years up to 1852, when Congress finally passed an effective regulatory bill, saw at least fifty such explosions on western rivers alone, with a death toll of more than 1,100.[7]

Even if the total number of explosions seems rather modest, given that thousands of marine, locomotive, and stationary steam engines had been put into use by 1860, the perception was that boilers exploded with shocking regularity. A New York newspaper account of an explosion aboard a steamboat in 1831, in what was a typical formulation, opened simply with the announcement of "Another Explosion." Nearly twenty years later, after more than three decades of efforts to prevent boiler explosions, a writer for *Scientific American* could still write that "scarcely a week, yea, scarcely a day passes over our heads without hearing of some terrible calamity, caused by the bursting of a steam boiler." One reason for the perception that boiler explosions were commonplace was that calamities like the *Reindeer* explosion were widely reported in the daily and weekly press. Newspapers and weekly periodicals, like *Niles' National Register* and the *New-Yorker*, were the most prolific in their coverage of boiler explosions. In fact, in the 1820s, *Niles'* made boiler explosions a regular feature of its "Chronicle" section, alongside crop reports and banking news. Readers interested in boiler explosions could also turn to more technical periodicals, like the *Journal of the Franklin Institute* and, by the middle of the 1840s, *Scientific American,* both of which devoted considerable attention to the question of how explosions might be prevented. Beginning in the 1840s, they could also read books like Samuel Howland's *Steamboat Disasters and Railroad Accidents in the United States* (which was updated several times between 1840 and 1846) or, later, James T. Lloyd's *Steamboat Directory, and Disasters on the Western Waters* (1856).[8]

Printed accounts of boiler explosions often included lavish descriptions of the injury and suffering caused to those caught in the explosion. Indeed, few subjects treated by antebellum writers seem to have given equal impetus or freedom to graphically depict violence. The report of a steamboat explosion that appeared in the December 28, 1826 edition of the *New-York Evening Post* is typical. According to an eyewitness, the steamboat *Union* had just gotten underway when a boiler exploded. "The boiler burst like a clap of thunder," recounted the witness, "and instantaneously the whole boat was a complete wreck." Readers could not fail to appreciate the enormity of the suffering that followed: "Four men sent instantaneously to eternity, seven persons dreadfully scalded—one a female, who, poor soul, never ceased screaming for nearly twenty hours after the accident happened." When the *New-Yorker* reported on the explosion of the *Moselle,* it reprinted an article from the *Cincinnati Whig* describing the terrible violence done to the victims of the explosion. "The fragments of human bodies are now lying scattered all along the shore," wrote the *Whig,* "and we saw the corpses of a number so mangled and torn, that they bear scarcely any resemblance to the human form." The gruesome catalogue continued: "We also saw several with their heads and arms entirely blown off; others with only a part of their head destroyed, and others with their lowest extremities shivered to an apparent jelly." Perhaps the most commonly described injury was the ghastly shedding of skin caused by the steam and boiling water. "Among the wounded," wrote James T. Lloyd of a steamboat explosion that occurred in 1816 on the Ohio River, "six or eight, under the influence of their maddening torments, had torn off their clothes, to which the entire skin of their limbs or bodies adhered; the eyes of others," he continued, "had been put out, and their faces were changed to an undistinguishable mass of flesh by the scalding water." Writers also made clear that boiler explosions tore apart families as well as bodies, as witnessed by the countless descriptions of "heart-rending" scenes of a surviving father searching fruitlessly for his missing children, or of a wife engulfed by grief after waving goodbye to her husband only to see the deck on which he was standing "shivered to atoms."[9]

Antebellum readers would have learned that most explosions occurred aboard steamboats, but they would also have known that steam engines were present in an increasing number of manufacturing establishments, and that danger resided there as well. In the Pittsburgh area by the 1830s, for instance, stationary steam engines were used in machine shops, tanneries, iron foundries, breweries, flour mills, saw mills, and a variety of other manufacturing settings. During that same decade, steam power became commonly used by manufacturers in Boston, Philadelphia, and most other sizeable cities in the North and West. One of the great benefits of steam power in comparison to water power was that it freed the manufacturer from having to locate his establishment along a steep and steady fall of water. Steam-powered manufacturing thus became much more of an "urban phenomenon," in the words of one study, in part because the unevenly mechanizing trades were already concentrated in cities, and in part because labor, fuel, and cheap transportation were more readily found there. When stationary steam engines exploded, then, they often imperiled unknowing city dwellers going about their daily lives. An explosion at an iron foundry in New York in 1830 reportedly threw a heavy piece of boiler more than fifty feet across a street and into the house of a Mrs. Jacobson, who remained uninjured even though the boiler piece passed within two feet of her, severely damaging her house and destroying her furniture. Thomas Reily was not so fortunate when another foundry boiler exploded in New York more than twenty years later. An account published in *Scientific American* in 1853 reported that Reily was "walking home,

smoking his pipe, in the broad blaze of the noon-tide sun" when the explosion occurred at an establishment on a nearby street, sending boiler fragments flying through the air. Almost to his door—and to his wife, who had
just turned her back after seeing him coming up the street—Reily was hit
in the head by a piece of metal and fell to the ground. He died two days later.[10]

As with accounts of explosions aboard steamboats, discussions of explosions that occurred at manufacturing establishments sometimes described in
horrifying detail the violence done to their victims. A brief account of an
explosion in Philadelphia published in the *Farmer and Mechanic* in 1848, for
instance, noted that a young boy working in the "factory" (as they were now
called) was decapitated by the explosion, that his head was carried with a
portion of the boiler and "dashed" against a nearby dwelling ("the wall being
bespattered with his brains and blood"), and that his "headless trunk" stood
"quivering ghastly" for a moment before falling to the ground. In general,
these accounts drew little if any distinction between stationary steam boiler
explosions and explosions aboard steamboats. An account in Philadelphia's
National Gazette of the 1830 iron foundry explosion in New York announced
simply, "Another Disaster from the Use of Steam," and concluded by noting
the total number of fatal boiler explosions that "season." When a writer for
Scientific American in 1852 finished his discussion of a recent explosion
aboard a steamboat, he moved seamlessly into the observation that "there
are steam boilers in many of the buildings in this city, . . . placed under the
side walks, and carrying steam of a very high pressure. It is a wonder to us,"
he continued, "that more explosions do not take place."[11]

The ruin and death caused by steam boiler explosions dramatized, more
than any other event in the antebellum period, the destructive potential of
mechanization. The great tool of the new productive order—steam-powered
machinery—could be vastly productive when kept to the narrow round of its
assigned task. But when the boiler burst, when the machine broke free from
the reins of human ingenuity, havoc and despair followed. Perhaps all the attention given to the exploding boiler derived not only from the dramatic and very
public nature of these calamities, but from the fact that the exploding boiler
mitigated or even undermined the notion that the "progress of the arts"
was progress at all. Indeed, the close attention to boiler explosions given by
the popular press painted the dawn of the mechanical age as fraught with new
dangers. The account of Thomas Reily's death in the streets of New York in
1853, for instance, concluded by ominously noting that "at the present moment
there are hundreds of these powder magazine boilers in our city, to the great
danger of the lives of our citizens." A writer for the *Farmer and Mechanic*
several years earlier had similarly noted that "boilers are placed under our

side walks, in the cellars, or basement stories of buildings, in the very centre of our greatest thoroughfares," adding that "we can scarcely pass through many of the streets, or into the larger workshops and offices of our city, without walking over these hidden volcanoes." Indeed, the very fear of calamity in some cases resulted in panic and tragedy. In June 1840, two men died on a steamboat excursion out of New York City after a "slight accident" befell the boiler of the boat they were on. But it was not injury from the accident that caused their deaths. Apparently fearful of an explosion, the two men jumped overboard and were drowned.[12]

In light of the seeming intractability of the problem of boiler explosions, some observers went so far as to suggest that steam engines operating at high pressures were simply too dangerous to use. An article published in the *Minerva* in early 1825 noted that explosions of "high-pressure" (meaning noncondensing) engines "had very generally produced a conviction, that the use of high-pressure engines should be altogether abandoned," although the article itself did not take this position. More than two decades later, a writer in *Scientific American* concluded that "there is no real safety apart from a low pressure condensing engine," adding that "40 lbs. pressure, in large boilers" was "as high as the law should allow any boat to carry." Others pointed out that explosions were not as common as the extensive and often sensational press coverage of boiler explosions suggested. "We have yet experienced far fewer accidents by steam," noted one writer for the *New-Yorker* in 1838, "than the minute detail of all their horrors in the newspapers, and the eager anxiety with which they are devoured and remembered, has led the public to believe." In fact, most antebellum writers who took up the question argued that the steam engine was a triumph of human ingenuity that would underwrite a most profound advance in civilization. Still, these proponents of steam power recognized that the problem of boiler explosions needed to be overcome. "The steam-engine has, no doubt, been retarded in its race of usefulness, and in its applicability to the mechanic arts, by its liability to explosions, accompanied as this accident usually is, by so great a sacrifice of life and property," admitted a contributor to the *Journal of the Franklin Institute* in 1836. "The existence of so great an evil," he continued, "should induce mechanical and scientific men to seek untiringly for the means of remedying so dangerous a defect."[13]

The disaggregation of power from its regulating principle, figured by the bursting boiler, had its analogy in the disaggregation of hand from head, or of mind from body, which was at the center of debates about the personal and social consequences of mechanization. Writers on health and human physiology, for instance, pointed up this analogy when, in arguing that the physical, moral, and social health of the nation would be assured as soon as men and women attuned their bodies to prescribed physiological laws, they evoked boiler explosions to depict the physical ruin that would ensue when bodies were improperly managed. A Cincinnati physician writing in 1856 argued that the diffusion of physiological knowledge was no less crucial to public safety and health than the diffusion of engineering knowledge. "You will admit," he wrote, "that it is absolutely necessary for an engineer to understand thoroughly the structure, the workings, and the strength of his engine, in order to run it profitably and safely." If the body is a machine, he continued, "how vitally important is it that its engineer, or mind, should understand as much as possible of its structure, its workings, and its strength?" Indeed, for this writer, tending the human body without knowing its governing principles was to court the same risks as tending a steam engine without the proper training. "It would be rather hazardous for a man to go on board a steamboat and begin to fire up," he wrote, "without knowing which screw to turn to let off steam when it gets too high; or to undertake to drive the boat ahead without knowing the channel." "No less hazardous," he continued, "is it for one to go round on the top of his own individual engine . . . without knowing the nature and operation of its machinery." For William A. Alcott, the skin—as a crucial purifying apparatus—stood in the "same relation" to the rest of the body as the safety valve stood in relation to the steam boiler. Both relieved the system of dangerously high levels of substances otherwise necessary to its normal functioning. Thus, were one to ignore the laws governing the care of the skin—when and how to bathe, how to dress, and so forth—the results could be akin to improper operation of the steam engine. "As the steamboat boiler, under heavy pressure, would often burst, were it not for the safety valve," Alcott wrote in 1853, "so will there be many explosions of the human body, if the skin ceases to perform its offices."[14]

Other observers, in turning from personal disorder to social disorder, suggested that men and women who lacked the moral and mental attributes necessary for self-governance posed the same dangers to society as did the exploding steam engine. Indeed, the analogy between a potentially explosive society and a potentially explosive machine was evident to antebellum observers. In June 1828, readers of the *Boston Daily Advertiser* found a comparison between social explosions and mechanical explosions in a brief article titled "Humorous Description of the Steam Engine," which was reprinted from the *Liverpool Albion*. Contemplating the unrelenting productivity of the steam engine, the author wryly noted that "if pressed too hard, it may sometimes make a 'blow up,'" before adding that "so will those living steam engines—the mob."

For this writer, the difference between a boiler explosion and a social explosion was significant in that the social explosion was much more difficult to arrest. "The burst once over, the machine becomes as tame and harmless as a child," he wrote, "whereas the people, when duly roused, go on thundering at the door of the legislature with an increasing force;—so that if you once indulge their importunity, by reforming the most inveterate abuse, you must go on till 'social order' is cut up into ribbons, and nothing remains for a tax eater to subsist on." Two years earlier, James Kirke Paulding pressed a similar analogy in a sketch satirizing Robert Owens's *New View of Society,* recently published in its first American edition. After professing a belief that "children are merely compounded of corporeal machinery," a character in the sketch (which Paulding titled "The Man Machine") compares the human machine with the steam engine. "As you may equally apply the powers of a steam engine to the manufactory of cotton or the destruction of mankind," he points out, in clear reference to boiler explosions, "so you may with equal ease direct the machinery of man to good or evil purposes." The character then suggests how the two kinds of machinery might be kept to good—or productive—purposes. In the case of the inanimate machine, he avers, "it is done by regulating the operation of the steam engine by certain rules of science and experience." In the case of the human/machine, it is done "by example and education." This twin correlation between humans and machines, and between education and the safe operation of a steam engine, would be crucial for those seeking to conceptualize the social relations of mechanized production in terms favorable to middle-class interests.[15]

An essay titled "Revolutions," published in 1847 in the radical periodical *Herald of Truth,* likewise used the exploding steam engine as a metaphor for social unrest, placing that unrest more explicitly in the context of mechanization. According to the essay's author, Joseph H. Moore, such a metaphor would be especially appealing to conservative interests. In Moore's assessment, changes in productive arrangements were creating vast social inequities that were "hastening national crises" throughout the world. "Multitudes now discern this," he wrote, "but, at present, by the lack of Organised Labor and Associated Interests, matters grow steadily worse." For Moore, the machine was deeply implicated in the widening gulf between modern-day serfs and princes. "Machinery," he implored, "destined, when redeemed, to be the material agent for brilliant spiritual results, annually dooms myriads to infamy and the grave. Iron monsters, of tireless limbs, and hot, exhaustless breath, crush into the lists to compete with the animated machinery, where expiring bodies quiver, and deathless spirits agonise." But while Moore saw a "progressive" revolutionary spirit coming out of the industrial setting—one that

would find remedies in "moral forces" rather than in the "crashes and con-
vulsions of physical forces"—he knew that others would be skeptical. For
those fearful of what "organised labor" might accomplish, the revolutionary
spirit looked more French than American, an invitation to chaos rather than
measured change. Here Moore used the exploding steam engine as a metaphor
for a conservative vision of revolutionary change as ruinous, pointing to a
position that equated "constitutional securities against revolutions" with
"political safety-valves" against the "horrid explosions that may ensue."[16]

Given the unique status of the steam engine as both an agent of social
change and a metaphor by which that change might be understood, discussions of boiler explosions and the means for their prevention had meaning
not only in relation to their immediate referent—the exploding steam engine—
but also to larger social conditions attendant on mechanization, conditions
that at times and to some seemed equally explosive. If so, then discussions
of steam boiler explosions might be understood as a venue in which a largely
technical discussion both obscured and engaged a deeply contentious social
discussion, whereby efforts to solve the problem of boiler explosions worked
as well to solve the social problem of how to structure the social relations of
mechanized production.

The widespread and enduring concern over boiler explosions spurred engineers, inventors, and others to determine and debate the cause of boiler explosions and the measures for their prevention. In order to understand the literal content of these discussions, it is important to know something about
the work of operating a steam engine. Unlike many other forms of machine-
tending in the antebellum period, the work of steam engineering was anything but rote. The work varied depending on a number of factors, including whether the engine was condensing or noncondensing, and whether it
was a stationary, marine, or locomotive engine. In addition, developments
in engine design and safety features meant that the work of a steam engineer
in 1820 was different than it was in the 1860s. Nevertheless, some generalizations can be made about the duties of those charged with operating a
steam engine. All steam engineers were responsible for maintaining an adequate supply of steam to drive the engine, an adequate supply of water to
generate the steam, and an adequate fire to boil the water. In monitoring the
steam pressure, engineers relied on the safety valve to ensure that the pressure did not climb too high. Many condensing engines were equipped as well
with a mercury steam gauge that worked like a barometer to indicate the
pressure of steam inside the boiler. In addition to monitoring the pressure
inside the boiler, engineers were responsible for maintaining an adequate
water supply. To do so, he had to frequently check the water level and, when

it was low, pump more water into the boiler. To enable the engineer to check the water level, steam boilers were equipped with valves called "gauge cocks" or "try cocks," located in a vertical row at the front end of the boiler. When the engineer opened or "tried" the cocks—most boilers had two or three, but some had four—he could tell the level of water inside the boiler by noting which cocks emitted steam and which emitted water. In addition to try cocks, some boilers had glass tube gauges that displayed the water level at all times. Because the water inside the boiler was constantly boiling off into steam, the engineer regularly added more water to the boiler using a pump. On steamboats through the 1830s, this pump was powered by the steam engine itself or by hand. By the end of the 1840s, many steamboats were equipped with an auxiliary engine, commonly called the "doctor," that the engineer could engage to drive the pump (or pumps) so that he did not have to be distracted with pumping by hand, and so that the pump could be worked even when the boat was at a stop. The engineer also had to periodically blow water out of the boilers to clean it of any sediment that might have gathered and, especially in the case of saltwater boats, to prevent the accumulation of mineral deposits that could weaken the boiler wall or diminish the heating efficiency. In addition to blowing out all of the water, the engineer had to periodically scrub the boiler interior. The work of tending and feeding the fire below the boilers, meanwhile, was done by a crew of "firemen" who were supervised by the engineer. Engineers aboard steamboats also had to engage the engine with the machinery that moved the paddle wheel, arrest the boat's motion whenever called upon, and change the direction of the paddle wheel or wheels, depending on whether the pilot wished to go forward or backward. In addition, steam engineers had to know their way around a blacksmith's forge, in case the machinery needed repairs. Aboard larger steamboats, the various tasks of the engineer were typically performed by a crew consisting of one or two chief engineers, several assistant engineers, and a few "cub" or apprentice engineers.[17]

Many writers acknowledged that boilers sometimes exploded for reasons that were largely or entirely beyond the control of the engineer. For instance, some observers credited particular explosions at least in part to faults in the boiler construction—poor design or workmanship, or the use of inferior parts—that left boilers unable to take pressures that would normally be considered safe. Some leveled particular criticism at boilers designed with flues passing through the interior of the boiler, a feature that was meant to increase the heated surface area to which the water inside the boiler would be exposed, and that became increasingly common through the 1830s. These flues, they insisted, were liable to become red-hot if exposed directly to the flames or if the water inside the boiler fell low enough to leave them uncovered, causing the metal to soften and—if the pressure inside the boiler were high enough—the flue to collapse, with an explosion immediately following. Others found particular danger in the poor quality of the wrought-iron plates used in the construction of most boilers. One writer, in an 1831 letter to the secretary of the treasury, went so far as to argue that "all accidents which have occurred in steamboats, are owing entirely to a defect in the iron from which the boilers are manufactured." Few observers were as definitive as this one, but many would have agreed that inferior boiler plate could and sometimes did lead to an explosion.[18]

But more often, the fault found in a boiler explosion rested not with the engine designer or manufacturer, but with the engineer. Writers, lecturers, survivors, witnesses, and investigating committees almost always found that some combination of an engineer's neglect, ignorance, and in some cases, criminal misbehavior, was the root cause of an explosion. Some pointed to the neglect or misuse of safety valves. When the safety valve was properly set, the pressure inside the boiler would lift the valve plate and release steam before the pressure inside the boiler rose to a dangerously high level. But if the engineer wished or was ordered to maintain a high steam pressure, he would sometimes restrain the valve with rope or additional weights. Whenever a steamboat was at a stop, for instance, the safe practice was to release steam through the safety valve, both to maintain the boiling activity inside the boiler (and thereby keep the walls and flues covered by water), and to prevent the pressure from gradually reaching an explosive level. But releasing steam in such cases increased the time needed to build up the necessary pressure for getting underway. For this reason, captains seeking to make good time would sometimes order their engineer to "hold onto" the steam, which he could do either by not lifting the safety valve or by actually holding the valve down. After the steamboat *General Jackson* exploded on the Hudson River in 1831, a New York newspaper reported that the captain had urged a woman on shore to hurry onto the waiting boat, as it was "under a high pressure of steam." The report continued that two men seated on shore were watching the proceedings and commenting on the "imprudence" of not letting off steam, when the explosion occurred. According to the dying captain, the explosion was not due to some technical problem, but rather was *altogether the result of carelessness or negligence.*[19]

Others argued that the dangerously high pressure almost always occurred when the engineer allowed the water inside the boiler to fall to a dangerously low level. For most observers, the danger from having too little water in the boiler was evident. When the water level inside the boiler was low, the portions of the boiler left dry were liable to reach much higher temperatures than the portions covered in water. Observers frequently argued that cold water pumped into such a boiler would hit the overheated metal and burst into steam, in some cases causing an explosion. The resumption of boiling that occurred when the engineer restarted the engine or raised the safety valve might similarly cause an immediate and treacherous burst of steam. Thus was the argument made by a writer for *Scientific American* in 1854: "When water is below the flues or tubes as the case may be, and the engine stationary, the pressure of steam keeps the water solid and below the flues." But, he continued, "upon the instant action of the engine, the pressure is released, and the water flows over the exposed surfaces of the flues, and the awful results of an explosion follow." This chain of events was an explanation for why steamboats tended to explode just after a stop. It could also account for those instances in which several boilers seemed to explode simultaneously, occurrences that confounded theories based on defective boiler plate or a gradual increase in steam pressure. Through the decades before 1860, low water in the boiler was probably the most common reason given for boiler explosions. "This subject of explosions has been mystified quite too much," implored the writer of a letter to *Scientific American* in 1853, who signed his letter "An Engineer" and who wrote to criticize a discussion of boiler explosions published several weeks earlier. Urging the influential journal to "proclaim the truth," the writer expressed a view common among participants in the popular discussion of boiler explosions: "In ninety-nine cases out of every hundred, explosions occur from negligence of the engineer, in letting the water get low in his boilers."[20]

Among antebellum observers, the most grievous cause for boiler explosions was the practice of steamboat racing. If two boats happened to be running alongside one another, a race might ensue simply because the first to reach the next landing would be most likely to receive the waiting passengers and cargo. In addition, steamboat captains sometimes staged races to attract business: as one history of steamboating on the western waters put it in 1926, "Shippers and passengers preferred the fast boats." Such races could place perilous burdens on steam engines, as engineers would typically stoke the fire, keep the water low, and hold down the safety valve with whatever heavy item was at hand. Because these dangerous practices were understood to be common in steamboat races, racing was frequently named as a cause of explosions. The explosion of the steamboat *General Brown* in 1839, for instance, was said to have stemmed from "the engineer holding on to the steam, with the intent, it is supposed, of overtaking the *Empress* [a rival boat] which was passing quietly on her way." Similarly, the captain of the *Moselle* reportedly wanted to confirm his boat's reputation as a "brag boat" when he attempted to race past a crowd gathered on the Cincinnati shore just prior to the boat's explosion. Newspaper and periodical writers roundly criticized the practice of steamboat racing as early as the 1820s. When the *Car of Commerce* exploded in 1828, *Niles' Weekly Register* noted that a Cincinnati newspaper had attributed the disaster to "the vile practice of 'racing,' by which hundreds of valuable lives are put in jeopardy to gratify the childish vanity of a steam-boat captain." A decade later, the *Family Magazine,* in reporting on the *General Brown* explosion, simply denounced steamboat racing as a "pernicious and atrocious practice."[21]

In the context of these discussions, inventors designed new safety valves, water gauges, warning devices, and other contrivances to ensure the safe operation of engines, creating by the late 1840s a virtual industry in safety devices. Such safety devices were put forward with such frequency that a skeptic as early as 1836 noted that "hardly a month passes, without some *new boiler* being produced, to be perfectly free from the danger of explosion." Some focused on boiler design. In 1817—one year after the first reported steamboat explosion in the United States—*Niles' Weekly Register* printed an account of a new safety boiler. While the article was not specific about details, it did report that the new boiler had been installed on the steamboat *Etna,* and that a recent incident in which a small aperture opened up on the side of the boiler, harmlessly releasing the steam, proved that the boiler "cannot be exploded." The promise of this early safety boiler, designed by Oliver Evans himself, came into doubt when the *Etna* exploded in New York harbor seven years later, killing upwards of a dozen passengers and crew members. Others sought to devise improved safety valves, agreeing with a writer in 1853 who insisted that a well-designed safety valve would render steam boilers "as harmless as a tea-kettle that is not soldered hard and fast." But more than a few observers expressed little confidence in safety valves, such as the contributor to the *Journal of the Franklin Institute* in 1831 who noted that "not a boiler has been burst, not a boat disabled, not a limb mangled, nor a life destroyed by steam, that has not been placed under the protection of this false guardian." For many of them, the key to preventing boiler explosions was maintaining an ample water supply. "*No boiler ever yet burst,*" wrote one emphatic observer in 1838, "*when sufficiently supplied with water!*" Through the antebellum decades, a host of mechanisms were proposed and implemented for indicating when the level of water in the boiler was low, so that the engineer would know to pump more water into the boiler. The *New-York Evening Post* reported in June 1831 that an "ingenious mechanic" in that city had constructed a device that combined a dial (which would be openly placed for anyone to see) that indicated the water level in the boiler with a bell that would sound if the water fell too low. Another common suggestion through the 1850s was to affix a steam whistle to the side of the boiler that would sound when the water dropped to the point of danger.[22]

But warning devices such as these required the attention and prompt response of the engineer, which many feared was not always reliable. Efforts were thus undertaken to devise means for boilers to be supplied with water without human intervention. What was needed, said a writer for the *American Magazine of Useful and Entertaining Knowledge* in 1835, was a device that would "provide a process for keeping the boiler in such a temperature, by a constant, gradual supply of water, as to prevent explosion, so destructive of human life." A number of inventors and promoters put forward self-feeding devices by the 1830s. In the 1840s, Daniel Barnum of Bridgeport, Connecticut received considerable attention for his "self-acting safety apparatus," by which a float inside the boiler acted as a switch for an auxiliary engine that would, when necessary, pump water into the boiler. An advertising circular published in 1848 contained a number of statements from individuals testifying to the value of Barnum's device. "I can say with confidence," wrote Roger M. Sherman in an 1843 letter to the secretary of the navy that was printed in the circular, "that if Mr. Barnum's self-acting pump is properly applied, no explosion will ever again accrue from a deficiency of water in the boiler—that most prolific source of calamity in the steam navigation." Other safety features were similarly designed to operate beyond the control of the engineer. Some engines, in addition to the typical weighted valve, were equipped with a "fusible plug" safety valve as a back-up. This was simply a valve opening placed in the side of the boiler and filled with an alloy that melted at a temperature determined to be the threshold between safety and danger. The expectation was that, when the plug melted, the steam would be quickly released, rendering the boiler inert. The only thing the engineer could do to prevent this from happening was to keep the boiler temperature safe by maintaining a sufficient supply of water. A more novel device could have been seen at the American Institute in late 1838, when Thomas Blanchard—already something of a celebrity for his lathe that could cut irregular forms—placed on display the model of an apparatus designed to control the fire in the furnace beneath the boiler. According to a description of the device, a float inside the boiler would cause the doors to the furnace to close if the water inside the boiler fell too low, and remain locked until more water was added. "Thus it is placed out of the power of the careless engineer to add any more fuel to the fire," the description observed, "until the required quantity of water is supplied." Steam engines equipped with a fusible plug valve, Barnum's pump, and Blanchard's furnace apparatus might have approximated the ideal imagined by one engineer in 1853, "so perfect in their self-adjusting action, as to defy the consequences of the most reckless carelessness."[23]

Discussions of boiler explosions during the decades before 1860 were characterized by uncertainty and disagreement. Writers advanced an "irreconcilable diversity of opinions" about the application of steam power, noted an observer in the *Journal of the Franklin Institute* in 1852, "particularly as to the dangers accruing in its use, and the best modes of avoiding these risks." In the case of a particular explosion, was the boiler poorly constructed? Had the water fallen too low? Had the engineer been careless? Had the safety valve been adequate to the engine? If consensus on these questions could not be reached, even after lengthy investigation, some observers went further, insisting that not even steam pressure was blameworthy in most if not all explosions. Some argued that explosions were caused by the build-up of an explosive element that was believed to be released either when water and steam were heated to a very high point, or when water came into sudden contact with red-hot metal. A few insisted that this dangerous element was a gas yet to be identified and characterized by scientists; one New York writer in the early 1850s suggested that this gas be called "stame." Others insisted that the explosive element was simply hydrogen gas, which they believed was released when super-heated water decomposed into its constituent elements of hydrogen and oxygen. A man named Joshua O. Blair, for instance, in a petition favorably received by a committee of the Louisiana state legislature and passed on to the U.S. House of Representatives in 1832, concluded that "it is impossible for steam to be the cause of boilers exploding from any pressure it could produce," and that hydrogen gas, "freed from its accompanying component of steam oxygen," was the true cause. A writer in *Scientific American* nearly twenty years later similarly argued that hydrogen—which he called "a full blooded-cousin to gun powder"—was the sole culprit in boiler explosions. "All this noise then, about explosions by steam, is a 'fal-de-ral,' and will not bear the light radiating from philosophy and mathematics." Others, like a writer appearing in the *Minerva* in 1824, argued that oxygen released by the decomposition of water would attach itself to the interior surface of the boiler, weakening the metal and heightening the danger of explosion.[24]

Seeking to place the subject on certain, scientific ground, the Franklin Institute in Philadelphia launched an ambitious investigation into the causes of boiler explosions late in 1830. Spurred by a recent and unusually deadly explosion aboard the *Helen McGregor* on the Mississippi River, leaders of the institute wanted to demonstrate that explosions were indeed avoidable, so that the public could be confident in the safety of steam power. They also wanted to settle the question of what caused boiler explosions, so that the means for their prevention could be agreed upon and perhaps even mandated in regulatory legislation. The investigation was funded by the Treasury Department—which had recently been asked by Congress to suggest measures for preventing boiler explosions—and was divided into two main parts, one of which would determine how steam pressure arrived at explosive levels, and the other test the strength of boiler plate under various conditions. Over the next several years, the institute carried out its study by gathering information on previous explosions and conducting experiments using models of steam engines and other apparatus. Its final report, which was published in 1836, arrived at a number of conclusions. The investigators found that explosions were indeed caused by steam pressure, and that explosive pressures could mount slowly or come on all at once, depending on the circumstances. In addition, they confirmed that boiler plate could overheat significantly if not covered with water in the interior of the boiler and that an explosion could occur as a result. They also offered a number of preventive recommendations concerning the number and size of safety valves, the use of self-acting feeding pumps, and the stopping and starting of engines. Although the authors of the report hoped that their findings would divert others from promoting "false hypotheses" concerning boiler explosions "which cannot furnish the remedies they are in quest of," they failed in this regard, as theories about hydrogen gas and other explosive agents continued to circulate for decades after the report's publication. Nonetheless, the report was a significant intervention in a discussion that at that point was nearly two decades old, and which seemed to most observers to have done little if any good in actually preventing explosions from occurring.[25]

The report probably exerted its greatest influence not with the general public but with the federal government in its efforts to draft regulatory legislation for preventing boiler explosions. Congress had first considered the problem of boiler explosions in 1824, after the *Etna* explosion, and had been discussing ever since what it might do. Legislation was slow in coming, however, in part because of resistance to regulating a nascent and increasingly important industry, and in part because of real disagreement about the causes of explosions and how to prevent them. The authors of the Franklin Institute report, hoping that their conclusions would remove the latter obstacle, appended to their report the full text of a proposed bill "for the regulation of the boilers and engines of vessels propelled in the whole or in part by steam." But it was not until the explosion of the steamboat *Moselle,* more than two years after the Franklin Institute released its report, that the former obstacle was overcome. The shockingly high death toll of the *Moselle* explosion, combined with the clear negligence of the captain in seeking to prove the speed of his boat, moved Congress to act. The bill that was finally passed and signed into law in July 1838 did not address some areas that were of real concern to the Franklin Institute, such as the safety features of steam engines and the specific qualifications of engineers. Nonetheless, it followed the bill proposed by the Franklin Institute in several key respects. As was recommended by the Franklin Institute, the new law required that the federal government empower inspectors to examine and certify the safety of steamboat hulls, boilers, and machinery, and that penalties be levied against steamboat owners who continued to operate without proper certification. In addition, both the Franklin Institute bill and the new law required certain safety practices at every steamboat stop (although they differed on which practices should be performed, the Franklin Institute recommending that water be constantly supplied to the boiler during the stop, while the law required that the safety valve be kept open). Finally, the new law, like the Franklin Institute bill, stated that anyone who caused a death by their misconduct in operating a steamboat would be guilty of manslaughter. "Here is legislation enough," wrote a contributor to the *New-Yorker* a month after the new law took effect. "It now remains with travelers and with juries to give it full effect, upon the first and every fitting occasion."[26]

But despite the 1838 law and the numerous safety measures and devices that were developed during the antebellum decades, boilers continued to explode. A steam tow boat, the *Henry Eckford,* exploded alongside Cedar Street in New York City in April 1841, killing or severely injuring several on board. The federal inspector had been "grossly unfaithful to his duty," a writer for the *New-Yorker* reported, because the boat was "old and worn-out" and should not have been allowed to continue operation. The following year, an explosion on the Missouri River aboard the steamboat *Etna*— reported in an article in the *Brother Jonathan* titled "Another Terrible Explosion"—killed several passengers and wounded dozens more. More than seventy such explosions occurred between 1841 and 1848 aboard steamboats alone, with a death toll of more than six hundred. Some criticized the new law almost immediately after it was passed, calling it "totally inadequate" because it failed to make requirements about engine safety features, or because it relied on an inspection system that was so vaguely defined that one writer dismissed it as "a matter of moonshine." Others, such as a contributor to the *New York Herald* who also wrote an article for *Scientific American* in 1850, noted that the ever-increasing number of safety devices simply failed to ensure safety. "The 'Anglo Norman,' " he wrote of a recent steamboat explosion just off New Orleans that killed a number of passengers and crew members, "was furnished with a low pressure condensing engine, constructed at one of the first foundries, and furnished with all known inventions." Nevertheless, he continued, "the boiler, weighing many tons, exploded, and disappeared from the boat."[27]

As explosions continued, and discussion of explosions continued, observers kept returning to the notion that the safety of the steam engine ultimately rested with the person charged with its operation. It was the competence of the engineer that made the difference between safety and ruin, they argued, much more than any safety device. By the early 1840s, many observers would have agreed with the writer for the *North American Review* who argued that no amount of mechanical ingenuity could safeguard against boiler explosions. "As long as the management of so tremendous an agent as steam shall be abandoned to the control of careless, ignorant, or intemperate engineers," he wrote in an article published in 1840, "no perfection of boiler or engine, no strictness of periodical examination, will insure any exemption from explosion." James Renwick, more temperate in his argument, made the same point several years earlier in his popular *Treatise on the Steam Engine.* "It is difficult to point out methods that are of themselves entirely to be relied upon to prevent explosions," he wrote. "However perfectly a boiler may be constructed or furnished with safety apparatus, it will still depend much upon the carefulness and intelligence of the persons entrusted with its management." Some participants in this discussion, like Oliver Evans's son Cadwallader, rued the growing tendency to blame engineers. In an 1850 pamphlet promoting a new safety device he had developed, Evans identified himself as "an engineer and practical man" and stated that his "strongest wishes and sympathies are with that class" before insisting that, in cases of explosions, "the evil lies more in the defects of the machinery, than in the management of it." But by the time he wrote, his voice was in a distinct minority. More typical was a writer for the *Journal of the Franklin Institute* in 1852 who noted in an account of a recent explosion aboard a steamboat that "new boats are heralded with many safety contrivances; but no one states, (nor could many with truth,) that they have competent engineers."[28]

Writers and lecturers who emphasized the importance of the engineer to safety in the "age of steam" recognized that mechanization was not simply about machinery, but rather about a relation between humans and machines. Steam engines could not be relied upon to operate safely on their own; they needed attentive and skillful engineers in order to serve their proper function. In the lexicon of the more general popular discourse on mechanization, observers who pressed this point urged that the regulated and productive machine depended on a properly constituted relation between the human machine tender and the machine, in which the former remained in complete control of the latter. The term "manage," which was so commonly used by those highlighting the importance of the engineer to the safety of the steam engine, was rarely used in reference to the operation of other machinery, but here it made sense, given the lifelike quality of the steam engine. The term codified the hierarchical nature of the relation between the competent engineer and his engine at the same time as it suggested a metaphoric meaning, whereby the engineer who managed the engine was analogous to the proprietor or foreman who managed the worker. A contributor to *Scientific American* in 1854, in discussing an explosion aboard a steamboat on the Missouri River earlier that year, evoked a similar metaphoric meaning when he reverted to an older language of social hierarchy in writing, "We hold to the opinion that steam is the servant, not the master of the engineer."[29]

But in spite of the importance of the work done by the engineer and the relative level of skill required to keep a steam engine running well and safely, the work of operating a steam engine was held in relatively low esteem through the 1850s. Aboard steamboats, the engineer occupied an uncelebrated position in relation to the captain—who was formally in command of the boat—and to the pilot, who was the trained navigator and the person to whom the captain generally deferred in matters of operation. Most observers associated the work of steam engineering with the grime, heat, and physical toil that was much more the province of manual labor than of mental labor. In 1824, a congressional committee considering regulatory legislation after the *Etna* explosion emphasized the physical and manual nature of operating steam engines when it reserved the term "engineer" for those who were knowledgeable about engine design and construction, referring to the men who operated the engines simply as "engine workers." Indeed, in the language of head and hand, the steam engineer was, particularly in the 1820s and 1830s, generally thought to be simply one of the hands that engaged in the work of tending machinery. A contributor to a Philadelphia newspaper in 1826, for instance, singled out "the engineers and other hands" in discussing who needed to be particularly careful in steam travel. Similarly, a minister whose sermon on the explosion of the steamboat *Pulaski* appeared in part in the *American Railroad Journal* in 1838 insisted that the "most fruitful source of evil" in causing boiler explosions was "the reposing of trust, where trust should never be reposed, with incompetent and reckless hands, with men that have no prudence, nor vigilance, nor self-control, and whose passions are their masters."[30]

As long as they were mere hands, engineers were understood to be liable to fail in two regards. First, they were likely to be morally unsound, governed by passion, meanness, or sloth, rather than by a considered desire to do what was right. Observers often pointed out that an engineer had to be reliable but in too many cases he was someone who, in the words of one writer in 1838, "drinks hard, swears loud, and brags strong, and neglects doing what little he does know." Stories abounded of engineers who drank on the job, or gambled, or whose arrogance or orneriness kept them from heeding the advice or warnings of others. Especially horrifying was the abrogation of safety evident in the steamboat race. Engineers known for their racing prowess were sometimes called "hot engineers," men whom one writer labeled a "worthless tribe." According to a writer for the *North American Review* in 1840, during a race a "mania" seized the captain and crew members, who were driven both by the excitement of the race and by the encouragement of some passengers equally possessed by the moment. A fictional account of a steamboat race published in the *New-Yorker* in 1836 described crew members slugging back rounds of drinks between cries for more steam, terrified female passengers begging the captain to pull out of the race, and finally an explosion aboard the opposing boat. When the steamboat *Ben Sherrod* burst into flames and exploded during a race in 1837, the captain's disregard for safety seemed especially shocking. One report stated that he had placed an open barrel of whiskey on deck "to stimulate the hands to exert themselves in making steam." The fire and series of explosions that followed reportedly killed well over one hundred passengers and crew members. The contempt reserved for irresponsible engineers found frequent expression in discussions of boiler explosions. One writer for *Niles' Weekly Register* in 1830, after giving a brief account of three recent boiler explosions aboard steamboats, observed that there was some justice in the world. "As these things result either from criminal carelessness or fool-hardiness, nineteen times out of twenty," he wrote, "there is something not altogether unpleasant in the melancholy fact, that in the four last explosions we have lately heard of, the four *engineers* were wretchedly mangled and killed."[31]

But other writers took the fact that engineers were so often among those injured or killed in explosions as evidence that their dangerous practices were due less to neglect or some larger moral failing than to ignorance. The author of the 1840 *North American Review* article argued as much when he noted that "the engineer on duty at the time of any catastrophe is almost without exception the first victim," which led him to conclude that "ignorance . . . more often than negligence, is the cause of these accidents." Indeed, writers often noted that not all men who called themselves steam engineers had the experience or formal training that the term popularly suggested. In an 1825 letter from the *Boston Evening Gazette* reprinted in the *Journal of the Franklin Institute* six years later, one observer claimed that "much of the evil" attendant on the use of steam power had arisen "from confidence in unqualified persons" who had been placed in charge of steam engines. "Has it not frequently happened," he wrote, "that men have been taken from the work bench, and, if they had barely understanding enough to oil a gudgeon, drive a wedge, or screw up a nut, have been thought adequate to a most responsible duty, on a faithful and intelligent discharge of which, depended the happiness of thousands?" Members of the committee investigating the *Moselle* explosion in Cincinnati concurred. "It is a lamentable fact," they wrote in 1838, "that many of our steamboat Engineers are only so in name, being entirely unacquainted with the nature or power of steam, and, of course, are unacquainted with the mode and manner of applying it with safety." A writer appearing in the *Journal of the Franklin Institute* in 1852 similarly found that "the place of engineer in charge of a steamboat, including as it does, the responsibility for the lives of hundreds of passengers at a time, is frequently . . . intrusted to persons, who are in no wise fitted either by previous education, or by mental or moral habits, to be entrusted with such responsibilities." Others noted that, even when a qualified engineer was employed, he was not always tending to the most dangerous aspects of the steam engine. James H. Ward pointed out in 1847 that "the boilers are the source both of power and of danger, and should therefore receive the frequent attention of the best intelligence in the steam department of a vessel," but that "engineers often confine their attention wholly to the starting bar, injections, throttles and other parts of the engine, and leave the water gauges, feed, and blow cocks of the boiler, entirely to the judgement and management of firemen." And some lamented that firemen sometimes became engineers without even the most fundamental knowledge of steam engineering principles. "Many there are," wrote one observer shortly after the *Moselle* explosion, "who descend the river in the humble capacity of firemen and shortly after take charge of an engine. These persons many of them know nothing of danger, they have no experience, no skill; . . . if you ask them what pressure they have, many of them will turn away; and if they do answer, there is as little likelihood of a correct answer as though you had asked them to calculate the return of some comet."[32]

When writers focused on the character and training of engineers rather than on the machine itself, they figured the problem of boiler explosions less as a technical problem and more as a social problem. According to this view, in order to safeguard against the destructive possibilities of the steam engine, it was important to morally and intellectually elevate those men charged with operating steam engines. Society as a whole, they urged, would benefit from ensuring that powerful machinery was under the guidance of knowledgeable men of good standing. "The interests of society . . . demand that men of the highest skill and most exalted characters, should receive the preference as engineers," wrote Cadwallader Evans in 1850.[33]

A number of observers argued that the competent engineer should exhibit certain moral qualities that were increasingly being identified as distinctly middle-class. In the first place, he should eschew the use of alcohol not only on the job, but at all times. In a letter to the editor of the *Boston Atlas,* reprinted in the *New-Yorker,* one writer called for the formation of a review board that would "examine *engineers* and *pilots* before they are employed, and require them to produce certificates of good moral character and sober habits." Cadwallader Evans also insisted that the good engineer "should be a man of sobriety and temperance in all things." Gambling was similarly unacceptable among those charged with regulating the power of steam. A writer for the *North American Review* in 1840 noted with approval the record of one captain who, in sixteen years of duty, had never had a serious accident. "*He never allows a man in his employ to play at cards on board of his boat,*" the writer observed by way of explanation, adding that the captain was "*careful to select men of temperate habits.*" In 1852, steamboat owners, captains, and engineers meeting in St. Louis passed a resolution stating that no captain or crew member could, while on board their vessel, drink alcohol "so as to become under its influence," or play cards. "Habitual drunkenness or gambling, either on board or on shore," the resolution read, "shall be good cause for revoking a license to any steamboat officer." In addition, the competent engineer would exhibit a certain fortitude and self-control. "He should possess firmness, courage and self-possession," wrote Cadwallader Evans in 1850. "He ought never, under any circumstances, to yield to excitement, no matter what the temptation or what the reward." A writer twelve years earlier similarly observed of the qualified engineer that "his control should be absolute," and that "he should be independent . . . and sober and watchful." The question of independence was especially important, as some boiler explosions were credited to timid engineers failing to insist upon a course of action they thought prudent. A report of a boiler explosion that appeared in the *New-York American* in 1826, for instance, noted that just prior to the explosion the "too obedient" engineer told the steamboat owners that the steam pressure could go no higher without danger. Nonetheless, the owners insisted that he raise more steam. "This was done," the report continued, "and the explosion was instantaneous."[34]

In addition to moral improvement, the elevation of "hands" would entail proper training for engineers. However, between 1820 and 1860, there was a marked shift in the popular conception of what constituted proper training. In the 1820s and 1830s, observers frequently argued that knowledge gained from "experience and observation" would be the chief requisite for the safe operation of steam engines. In 1831, for instance, the *Journal of the Franklin Institute* published a letter from an Indiana steamboat builder named Matthew Robinson who professed that all boiler explosions proceeded either from the carelessness of engineers or from failures in boiler design and manufacture, and that "the power of steam may be completely under the control of the careful and experienced artist." A second letter from Robinson appearing several pages later pointed again to experience as the key characteristic of the ideal engineer. High-pressure steam engines, he wrote, needed to be operated by "experienced engineers, who shall have the whole control of the engine."[35]

But by the early 1840s, many observers were urging that engineers base their work as well in theoretical knowledge acquired through study, and that this was at least as important as the "practical skill" acquired through experience. "Accidents have happened," noted a contributor to *Scientific American* in 1850, "when those having charge of the engine were men known to have been possessed of all the requisites, so far as practical and experienced mechanics can have, and yet relying upon their experience, based upon well known principles, were suddenly launched into eternity." For this writer, engineers needed to know more about the "nature of steam"; they needed to be able to answer questions such as " how much does water expand into its elementary gasses?" The writer for the *North American Review* in 1840 argued that the lack of theoretical knowledge among engineers—rather than their negligence or inexperience—accounted for most boiler explosions. The problem, he wrote, was that there were far too many engineers "who know nothing, or next to nothing, about the nature and properties of the mysterious and powerful agent"—by which he meant steam—"which is as yet in some respects an enigma even to the learned." A writer appearing in the *Farmer and Mechanic* eight years later agreed that steam engines should be operated only by engineers who had "a sound, practical, scientific and mechanical education in the profession of Engineering," an education that would include not only "the science of steam," but "the science of chemistry and mechanics" as well. Joining these calls for more theoretical training for engineers were calls for the government to establish engineering schools, or for other institutions—such as mechanics' institutes—to establish courses of study on steam and steam engines.[36]

In 1851, a *Journal of the Franklin Institute* article titled "What Constitutes an Engineer?" clearly expressed this new emphasis on theoretical knowledge. Noting several recent explosions aboard steamboats, the author of the article argued that ignorance among engineers "of the first principles of mechanics, either practical or theoretical" stood behind most boiler explosions. According to this writer, men who asserted their engineering qualifications by highlighting their practical experience and setting themselves apart from theory too often won the confidence of a misguided public. "If a man has a greasy jacket, and rails at anything like theoretical knowledge," he wrote, "he is immediately set down as a *sound practical man*." But to deny the value of theoretical knowledge was, he continued, foolish. "We say the general diffusion of knowledge prevents crime . . . and at the same time employ engineers who know nothing of the principles of steam or practical mechanics." Eager not to malign all engineers who based their practice in the rule of experience rather than the rule of theory, the author noted that "I am acquainted with some who, by years of practice, have become well worthy of confidence." But, he added, "these men are now the last to deny, and the first to appreciate the value of proper theoretical or mechanical knowledge."[37]

In spite of the call for increased theoretical training among engineers, it is difficult to say precisely in what way knowledge of the "nature of steam," or of the chemical and mechanical properties of water, helped the engineer in the engine room. And if writers appearing in prominent periodicals like *Scientific American,* the *Farmer and Mechanic,* and the *Journal of the Franklin Institute* urged the priority of theory over experience, some men who identified themselves as engineers and published pamphlets on their own asserted that the knowledge imparted by experience was, in fact, more useful than anything that theorists might have to offer. The author of a pamphlet published in Louisville, Kentucky in 1839, Robert M'Lane, wrote that "the knowledge of the principle by which steam is generated, is of very little use to the practical engineer," insisting that he know instead how to make the steam work safely upon the machinery. M'Lane mocked the pretensions of those who would "tell you how many cubic feet of steam one of water will make, and weigh it out to you as though it were a substance they could hold in the palm of their hand." Experience and "good sound reason," he went on to say, "will teach us that the most of theorists hold very wrong ideas respecting steam, and the best principle by which it can be made to act on machinery." Cadwallader Evans argued a similar point in his pamphlet *A Short Treatise on the Causes of Explosions of Steam Boilers,* published in 1850. Referring to continued efforts by the government to address the problem of boiler explosions, Evans wrote that "government should not always employ in its experiments and offices the merely scientific professor, to the exclusion of men of enlarged practice and experience." Indeed, in the introduction to the pamphlet, Evans made clear his preference for experience over theory. "I aim at nothing polished in style or abstruse in principle," he wrote. "A higher object is to impart, in familiar language, the results of my own observations and experience."[38]

But if theoretical training had little to offer the steam engineer in terms of his practice, it had much to offer him in other terms. The subordination of experience to theory was a means of elevating the authority and social status of the steam engineer by figuring his work as a form of mental labor more than a form of manual labor. The distinction between experience and theory was analogous to that between head and hand, mind and body. Experience was bodily—the experienced engineer relied on knowledge he gained from looking at the color of steam, listening to the sound of the safety valve, and so on. Theory was cerebral—it was understood to be gained, not from sensual engagement with the world, but from classroom study. Experience was the work of the hand; theory, the work of the head. As writers and lecturers highlighted the theoretical training believed to be necessary for steam engineering competency, they began explicitly to place the engineer among members of the professions. A writer for the *Farmer and Mechanic* in 1848, for instance, urged that the educational requirements for the competent engineer made his position equal to that of the physician "or any other scientific professor." "The situation of Chief Engineer on board a steam vessel is manifestly one of great responsibility," he wrote, "and enough is already known of this explosive element, to demand that the head or chief of this department should be educated in the science of his profession." Ten years earlier, the author of the report on the *Moselle* explosion had argued that engineering, given its importance to human life, needed to be placed alongside the more traditional professions. "We know of no class of men, upon whose intelligence and skill the safety of so many lives depend, as upon those of Engineers," he averred, before comparing engineers with physicians, lawyers, and teachers. When the New Orleans Chamber of Commerce published a report on boiler explosions in 1851, it called for a law that would "provide for the rigid examination, and licensing" of engineers, pointing out that "surely as much human life is dependant [sic] upon their skill and prudence, as upon the skill of army surgeons," before asking, "Why should not the former be examined and commissioned, as well as the latter?"[39]

Finally, in the face of increasing demand for more action, Congress passed a new regulatory law in August 1852 requiring the examination and licensing of engineers aboard passenger steamboats. The language of the law identified competency in broad terms, pointing to the moral character of the engineer, his knowledge, and his experience. "Whenever any person claiming to be qualified to perform the duty of engineer upon steamers carrying passengers, shall apply for a certificate," the law read, the area board of inspectors must "examine the applicant" in order to evaluate his "character, habits of life, knowledge, and experience in the duties of an engineer." If satisfied, they could then issue him a license for one year. While this was only one of a number of provisions of the new law, it did the most to address the concern that accidents frequently were due to incompetent engineers who failed to properly "manage" their engines. The idea of licensing engineers had been around a long time but had never been enacted into law. The Franklin Institute, in its 1836 report, had recommended a law requiring that engineers serve two years "in a steam engine factory, or general machine making establishment" before being hired, and that they have "a thorough knowledge of the working of an engine" and provide "satisfactory testimonials of steady habits." But this was not the same as requiring a license, and even these provisions—which clearly placed experience over "theory" as a basis for competent practice—were not written into the 1838 law, which stipulated only that owners of steamboats employ "experienced and skilful" engineers. Over the next decade, however, a shift to emphasizing theoretical or "scientific" knowledge occurred, so that in 1848 a writer for the *Farmer and Mechanic* could cite approvingly a proposal to require that "no person should be entrusted with the working of a steam engine on board a steam vessel, but a practical scientific mechanic, one who had a thorough knowledge of steam and the steam engine." The competency of this engineer, the proposal continued, would be indicated by "a proper uniform or badge, with a diploma . . . obtained from a board of practical scientific professors in the science of steam and the working of the steam engine." The examination and licensing provision of the 1852 law, which many practicing engineers had supported for years, expressed this essential sentiment. The steam engineer, aboard passenger steamboats and in the popular imagination, would no longer simply be a "hand."[40]

By most accounts, the 1852 law—which went into effect January 1, 1853—helped dramatically reduce the number of boiler explosions in America. According to a government inspectors' report published in 1861, fifty explosions occurred on western waterways alone from 1848 to 1852, with more than 1,100 lives lost. The number of explosions on western and eastern waters combined was less than half that in the five years from 1854 to 1858, with the number killed reduced even more dramatically, to 224, on both western and eastern waterways. Another study, pointing to the general increase in the safety of steam travel following the 1852 law, found that the eight years after the passage of the new law saw a 35 percent reduction in the loss of life aboard steamboats from all accidents (which would include, for instance, fires and collisions as well as explosions), in comparison to the eight years prior to the passage of the new law. By the middle of the 1850s, observers were noting the effectiveness of the new law. A writer for *Scientific American* in 1855, for instance, wrote of the "new steamboat law" that "it gives us great pleasure to inform our readers that the law has operated well since it went into force," noting that government inspectors were being "very" strict regarding "the character of engineers and pilots." "We all remember how that the Ohio and Mississippi rivers used to run red every week with the blood of slaughtered victims," he wrote. "Now all this is changed." While boilers would continue to explode aboard steamboats and in steam-powered manufactories, these disasters on the whole were much less frequent—even with the significant increase in the use of steam power—so that the general sense of crisis that had pervaded the decades before the Civil War passed.[41]

Steam boiler explosions were not only common occurrences in America's early industrial period; they were commonly discussed, spawning countless inquiries, reports, protestations, suggestions, and purported technical improvements. "We believe we are not saying too much," claimed a writer for *Scientific American* early in 1850, "when we assert that no subject . . . has engaged so much attention and has been the object of so much investigation as that of 'Steam Boiler Explosions.'" But in spite of endless investigation and repeated cries for something to be done, the popular conception year after year was that little progress was being made. "Whenever a steam boat is blown up and a number of lives lost," observed a writer for a New York newspaper in 1832, "the excitement is prodigious, and inquiries are every where put forth, 'can nothing be done to prevent the recurrence of these dreadful accidents?'" Such attention was relatively short-lived, he continued. "After a while, however, we subside into comparative apathy, until aroused by a new explosion, when we go over the same ground and end as we begun." But if going over the same ground again and again seemed to make little headway in addressing the problem explicitly at hand, it served another, more subtle purpose. As editors, inventors, boat captains, engineers, poets, ministers, mechanics, and others discussed and wrote about the problem of boiler explosions, they articulated a conception of mechanized society in terms of a critical relation, that between machine tender and machine. If steam engines were going to be used to good effect, they urged, then they needed to be managed by men who possessed certain technical knowledge and exhibited certain elevated qualities. No interests in society would be served by contravening the authority of engineers over engines. Given the metaphoric relation

between a potentially explosive steam engine and a potentially explosive society, the figure of the professional engineer took on added meaning: he was
the disinterested authority whose special knowledge meant that his direc-
tions should be heeded for the safety of all society. The image of the steam
engine properly regulated by the qualified engineer thus enabled antebellum
Americans to conceptualize the relation between human and machine, between
head and hand, and between manager and worker in terms that would ensure
the authority of the former over the latter. In writing the social problems
of industrial development onto the problem of boiler explosions, participants in the popular discourse on mechanization saw themselves to be on
impartial ground, even as they elaborated a set of relations that helped to
conceptualize the cooperative relation between managers and workers, thereby
furthering middle-class interests without seeming to do so.[42]

Epilogue

The making of the American middle class was as much a conceptual undertaking as it was a social undertaking. New modes of labor-divided and mechanized production in the first decades of the nineteenth century created a division between "headwork" and "handwork" in a way that had not been seen before. Proprietors, manufacturers, managers, and overseers, along with a growing number of clerks, bookkeepers, bankers, and retail merchants, joined lawyers, physicians, teachers, and ministers to constitute a new and unprecedentedly large nonmanual workforce. In the course of their work, these men invariably used their hands—to write a check, emphasize a point, close a deal, feel a pulse—but the popular understanding was that theirs was headwork, not handwork. Those who performed this mental labor, going to offices where they were paid to sit and write and talk and think, or to shop floors where they were paid to oversee the work of others, distinguished themselves socially from those who went to work at building sites, on wharves, in craft shops, or on mechanized shop floors, where they were generally paid much less to perform labor now seen as distinctly manual. In the clothes they wore and the manner in which they spoke, in the homes they built and the things they bought and the books they read and their leisure pursuits, members of this nascent middle class found ways large and small to make real their elevated status and authority.

But their ascent did not go unchallenged. Just as unprecedented as the social presence of this new middle class was the social presence of a working class of men and women who worked with their hands for wages in jobs and settings that seemed to offer little opportunity for advancement. Some of these wage-workers agreed that their interests were fundamentally opposed to the interests of their employers (and anyone else who benefited from what they considered to be their exploitation), and they resisted collectively and individually—also in ways large and small—the inequities of the new industrial age. This book has argued that those who were interested in stabilizing their middle-class authority worked to mitigate class tensions by promoting a series of conceptual frameworks that effectively undermined oppositional notions of class. More specifically, this book has examined how these nonoppositional conceptions of class circulated, not through explicit pronouncements by ministers, college professors, or business owners, whose class interests were clearly on display, but implicitly, by observers anonymous and known, who seemed to be talking about things far removed from scenes of class conflict. In the mechanics' institute movement and the manual labor school movement, in popular health reform activities and discussions of the problem of steam boiler explosions, men and women in antebellum America conceptualized a series of relations and called for their proper arrangement: the head needed to govern the hand, as the mind needed to govern the body, as the human needed to govern the machine. Because each of these relations figured the relation between proprietors or managers and wage-workers, the lines of deference and authority in the one realm extended to the other. If the hand should submit to the head, if the body needed to be worked by the rule of the mind, if the machine needed to be checked by the human, then wage-working "hands" needed to defer to the authority of the "heads" of the shops that employed them. While it seems evident that some people remained unpersuaded by the conclusions of these movements and discussions—the wage-workers in the early 1850s, for instance, who preferred to spend their leisure hours outside the purview of the Mechanics' Institute of the City of New-York, or that portion of the "laboring public" (in George Junkin's words) who resented the activities of manual labor schools, or possibly the "mob" that greeted Sylvester Graham in Portland, Maine in 1834—their general formulations clearly were compelling to many participants in the antebellum popular discourse on mechanization.

Although this popular discourse on mechanization continued to fill newspapers, periodicals, lecture halls, and other venues through the remainder of the nineteenth century, developments in the 1860s gave new direction and meaning to some of the activities and discussions that have been considered here. Steam boiler explosions in the decades before 1860 often were terribly destructive, for instance, but none could compare with the most dramatic and deadliest boiler explosion of the century, which occurred in April

1865, in the waning weeks of the Civil War, aboard a steamboat on the Mississippi River. Heading north just days after Robert E. Lee's surrender at Appomatox, the steamboat *Sultana* was packed with more than two thousand Union soldiers who had recently been released from prisoner of war camps and were returning home to Tennessee, Indiana, Ohio, Michigan, and other western states. Early in the morning of April 27, a boiler exploded as the boat passed several miles north of Memphis. The results were catastrophic—those who survived the explosion, which would have been most of the passengers and crew members, found the boat engulfed in flames and sinking. The poor physical condition of many of the newly released prisoners, along with the darkness and the cold, swift water, compounded the tragedy. When all was told, more than 1,700 persons were dead. Events of the day, however, in combination certainly with the awful familiarity of printed numbers of dead, prevented the *Sultana* disaster from receiving anything like the national attention that earlier explosions had received. The war's end, Lincoln's assassination and funeral cortege, and the search for John Wilkes Booth and other conspirators dominated the news during the weeks before and after the explosion. The official army investigation into the incident, released less than a month after the explosion occurred, had much more to say about the overcrowding of the boat than it did about the possible cause of the explosion. Those investigations that did focus on the cause differed in their conclusions: the federal steamboat inspector found that a recent and poorly done patch job on one of the boilers was to blame, while an investigation conducted several years later found that the explosion resulted from a boiler design that was unsuited to the silty waters of the Mississippi River.[1]

The *Sultana* tragedy, enormous as it was, did little to change how people used and discussed steam engines, but other developments during the Civil War had a dramatic impact on important aspects of the popular discourse on mechanization. In 1862, during the difficult early years of the war, Abraham Lincoln signed into law the Morrill Land-Grant College Act. The Morrill Act provided each state with land that would be used to raise money for establishing colleges that would stress studies in "agriculture and the mechanic arts." The spirit of the law was twofold: it was intended both to promote the study of practical knowledge and to provide educational opportunities for farmers, mechanics, and—in the words of the act's tireless proponent, Senator Justin Morrill of Vermont—members of "the industrial classes" more generally. The results for those seeking training in engineering were clear: the generally unsystematic popular educational programs of surviving mechanics' institutes, and the relatively inaccessible science and technical programs offered at traditional liberal colleges, or at schools such as Rensselaer Polytechnic Institute or the

Massachusetts Institute of Technology that were devoted to science and engineering education, would be joined by a rapidly growing number of public colleges and universities offering full degree programs in science and engineering. Those seeking to enter the ranks of headworkers by acquiring formal training in engineering would now have much greater opportunity to do so, and with the support of the federal and state governments. For proponents of the educational efforts of mechanics' institutes, or for those concerned about the training of engineers designing and operating steam engines, this would have been an auspicious and even vindicating development.[2]

If the passage of the Morrill Act in 1862 carried forward some of the imperatives of the waning mechanics' institute movement, the founding of Hampton Institute in Virginia in 1868 carried forward some of the imperatives of the practically defunct manual labor school movement. The founder of Hampton Institute, Samuel Chapman Armstrong, became familiar with the manual labor system at a very young age. Born in Hawaii in 1839 to missionary parents, Armstrong saw the manual labor system in action at the two schools for Hawaiians overseen by his father. Armstrong came to Massachusetts for college in 1860, joined the army and led a regiment of black soldiers during the Civil War, and then took a position with the Freedmen's Bureau in Virginia. There he recognized the importance of education for freed blacks, and settled on the manual labor system as the best means for providing that education. With the help of the American Missionary Association, Armstrong opened Hampton Institute in the spring of 1868 as a school of higher education for black students. As with the manual labor schools of the 1820s and 1830s, students divided their time between labor and study. For Armstrong, the "plan of combining mental and physical labor" was of central importance to the school, for reasons that were commonly voiced by antebellum proponents of the manual labor system: physical labor would enable students to pay for their schooling, it would teach them the virtues of discipline and hard work, it would provide them with useful knowledge, and it would help them excel in their studies. Armstrong's notion of "industrial education" became the model not only for other schools for black students in the South, but for a number of "off-reservation" Indian boarding schools, the first and most famous of which was the Carlisle Indian School, founded in Pennsylvania in 1879. The prevailing rhetoric surrounding these postbellum manual labor schools was not that labor was necessary to preserve the health of students who might otherwise grow sickly from their studies. Instead, it was that labor was necessary to improve the lives of students who were disadvantaged by race and custom and who would find in their labor—as much as in their study—the path upward.[3]

The Civil War was not the only engine of change for the popular discourse on mechanization. Prior to the war, in laboratories, science journals, and lecture halls overseas, a new set of scientific ideas came into focus that explained the fundamental relation between heat, energy, and mechanical work. These ideas about the "correlation of forces"—eventually they would be called the principles of thermodynamics—held that heat and work were simply different forms of energy, and that known and inviolable laws governed the transfer of one form of energy into the other. More specifically, the laws of thermodynamics found that energy could be neither created nor destroyed, but simply held in one state and transferred to another. The energy of the sun, for instance, was stored in wood, or in coal, and then released when burned. A steam engine, then, did not produce energy, it simply converted it from one form to another. This principle of the conservation of energy was joined by a second principle, entropy, which stated that a portion of energy was effectively lost whenever it passed from a warm state to a cool state, as in a steam engine. Discussions of the "correlation of forces," or of the "dynamical theory of heat," began to appear in popular magazines in America by the late 1850s. For participants in the popular discourse on mechanization, the implications of these principles were several. First, they provided a framework not only for designing and using new, theoretically informed steam engines, but also for conceiving other kinds of engines for converting heat into mechanical work. Second, they pointed to both the need for and the means of developing more efficient engines. Since there was a limit to the supply of energy that could be transformed into work, since the exhaustion of energy was a real endpoint on some distant horizon, waste was now anathema. Finally, the principles of thermodynamics suggested that the human body was not simply analogous to a machine—it literally was a machine, to the extent that it was an apparatus for converting heat into mechanical work, in just the same way that a steam engine was an apparatus for converting heat into mechanical work. Food was not like fuel, it *was* fuel; the body was not like an engine, it *was* an engine. In this way, human bodies—in their ability to perform work—were bound by the same laws of nature that bound steam engines. If the use of the latter could be improved by the study of those laws, so too could the use of the former.[4]

This new understanding of the correlation of forces found its way into a series of articles titled "Strength, and How to Use It," published in *Lippincott's Magazine* beginning in October 1868. Written by Walter Wells, a popular lecturer and writer living in Maine, the four articles explored the multitude of ways in which Americans made poor use of their physical energy, and the ways they could correct this national problem. "The great social or industrial sin of our American people," the first article stated at the outset, "is, that they habitually do too much." Craftsmen worked harder than did their counterparts overseas, factory workers worked twelve-hour days, students toiled through "overwhelming" demands, businessmen planned and worried without end, housewives labored ceaselessly, and members of the professions—if any good—were "tasked beyond endurance." This overwork, Wells continued, was unfortunate not only because it diminished the pleasures of life, but because it led to a host of diseases. In fact, for Wells, various "nervous diseases and ailments"—dyspepsia and consumption being chief among them—had become "characteristic national infirmities." What is more, the endemic ill-direction of strength in the workplace and in all arenas of human activity was unnecessary, which meant that the baleful consequences of overwork were avoidable. For Wells, the solution to the "great evil of intemperate labor" was simple: work needed to be done with greater "efficiency," and this could be accomplished only through study and "careful adjustments of labor." The ideas of entropy and the conservation of energy suffused Wells's argument. "Every worker should bear constantly in mind the fact that his strength is a constantly-evanishing possession. With every word we utter and breath we draw it passes from us to mingle with the universe of power," he wrote. "The strength that now moves in us was a little while ago a part of the brute force of Nature in the sunbeam, in the electric flash, or pulsating in the arteries of animals." Fatigue was unavoidable, he urged, but true exhaustion was not only unnecessary but profoundly damaging. Waste, therefore, should be avoided in all human efforts, and efficiency should be the overriding goal.[5]

The continuities between the antebellum popular discourse on mechanization and this series of articles are several. Wells's articles argued that the most salient divide in the world of work was between headwork and handwork, and that the relation between the two was an important social relation (at one point he applauded the effectiveness of an overseer who, "with both hands in his pockets" and "keeping up a thinking all the time," put "intelligence and one purpose into the stupid workmen," workmen who "could lift but could not think"). Like proponents of manual labor schools, he insisted that mental labor took a high toll on those who worked with their heads, arguing that it was even more taxing than manual labor, that indeed "head-workers need more rest than hand-workers." He also evoked the specter of the "diseases of a literary life"—although he did not use the phrase—arguing that "in by far the larger proportion of all cases of extraordinary mental endowment . . . there is a decided tendency toward morbid if not absolutely diseased bodily condition." In addition, like proponents of mechanics' institutes, he argued that scientific study had much to offer those seeking to understand how best to do their work, and that while general education was important, schools should be seen as places for sorting those suited to headwork from those suited to handwork. Finally, like the popular physiologists of the 1840s and 1850s, Wells emphasized the deleterious health effects of what he saw to be particularly modern ways of life, argued for the importance of judicious physical exercise, and highlighted the importance of diet to health and productive living.[6]

At the same time, these articles pointed to new trajectories that would become quite familiar to Americans in the decades ahead. What Wells called "nervous diseases" that resulted from overwork and had become "characteristic national infirmities" would, in 1869, be codified under the single medical diagnosis of "neurasthenia," one of the most discussed diseases of the postbellum decades. The symptoms of neurasthenia—also called "nervous exhaustion" and "nervous prostration"—included a variety of physical and psychical complaints, ranging from headaches to insomnia to fear of being alone. One of its most characteristic symptoms was profound physical exhaustion. As described by physicians, the underlying condition to neurasthenia was a depletion of the vital energy (or nerve force) that animated the various functions of the body. Physicians explained that normal physical activity occurred in a dynamic of "waste and repair," whereby energy expended in a day's activity needed to be replenished before more activity could be undertaken. Health was preserved when men and women were careful to regulate their activity according to physiological laws. Neurasthenia ensued when an individual used more nerve force than he or she had in store, much like depleting a battery or overdrawing a bank account (two favorite metaphors in discussions of the illness). Physicians and others generally understood this "nervous exhaustion" to be a pathology specific to the pace and complexity of industrial society. In his 1881 book *American Nervousness,* one of the most popular works on the subject, George Beard included in his list of causes of neurasthenia three relatively recent technologies—steam power, the periodical press, and the telegraph—that set modern civilization apart from civilizations of old and pushed modern life to such a heightened pace that neurasthenia ensued. Treatments were almost as varied as the symptoms. Most were intended to strike the right balance between waste and repair by restoring enough of the body's supply of nerve force to enable the patient to resume normal activity. Common restorative therapies included enforced rest, electrotherapy, massage, and hydrotherapy. Exercise and travel could, if moderately pursued, also serve to replenish nervous energy, and drugs were sometimes prescribed to alleviate specific symptoms. Americans responded to this medical framework for enervation and anxiety with intense and widespread interest. Silas Weir Mitchell's 1869 article for *Lippincott's Magazine* titled "Wear and Tear," which took up the question of whether "the nervous system of the American is being sorely overtaxed," served as the basis for a book by the same title published in 1871, which almost immediately sold out and appeared in five editions in the first decade after its publication. Mitchell, the son of John Kearsley Mitchell of the Franklin Institute (one of the purchasers of Maelzel's automaton chess-player), popularized the so-called "rest cure" for neurasthenic patients and became perhaps the most famous "nerve doctor" of the late nineteenth century.[7]

Discussions of neurasthenia clearly echoed antebellum popular physiologists, both in their ascription of disease to the demands of modern life and in the call to accord behavior with inviolable physiological laws. They also echoed the manual labor school movement, primarily in their general association of mental exertion and disease. Especially in their popular writings on the disease, some of the most prominent neurasthenia physicians held that "American nervousness" was found principally among headworkers rather than handworkers. In "Wear and Tear," for instance, Mitchell distinguished between the "physical worker" who occupied himself with "pure mechanical labor" and those employed in "brain-work." He argued that nervous exhaustion resulted from an excess of brain work rather than physical work, insisting on the overall health benefits of physical work. For Mitchell, the difference between the two kinds of work was clearly a matter of class. "If the strictures I have to make applied throughout the land," he wrote, "to Oregon as to New England, to the farmer as to the business man, to the women of the artisan class as to those above them socially—then indeed I should cry, God help us and them that are to come after us!" But doctors who wrote about neurasthenia in the popular press as if it were almost exclusively an ailment among people who worked with their heads would have known from reading medical journals (and probably from their own practices) that such was not the case. From the very beginning of the diagnosis, case studies appearing in medical journals showed neurasthenia occurring among not only lawyers, clergymen, and merchants, but also farmers, carpenters, butchers, brass polishers, and unskilled laborers. For these poorer patients, men and women who could afford neither the cost of expensive therapies nor the time necessary for the "rest cure," a different set of imperatives prevailed, imperatives that looked more to the prevention of disease than to the cure.[8]

It was, perhaps, this different set of imperatives that helped give ascendancy to the postbellum movement for efficiency in the workplace. When Walter Wells called for greater efficiency in work so that people could avoid

exhaustion and disease, he lamented the fact that while there was much discussion and debate over such questions as the proper length of the workday,
"no scientific basis for general and intelligent action exists." Less than a
decade later, Frederick Winslow Taylor began working at the Midvale Steel
Company outside Philadelphia, where he set out to establish such a basis.
Taylor—who received a degree in mechanical engineering from the Stevens
Institute of Technology in 1883—commenced a series of experiments and
changes in workplace practices at Midvale designed (according to Taylor) to
increase the productivity and efficiency of the shop. In the mid 1890s, after
having left Midvale, he began presenting papers before the American Society of Mechanical Engineers—founded in 1880—on a new system of management that Taylor argued would both maximize the productive efficiency of working men and women and foster greater cooperation between
workers and managers. Taylor refined and promoted his managerial system
through the first decade of the twentieth century and pulled together all of
its elements in 1911 with the publication of *The Principles of Scientific Management*. According to Taylor and others, the "human element" of production, meaning all of the variability and uncertainty that accompanied
workers who were guided by habit or tradition rather than by science, was a
realm of inefficiency that could no longer be tolerated or afforded. For Taylor, one of the chief hindrances to productivity was "soldiering," or the conscious (and sometimes unconscious) slowing of output by workers. Through
"time study" and "motion study," the work done by men and women in practically any setting could be made most efficient by eliminating soldiering and
all forms of waste and arriving at the "one best way" to do work. At the same
time, greater harmony between workers and employers would be achieved
by basing workplace decisions—about how best to complete a particular
task, for instance, or about the pace of work—in the objective, scientific
knowledge possessed by managers rather than in interest-group politics or
"rule of thumb" knowledge. Taylor's book was something of a sensation,
and the professed ideals of scientific management—efficiency, the elimination of waste, maximal productivity, the rationalization of work, and social
harmony—captured the imagination of an American public that came to
embrace a new "gospel of efficiency."[9]

   While Taylor himself had little to say about preventing the exhaustion
and fatigue that were at the center of Wells's discussion and the neurasthenia diagnosis, other figures in the efficiency movement did. Frank and Lillian Gilbreth, who next to Taylor were perhaps the best-known leaders of
the scientific management movement, were among the most explicit in addressing the problem of worker fatigue. In *Applied Motion Study* (1917), for

instance, the Gilbreths insisted that the "worst form of waste" in the work setting was "undue and unnecessary fatigue," not soldiering. They argued that the elimination of worker fatigue—which would be accomplished by better lighting, better seating for workers, the removal of wasted motions, the introduction of rest periods, and other reforms—was crucial to the twin aims of scientific management: productive efficiency and harmonious relations between workers and managers. Even more vocal on the problem of worker fatigue was Frederic Schiller Lee, a professor of physiology at Columbia University from 1891 until his retirement in 1938. Lee, who wrote and lectured extensively on how physiological knowledge could be applied to workplace decisions, pointed to general physical and psychical fatigue among industrial workers as a pernicious but avoidable effect of industrial life. Indeed, fatigue in what he called the "human machine" was for Lee one of the chief obstacles to "physiological efficiency," and it was this efficiency that every worker should strive to obtain by working according to the physiological laws discerned by scientific research. In 1916, Lee weighed in on the contentious issue of the eight-hour day by arguing that the length of the workday was "primarily a problem of physiology" and needed to be determined not by the "mere opinions" of employers or labor leaders but by a "rigidly scientific study of the question." Although Lee favorably mentioned Taylor in his discussion of the eight-hour workday, he became increasingly critical of the scientific management movement, arguing that scientific managers seemed to know little of the physiology of fatigue, so that their managerial reforms were not truly scientific. Nonetheless, like Taylor and other scientific managers, Lee argued that maximal efficiency in the workplace was an ideal, and one that could be accomplished only under the guidance of experts armed with scientific knowledge.[10]

These developments—the establishment of land grant colleges and universities, the promotion of "industrial education" for black and Native American students, the popularization of thermodynamic principles, the elaboration of the diagnosis and treatment of neurasthenia, and the spread of the efficiency movement—occurred in the context of unprecedented class conflict in America. If the antebellum period saw the general introduction of powered machinery to the workplace and the beginning of the organized labor movement, the decades after the Civil War saw the consolidation and spread of the "factory system" of production and the organization of a national labor movement. The acts of collective resistance among wageworkers—most dramatic in the several decades after the railroad strike of 1877, the first national strike the country had seen—were the chief measure of the period's "unrest" (a term that was frequently used in the popular press and which most likely had special meaning for those who understood "rest" to be conservative and healthful). As the discussions and activities that were part of the antebellum popular discourse on mechanization changed and became more diffuse in the midst of the postbellum labor struggle, they generally lost their more subtle rhetorical power. In the place of implicit languages of class emerged quite stark and confident claims to social authority.

Notes

1. "Effects of Machinery," *North American Review* 34 (January 1832), 221, 226, 225, 236, 237, 238, 243.

2. Seth Luther, *An Address to the Working-Men of New-England, on the State of Education, and on the Condition of the Producing Classes in Europe and America:* . . . (Boston, 1832), 10, 22, 15, 28, 31.

3. Ibid., 21n*, 19.

4. The literature on industrial development, the reorganization of work, and class formation in the nineteenth century is substantial. Two excellent works of synthesis are Walter Licht, *Industrializing America: The Nineteenth Century* (Baltimore, Md., 1995); and Bruce Laurie, *Artisans into Workers: Labor in Nineteenth-Century America* (New York, 1989). The clearest treatment of the salience of the division between "headwork" and "handwork" is Stuart M. Blumin, *The Emergence of the Middle Class: Social Experience in the American City, 1760–1900* (New York, 1989).

5. On nineteenth-century ideas about mechanization and work, see David A. Zonderman, *Aspirations and Anxieties: New England Workers and the Mechanized Factory System, 1815–1850* (New York, 1992); Jonathan A. Glickstein, *Concepts of Free Labor in Antebellum America* (New Haven, Conn., 1991); Carl Siracusa, *A Mechanical People: Perceptions of the Industrial Order in Massachusetts, 1815–1880* (Middletown, Conn., 1979); Daniel T. Rodgers, *The Work Ethic in Industrial America, 1850–1920* (Chicago, 1978); and Hugo A. Meier, "Technology and Democracy, 1800–1860," *Mississippi Valley Historical Review* 43 (March 1957), 618–40. Two influential cultural histories of technology in America in the nineteenth century are John F. Kasson, *Civilizing the Machine: Technology and Republican Values in America, 1776–1900* (New York, 1976); and Leo Marx, *The Machine in the Garden: Technology and the Pastoral Ideal in America* (New York, 1964). See also Julie Wosk, *Breaking Frame: Technology and the Visual Arts in the Nineteenth Century* (New Brunswick, N.J., 1993). On cultural expressions of ideas about work in the nineteenth

century, see Melissa Dabakis, *Visualizing Labor in American Sculpture: Monuments, Manliness, and the Work Ethic, 1880–1935* (New York, 1999); Laura Rigal, *The American Manufactory: Art, Labor, and the World of Things in the Early Republic* (Princeton, N.J., 1998); and Nicholas K. Bromell, *By the Sweat of the Brow: Literature and Labor in Antebellum America* (Chicago, 1993).

6. For a useful brief discussion of the term, see "Class" in Raymond Williams, *Keywords: A Vocabulary of Culture and Society* (New York, 1983), 60–69. Martin Burke, in *The Conundrum of Class: Public Discourse on the Social Order in America* (Chicago, 1995), traces some of the different ideas about class in nineteenth-century America. In seeking to take up a "history of concepts" by studying what he calls in his subtitle "public discourse on the social order," Burke's approach to the study of class similarly focuses on language and perception rather than on some purported material reality. The passage appears on p. xvi.

7. Sven Beckert questions the usefulness of the phrase "middle class" in "Propertied of a Different Kind: Bourgeoisie and Lower Middle Class in the Nineteenth-Century United States," in Burton J. Bledstein and Robert D. Johnston, eds., *The Middling Sorts: Explorations in the History of the American Middle Class* (New York, 2001), [285]–95. On middle-class refinement, see Timothy R. Mahoney, *Provincial Lives: Middle-Class Experience in the Antebellum Middle West* (New York, 1999); Richard L. Bushman, *The Refinement of America: Persons, Houses, Cities* (New York, 1992); John F. Kasson, *Rudeness and Civility: Manners in Nineteenth-Century Urban America* (New York, 1990); John S. Gilkeson, Jr., *Middle-Class Providence, 1820–1940* (Princeton, N.J., 1986); Karen Halttunen, *Confidence Men and Painted Women: A Study of Middle-Class Culture in America, 1830–1870* (New Haven, Conn., 1982); and Paul E. Johnson, *A Shopkeeper's Millennium: Society and Revivals in Rochester, New York, 1815–1837* (New York, 1978). For a recent book that finds middle-class men and women resisting the imperative of respectability, see Brian Roberts, *American Alchemy: The California Gold Rush and Middle-Class Culture* (Chapel Hill, N.C., 2000). The principal study on family life and the middle class in the nineteenth century is Mary P. Ryan, *Cradle of the Middle Class: The Family in Oneida County, New York, 1790–1865* (New York, 1981). See also Blumin, *The Emergence of the Middle Class*, ch. 5. On the importance of occupation to middle-class standing, see Blumin, *The Emergence of the Middle Class*; and Burton J. Bledstein, *The Culture of Professionalism: The Middle Class and the Development of Higher Education in America* (New York, 1976). Two very useful surveys of the concept of the middle class more generally and of the scholarship on the American middle class are Burton J. Bledstein, "Introduction: Storytellers to the Middle Class," in Bledstein and Johnston, eds., *The Middling Sorts*, [1]–25; and Blumin, *The Emergence of the Middle Class*, ch. 1.

8. Blumin, in *The Emergence of the Middle Class*, does focus in detail on middle-class formation. The general tendency among labor historians to say little about middle-class formation comes in spite of E. P. Thompson's injunction that "the notion of class entails the notion of historical relationship." See E. P. Thompson, *The Making of the English Working Class* (New York, 1966), 9. One excellent study of labor and industrial development that does examine both working-class and middle-class formation is Judith A. McGaw, *Most Wonderful Machine: Mechanization and Social Change in Berkshire Paper Making, 1801- 1885* (Princeton, N.J., 1987).

9. Gareth Stedman Jones, *Languages of Class: Studies in English Working Class History, 1832–1982* (Cambridge, 1983), 101, 102. For more on language and class analysis, see Lenard R. Berlanstein, ed., *Rethinking Labor History: Essays on Discourse and Class Analysis* (Urbana, Ill., 1993); Patrick Joyce, *Visions of the People: Industrial England and the Question of Class 1848–1914* (Cambridge, 1991); and Joan Wallach Scott, "On Language, Gender, and Working-Class History," in *Gender and the Politics of History* (New York, 1988), [53]–67. Daniel T. Rodgers, *Contested Truths: Keywords in American Politics Since Independence* (New York, 1987), 5.

10. The phrase "language is not life" is from Bryan D. Palmer, *Descent into Discourse: The Reification of Language and the Writing of Social History* (Philadelphia, 1990), xiv. For an extended debate over the discursive approach to social history, see David Mayfield and Susan Thorne, "Social History and its Discontents: Gareth Stedman Jones and the Politics of Language," *Social History* 17 (May 1992), [165]–88, and the series of articles that followed.

11. T. J. Jackson Lears traces a similar relation between culture and social authority in "The Concept of Cultural Hegemony: Problems and Possibilities," *American Historical Review* 90 (June 1985), 567–93. "The concept of cultural hegemony," Lears writes, "can aid intellectual historians trying to understand how ideas reinforce or undermine existing social structures," 568. While I have chosen not to employ the terms "hegemony" or "hegemonic" in this book, I am indebted to the essential framework suggested by Lears. Somewhat similarly, JoAnne Brown explores what she calls "the phenomenon of linguistic modeling" or "the use of metaphor to found a new enterprise upon the cultural authority of an old one" in "Professional Language: Words That Succeed," *Radical History Review* 34 (January 1986), [33]–51. The passage appears on p. 39. Two studies on how specific popular discourses in nineteenth-century America worked to consolidate the social authority of particular groups are Michael O'Malley, "Specie and Species: Race and the Money Question in Nineteenth-Century America," *American Historical Review* 99 (April 1994), 369–95; and David Scobey, "Anatomy of the Promenade: The Politics of Bourgeois Sociability in Nineteenth-Century New York," *Social History* 17 (May 1992), [203]–27.

CHAPTER 1: THE ANTEBELLUM POPULAR DISCOURSE
ON MECHANIZATION

1. "Automaton Chess-Player," *New-York Evening Post* (April 14, 1826), 2; "Maelzel's Automatons," *New-York Evening Post* (April 14, 1826), 2; "Automaton Chess-Player," [New York] *Commercial Advertiser,* (April 14, 1826), 2; ibid; "Maelzel's Automatons," 2.

2. "The Automaton," *New-York American* (April 22, 1826), 2; "Automaton," *New-York Evening Post* (May 27, 1826), 2. Anyone who read the newspaper accounts of Maelzel's show would have learned that the chess-player's career began more than fifty years prior to its arrival in America. Constructed in 1769 by Wolfgang von Kempelen, the chess-player was devised as a "bagatelle" to amuse members of the Viennese royal court. Kempelen won wide acclaim for his puzzling invention, but he showed little interest in making a career out of exhibiting it. By the first decade of the nineteenth century, the chess-player had come under the proprietorship of Johann Maelzel, a Bavarian musician and inventor. More of a showman than Kempelen was, Maelzel

improved the device and exhibited it throughout Europe. In 1825, Maelzel decided to take his show to America, and in December of that year, he boarded a ship bound for the New World.

3. "Chess Player," [Boston] *Evening Gazette* (August 17, 1833), 2; "Automaton Chess-Player," *New-York Evening Post* (April 24, 1826), 2.

4. [Henry Baldwin], "Judge Baldwin's Address," *Register of Pennsylvania* 6 (October 23, 1830), 262. Similarly, a writer for the *Democratic Review* in 1848 imagined a future where "the human race are to live by machinery" and "steam is to perform all the operations of thought." See "Influence of the Telegraph Upon Literature," *Democratic Review* 22 (May 1848), 413. The automaton chess-player has received recent attention from historians and others. See Tom Standage, *The Turk: The Life and Times of the Famous Eighteenth-Century Chess-Playing Machine* (New York, 2002); Gerald M. Levitt, *The Turk, Chess Automaton* (Jefferson, N.C., 2000); James W. Cook, *The Arts of Deception: Playing with Fraud in the Age of Barnum* (Cambridge, 2001), ch. 1; James W. Cook, Jr., "From the Age of Reason to the Age of Barnum: The Great Automaton Chess-Player and the Emergence of Victorian Cultural Illusionism," *Winterthur Portfolio* 30 (winter 1995), 231–57; Stephen P. Rice, "Making Way for the Machine: Maelzel's Automaton Chess-Player and Antebellum American Culture," *Proceedings of the Massachusetts Historical Society* 106 (1994), 1–16; and John T. Irwin, "Handedness and the Self: Poe's Chess Player," *Arizona Quarterly* 45 (spring 1989), 1–28. For earlier studies, see Charles Michael Carroll, *The Great Chess Automaton* (New York, 1975); Joseph Earl Arrington, "John Maelzel, Master Showman of Automata and Panoramas," *Pennsylvania Magazine of History and Biography* 84 (January 1960), 56–92; W. K. Wimsatt, Jr., "Poe and the Chess Automaton," *American Literature* 11 (March 1939–January 1940), 138–51; and Henry Ridgely Evans, *Edgar Allan Poe and Baron von Kempelen's Chess Playing Automaton* (Kenton, Oh., 1939). The most detailed nineteenth-century account of the chess player is G[eorge] A[llen], "The History of the Automaton Chess-Player in America," in Daniel Willard Fisk, *The Book of the First American Chess Congress* (New York, 1859), 420–84.

5. "Effects of Machinery," *North American Review* 34 (January 1832), 225.

6. On Samuel Slater and the beginning of mechanized textile manufacturing in America, see Barbara M. Tucker, *Samuel Slater and the Origins of the American Textile Industry, 1790–1860* (Ithaca, N.Y., 1984). For a good brief overview of the early history of Lowell, see Steve Dunwell, *The Run of the Mill: A Pictorial Narrative of the Expansion, Dominion, Decline, and Enduring Impact of the New England Textile Industry* (Boston, 1978), 29–42. For a more extended study, see Thomas Dublin, *Women at Work: The Transformation of Work and Community in Lowell, Massachusetts, 1826–1860* (New York, 1979). Statistics on Lowell's output are from Walter Licht, *Industrializing America: The Nineteenth Century* (Baltimore, Md., 1995), 27. On Philadelphia area textile manufacturing, see Cynthia Shelton, *The Mills of Manayunk: Industrialization and Social Conflict in the Philadelphia Region, 1787–1837* (Baltimore, Md., 1986); Philip Scranton, *Proprietary Capitalism: The Textile Manufacture at Philadelphia, 1800–1885* (New York, 1983); and Anthony F. C. Wallace, *Rockdale: The Growth of an American Village in the Early Industrial Revolution* (New York, 1978). For an excellent overview of antebellum textile machinery, see Wallace, *Rockdale,* ch. 4.

7. The point about printing and the woodworking trades is in Sean Wilentz, *Chants Democratic: New York City and the Rise of the American Working Class, 1788–1850* (New York, 1984), ch. 3; "Improvements in Mechanics," *Farmer and Mechanic*, n.s., 4 (February 21, 1850), 90; review of *Appleton's Dictionary of Machines, Mechanics, Engine-Work and Engineering*, in *New-Englander* 9 (November 1851), 625.

8. [George Tucker], "Progress of Population and Wealth in the United States, in Fifty Years," *Merchants' Magazine* 9 (July 1843), 57; "Ollapodiana," *Literary Harvester* 2 (February 15, 1843), 160; "Steam and Other Matters," *Pearl and Literary Gazette* 3 (January 4, 1834), 90.

9. "Statutes Made by Steam," *Supplement to the Courant* 12 (July 31, 1847), 118; "Steam and Other Matters," 90; Charles Fraser, "The Moral Influence of Steam," *Hunt's Merchants' Magazine* 14 (June 1846), 512.

10. See H. W. Slater to Mssrs. William Tiffany and Co., March 5, 1830, Letter-book (1827–1836), vol. 14, Slater Companies Collection, Baker Library, Harvard Business School; "Steam and Its Effects," *American Monthly Magazine* 1 (May 1833), 179; "On the Probable Application of Steam Power to Various Purposes," *Mechanics' Magazine, and Register of Inventions and Improvements* 1 (March 1833), 118; "Portable Steam Engine," *Scientific American* 9 (December 3, 1853), [89]; James L. Baker, *Men and Things; or, Short Essays on Various Subjects* (Boston, 1858), 42. Some writers made light of the pervasive use of—or at least enthusiasm for—steam power. An almanac published for the year 1837, for instance, included a series of comical engravings and descriptions of steam-powered machines for shaving, fishing, pulling teeth, and walking. The depiction of a steam boiler explosion appeared on the cover. See *Uncle Sam's Comic Almanack for 1837* (Wheeling, [1837]).

11. Elihu Burritt, "Why I Left the Anvil," *Supplement to the Courant* 15 (April 20, 1850), 62; Baker, *Men and Things*, 41; "The Steam-Engine," *American Quarterly Review* 6 (December 1829), 409. Not all observers marveled at the steam engine. The southern editor J. D. B. DeBow, for example, wrote in 1846 that "the steam engine appears to be a wonderful result of combined art and science; we consider it such, and honor its projectors; but there is nothing in it which refuses to accord with our preconceived notions of the possible, and of the powers and resources with which the intellect of man is endowed." See [J. D. B. DeBow], "Morse's Electro-Magnetic Telegraph," *Commercial Review* 1 (February 1846), 134. For a discussion of how the steam engine blurred the boundary between mechanism and organicism, see David F. Channell, *The Vital Machine: A Study of Technology and Organic Life* (New York, 1991), 78–79. For a fascinating discussion of how different machines have served as metaphors for competing notions of authority and liberty, see Otto Mayr, *Authority, Liberty and Automatic Machinery in Early Modern Europe* (Baltimore, Md., 1986).

12. James R. Leib, *Lecture on the Nature and Objects of the Modern Philosophy . . .* (Philadelphia, Penn., 1830), 14; "Effects of Machinery," 244; [Samuel Griswold Goodrich], *Enterprise, Industry, and Art of Man; . . .* (Philadelphia, Penn., [1845]), 327. The metaphor of harnessing or saddling nature was also commonly used in reference to the telegraph. See, for instance, the poem by Amadis De Gaul titled "The Age We Live In. No. 1" in *Democratic Review* 40 (August 1857), 174: "We 'advance' beyond all measure— / How we go by rail and paddle! / Ay! and we have learned to saddle / Even the lightnings for our pleasure!" See also the poem "The Atlantic Telegraph," published in 1858 in *Knickerbocker:* "The subtle fluid that was tamed / By

Franklin's magic skill; / That Morse by Science has enchained, / To serve the human will: / Whose lightning course has banished Space, / And leaves slow Time behind, / Is destined soon two kindred lands / By closer ties to bind." Robert T. Maccoun, "The Atlantic Telegraph," *Knickerbocker* 52 (August 1858), 187.

13. "Effects of Machinery," 245; [Timothy Walker], "Defence of Mechanical Philosophy," *North American Review* 33 (July 1831), 125; "Steam," *Harper's New Monthly Magazine* 1 (June 1850), 50; "Fulton and Steam Engines," *American Magazine of Useful and Entertaining Knowledge* 2 (November 1835), [89]; Henry T. Tuckerman, "Robert Fulton," *Graham's Magazine* 38 (March 1851), 235.

14. "Effects of Machinery," 244, 233; E. L. Magoon, *Oration . . . Delivered July 4th, 1848, at the Laying of the Corner Stone of the Ohio Mechanics' Institute, Cincinnati* (Cincinnati, Oh., 1848), 20; "The Railway System in Europe," *American Review* 4 (November 1846), 486; "The Iron Horse," *Knickerbocker* 14 (November 1839), 413.

15. "Manufactory of Pins," *New-Yorker* 7 (May 25, 1839), 158. While the article appeared in the *New-Yorker* uncredited, the *Supplement to the Connecticut Courant* printed a longer version of the same article one month earlier, crediting the selection to the *New Haven Record*. See "Manufactory of Pins," *Supplement to the Connecticut Courant* 5 (April 27, 1839), 255; Joseph Story, "A Discourse Delivered before the Boston Mechanics' Institution, at the Opening of their Annual Course of Lectures, November, 1829," *American Library of Useful Knowledge* 1 (Boston, 1831), 27. Carding machinery struck another observer in 1845 the same way. "The card machine is another ingenious contrivance, where machinery is made to work like the human hand, and to think like the human mind." Several paragraphs earlier, the same author wondered at the "almost intelligent machinery" used at Lowell for manufacturing carpeting. See T.S.K., "A Visit to Lowell," *Supplement to the Courant* 10 (April 5, 1845), 51, 50. In 1857 a speaker before the Metropolitan Mechanics' Institute in Washington, D.C., Fred P. Stanton, turned to the same conceit to describe the wonderful abilities of machines. "With machinery, endued with immense power, and *almost with conscious intellect,"* Stanton averred, "[man] cuts, stamps, presses, or rolls the useful metals into all desirable shapes, and for every imaginable purpose." See Fred P. Stanton, "Address," *A Record of the Third Exhibition of the Metropolitan Mechanics' Institute* (Washington, 1857), 6; "Mechanism," *New-Harmony Gazette* 2 (December 6, 1826), 78; "Babbage's Calculating Engine," *American Magazine of Useful and Entertaining Knowledge* 1 (October 1834), 88. A speaker before a mechanics' institute in Ohio two years earlier similarly marveled at the promise of Babbage's machine, one reported feature of which was an ability to discern mistakes when printing the results of a calculation. "The intellectual part of this machine, (if I may be allowed the expression) integrates partial equations of finite differences, and this with an assured accuracy, of which no human being is capable, and if like all the works of man, (are we indeed speaking of the works of man?), it may fall into mistakes in printing the results of its profound calculations, it possesses the divine property, if not of seeing, at least of rectifying them." The speaker then went on to describe a carpet-weaving loom said to be in use at Lowell that had a similar capacity to monitor its operations. See Benjamin G. Leonard, *An Introductory Discourse, Delivered before the Chillicothe Lyceum and Mechanics' Institute, on the 1st of November, 1833* (Chillicothe, Oh., 1834), 48. Fred P. Stanton surely had Babbage's device in mind when he

marveled that modern man "even calculates" by machinery: "He actually performs the labor of the intellect by means of the mechanical operations of mere material parts." See Stanton, "Address," 6. Other observers saw that Babbage's machine would not qualify as a thinking machine. Edgar Allan Poe argued as such in an essay he published in 1836 on Maelzel's chess-player. Poe recognized that the solution to any mathematical problem was univocal and could be subject to the singular purposefulness of machinery. "We can without difficulty," he wrote in discussing Babbage's machine, "conceive the *possibility* of so arranging a piece of mechanism, that upon starting it in accordance with the *data* of the question to be solved, it should continue its movements regularly, progressively, and undeviatingly towards the required solution, since these movements, however complex, are never imagined to be otherwise than finite and determinate." See [Edgar Allan Poe], "Maelzel's Chess-Player," *Southern Literary Messenger* 2 (April 1836), 319; "Statues Made by Steam," 118. For an extended treatment of Blanchard's invention, see Carolyn C. Cooper, *Shaping Invention: Thomas Blanchard's Machinery and Patent Management in Nineteenth-Century America, 1820–1870* (New York, 1991); "Influence of the Telegraph upon Literature," 413; "The Railway System in Europe," 492. For an interesting discussion of how machinery in the nineteenth century was "swiftly redefining the parameters of human identity," see Julie Wosk, *Breaking Frame: Technology and the Visual Arts in the Nineteenth Century* (New Brunswick, N.J., 1993), ch. 2. The passage is on p. 68. See also Bruce Mazlish, *The Fourth Discontinuity: The Co-Evolution of Humans and Machines* (New Haven, Conn., 1993).

16. See, for example, W. S. C[hace], "Andraud's New System of Railroad Locomotion," *Merchants' Magazine* 17 (July 1847), 40; Burritt, "Why I Left the Anvil," 62; [J. D. B. DeBow], "American Legislation, Science, Art, and Agriculture," *Commercial Review* 2 (September 1846), 103.

17. "The Iron Horse," 413; [Baldwin], "Judge Baldwin's Address," 262; Fraser, "The Moral Influence of Steam," 503; Daniel Webster, "Mr. Webster's Introductory Lecture, before the Mechanics' Institution," *American Library of Useful Knowledge* 1 (Boston, 1831), 51.

18. Judith A. McGaw, *Most Wonderful Machine: Mechanization and Social Change in Berkshire Paper Making, 1801–1885* (Princeton, N.J., 1987), 98–99.

19. "The Iron Horse," 413–14; David A. Zonderman, *Aspirations and Anxieties: New England Workers and the Mechanized Factory System, 1815–1850* (New York, 1992), 25; Sui Generis [Thomas Man], *Picture of a Factory Village: . . .* (Providence, 1833), 8; Thomas P. Jones, *An Address on the Progress of Manufactures and Internal Improvement, in the United States; . . .* (Philadelphia, Penn., 1827), 11, 10–11.

20. "The Iron Horse," 413; Webster, "Mr. Webster's Introductory Lecture," 51; Stanton, "Address," 6; [Thomas Carlyle], "Signs of the Times," *Edinburgh Review* 49 (June 1829), 442; Story, "A Discourse Delivered before the Boston Mechanics' Institution," 25; [DeBow], "American Legislation, Science, Art, and Agriculture," 102. In a remarkable anticipation of the scientific management movement that began toward the end of the century, one contributor to the *Mechanics' Magazine* urged that it was a matter of "the highest importance" to both workers and their employers "to ascertain the way in which the greatest quantity of work can be obtained from their [workers'] exertions, with the least quantity of bodily fatigue, or with such a quantity of fatigue as they can easily bear from day to day, without injuring their corporeal

functions." See "On the Strength of Men and Animals," *Mechanics' Magazine, and Register of Inventions and Improvements* 1 (February 1833), 81.

21. Charles Gayarré, *Influence of the Mechanic Arts on the Human Race* (New York, 1854), 66, 68. More than a dozen years earlier, a writer appearing in the *New-Yorker* urged a similar point about the degrading effects of unremitting work. "That man or woman who is compelled to toil incessantly for the bare necessaries of life," he wrote, "has of course no real opportunities for Self-Culture, which in the plan of Divine Wisdom is the great end of his being." For this observer, incessant labor posed a real threat to the status of the worker as fully human. "He who delves in a mine or digs in a trench from daylight to dark for a bare subsistence," he continued, "is virtually restrained from becoming a whole Man—a thinking, reasoning, observing, independent being." See "What Shall Be Done for the Laborer?" *New-Yorker* 11 (July 24, 1841), 297; [Theodore] P[arker], "Thoughts on Labor," *Dial* 1 (April 1841), 512. See also [Theodore] P[arker], "Thoughts on Labor," *New-Yorker* 11 (May 8, 1841), 119–20. The development of technologies that divided head from hand was not limited to production machinery. James W. Carey has made the suggestive argument that telegraphy, by making communication possible without the transportation of documents, marked the development of what he calls a "thoroughly encephalated social nervous system" in which "signalling was divorced from musculature." See James W. Carey, "Technology and Ideology: The Case of Telegraphy," *Prospects* 8 (1983), 314.

22. "Effects of Machinery," 239; Stuart M. Blumin, *The Emergence of the Middle Class: Social Experience in the American City, 1760–1900* (New York, 1989), chs. 3 and 4. See also Nicholas K. Bromell, *By the Sweat of the Brow: Literature and Labor in Antebellum America* (Chicago, 1993); and Jonathan Glickstein, *Concepts of Free Labor in Antebellum America* (New Haven, Conn., 1991), for extended treatments of antebellum ideas about mental and manual labor. Mechanized production was not the only new form of production in which manual laborers were separated from their shop owners. In his study of shoemaking in Lynn, Massachusetts in the early nineteenth century, Paul Faler writes that the "outstanding feature" of the new system of "putting out" was "the physical separation of journeymen from employer at the workplace." According to Faler, this physical separation proved instrumental to the formation of working-class consciousness among the shoemakers of Lynn. See Paul G. Faler, *Mechanics and Manufacturers in the Early Industrial Revolution: Lynn, Massachusetts, 1780–1860* (Albany, N.Y., 1981), 166.

23. Horace Greeley, "Labor—Elegant Extract," *Supplement to the Courant* 10 (January 11, 1845), 8; Charles Quill [James Waddel Alexander], *The Working-Man* (Philadelphia, Penn., 1843), 215, 216, 217; F[rederic] D[an] Huntington, *Hands: Brain: Heart. . . .* (Boston, 1856), 15.

24. Juvenis, "Empire of Mind," *Hartford Pearl and Literary Gazette* 4 (August 20, 1834), 7, 8; James Madison Porter, *An Address to the Mechanics of Easton, Pennsylvania, . . .* (Easton, Penn., 1835), [5]; "The Human Mind," *The Bouquet: Flowers of Polite Literature* 1 (September 24, 1831), 62.

25. "Education," *American Quarterly Review* 6 (September 1829), 146; "Evil Effects of the Division of Labor," *Supplement to the Connecticut Courant* 4 (November 2, 1835), 159. Several years earlier, a speaker in Boston argued that America remained distinct from Europe in that it was characterized by "the non-existence of

the almost infinite subdivisions of labour, by which, though more perfection in the result is sometimes obtained, the process has an almost uniform tendency to reduce human beings to mere machines." See Story, "A Discourse Delivered before the Boston Mechanics' Institution," 34; Walter R. Johnson, *A Lecture on the Mechanical Industry and the Inventive Genius of America*. . . . (Baltimore, Md., 1849), 4. John K. Mitchell evoked a similar image more than a decade earlier when he stated in a lecture before a group of mechanics in Philadelphia, "I feel assured that no American man or boy who now hears me, will be content to be turned into a mere machine, distinguished perhaps for its precision, but unfitted for progression, and hopeless of improvement." See John K. Mitchell, *The Value of the Practical Interrogation of Nature;* . . . (Philadelphia, Penn., 1834), 21; [Andrew Preston Peabody], "The Future of Labor," *North American Review* 74 (April 1852), 456–57.

26. Robert Dale Owen, "Wealth and Misery," *Popular Tracts* 11 (1830), 4; Daniel Webster, "Second Speech on the Sub-Treasury Bill, Delivered in the Senate of the United States, March 12, 1838," in Daniel Webster, *Speeches and Forensic Arguments,* vol. 3 (Boston, 1843), 289, 289–90; "What Are We Going to Make?" *Atlantic Monthly* 2 (June 1858), 95; Thomas Ewbank, *Inorganic Forces Ordained to Supercede Human Slavery* (New York, 1860), 21, 26. See also George P. Marsh, *Address Delivered before the Burlington Mechanics Institute,* . . . (Burlington, Vt., 1843), 25: "Now, the kind of labour anciently performed by slaves is precisely that which is now executed by machinery, the dead unconscious engine being substituted for the living and suffering man."

27. Robert Owen, "The Social System," *New Harmony Gazette* 2 (February 7, 1827), [145]; Seth Luther, *An Address Delivered before the Mechanics and Working-Men, of the City of Brooklyn,* . . . (Brooklyn, N.Y., 1836), 17; T. Throstle, "Factory Life in New-England," *Knickerbocker* 30 (December 1847), 512; [Herman Melville], "The Paradise of Bachelors and the Tartarus of Maids," *Harper's New Monthly Magazine* 10 (April 1855), 678, 675. Antebellum uses of the language of enslavement with regard to industrial production would in every case have had meaning as well in reference to the slavery that prevailed in southern states. For an interesting discussion of how white workers in the early nineteenth century used racial distinctions and the language of slavery to construct working-class identity, see David R. Roediger, *The Wages of Whiteness: Race and the Making of the American Working Class* (New York, 1991).

28. "Effects of Machinery," 237; Robert Dale Owen, "Labor: Its History and Prospects," *Herald of Truth* 3 (March 1848), 195, 194; "What Are We Going to Make?" 96, 95, 96. A writer for *Hunt's Merchants' Magazine* in 1852, in discussing a newly proposed alternative to steam power, used similar language when he wrote of steam that "if it has been a useful slave, it has also been a costly and dangerous one." See "Ericsson's Caloric Engine," *Hunt's Merchants' Magazine* 27 (July 1852), 20.

29. T.S.K., "A Visit to Lowell," 50; Andrew Ure, *The Philosophy of Manufactures* (London, 1835), quoted in [Henry Adolphus Miles], "The Cotton Manufacture," *North American Review* 52 (January 1841), 44. A writer for *The Merchants' Magazine* in 1847 concurred on the relation between moral order and productivity. Writing about Lowell, he noted that "the moral police which is established, also appears to be one of the greatest value, so far as it insures virtuous character and correct deportment, these lying at the foundation of the only solid and genuine prosperity." See "Lowell: And Its Manufactures," *Merchants' Magazine* 16 (April 1847), 360.

Another writer for the *Merchants' Magazine* made sure to ascribe moral supervision to goodwill rather than simple business. "We do not doubt that higher motives have had their influence with the Lowell proprietors, motives of benevolence and good will to the thousands in their mills, but we say, as a mere business calculation, it was a wise one, in the very outset of their enterprise to provide for a careful moral supervision, and guarantee ample sources of improvement for the minds under their control." See "Morals of Manufacturing Towns," *Merchants' Magazine* 19 (December 1848), 661; See Faler, *Mechanics and Manufacturers,* ch. 7.

30. "Machinery and Hand Labor," *Scientific American* 10 (August 18, 1855), 387.

31. "What Are We Going to Make?" 99, 99, 100; "Machinery, for Machine Making," *Graham's Magazine* 41 (November 1852), 469, 470, 471.

32. In 1794, audiences in Philadelphia gathered to see Blanchard's "Mr. Aristocrat" and "Citizen Sans Culotte," two "artificial persons" that danced and performed tricks on stage. See Ezekial Forman, "Amusements and Politics in Philadelphia, 1794," *Pennsylvania Magazine of History and Biography* 10 (1886), 185. New Yorkers interested in such fare could have gone to see Mr. Maffey's display of mechanical figures in 1818, Mr. Vogel's mechanical men and animals shown in 1820, and the exhibition of a "military Automaton or Mechanical Trumpeter" in January 1826. See George C. D. Odell, *Annals of the New York Stage* (New York, 1927–1949), vol. 2, 511 and 601, and vol. 3, 214; "The Automaton Chess-Player," [New York] *Commercial Advertiser* (April 21, 1826), 2; [Goodrich], *Enterprise, Industry, and Art of Man,* 328; the two phrases "an extraordinary piece of mechanism" and "machine for thinking" appear respectively in "The Automaton Chess-Player," [New York] *Truth Teller* (April 22, 1826), 6; and Burlington Chester, "To The Automaton Chess Player," *Philadelphia Gazette and Daily Advertiser* (February 10, 1827), 2; "Curiosities of Mechanism," *Scientific American* 3 (June 3, 1848), 296; "Hannington's Diorama," *Journal of the American Institute* 2 (June 1837), 504. A writer appearing in the same journal the following year similarly referred to the steam locomotive as a "magic *automaton*" and a "mighty automaton." See James Johnson, "The Rail-road Steamer," *Journal of the American Institute* 3 (June 1838), 490, 491.

33. [Poe], "Maelzel's Chess-Player," 318; "From the Baltimore Gazette," *Southern Literary Messenger* 2 (July 1836), 519; "Automaton Chess Player, etc.," [Boston] *Columbian Centinel* (September 16, 1826), 2; for a description of how, precisely, the chess-player worked, see [Silas Weir Mitchell], "The Last of a Veteran Chess Player," *Chess Monthly* 1 (February 1857), 41–45. See also Standage, *The Turk,* ch. 7; Cook, *The Arts of Deception,* 66–67; and [Poe], "Maelzel's Chess-Player," 319.

34. [Poe], "Maelzel's Chess-Player," 319; "The Automaton Chess-Player," [New York] *Commercial Advertiser,* 2; [Poe], "Maelzel's Chess-Player," 319.

35. "John Maelzel," *American Magazine of Useful and Entertaining Knowledge* 3 (February 1837), 196.

36. "Automaton Exhibition in Julien Hall," [Boston] *Columbian Centinel* (September 20, 1826), 2; [Poe], "Maelzel's Chess-Player," 319; "The Chess Player," [Philadelphia] *American Sentinel* (January 6, 1827), 2; "The Chess-Player," [New York] *Commercial Advertiser* (April 25, 1826), 2. Diarists who recorded attending Maelzel's show include Robert Gilmor, a wealthy Baltimore merchant and art patron, Benjamin Brown French, a New Hampshire legislator who went to see the chess-player while on a visit to Boston, and Bradley N. Cumings, an ambitious young clerk in a

Boston dry goods store who saw Maelzel's show in 1828, when he was sixteen years old, and again in 1833. See Robert Gilmor, "The Diary of Robert Gilmor," *Maryland Historical Magazine* 17 (September 1922), 231–68, and (December 1922), 319–47; Benjamin Brown French, *Witness to the Young Republic: A Yankee's Journal, 1828–1870,* edited by Donald B. Cole and John J. McDonough (Hanover, N.H., 1989); and the Bradley Newcomb Cumings Journal, Massachusetts Historical Society.

37. "For the American," *New-York American* (May 2, 1826), 2; "From the United States Gazette," *Southern Literary Messenger* 2 (July 1836), 522; On the Baltimore account, see "The Chess Player Discovered," [Washington, D.C.] *Daily National Intelligencer* (June 4, 1827), 3; [Gamaliel Bradford], *The History and Analysis of the Supposed Automaton Chess Player, of M. De Kempelen, . . .* (Boston, 1826), 22. Neil Harris has argued that antebellum Americans shared a passion for "observing process and examining for literal truth," a passion capitalized on by showmen like P. T. Barnum and Johann Maelzel, and by various perpetrators of popular hoaxes. According to Harris, this "operational aesthetic" derived in part from the experience of new production and transportation machines that were at once unbelievable and quite real. See Neil Harris, *Humbug: The Art of P. T. Barnum* (Chicago, 1973), 79.

38. "For the American," 2; *Philadelphia Gazette and Daily Advertiser* (March 17, 1827), 2.

39. A[llen], "The History of the Automaton Chess-Player in America," 473.

40. A list of the shareholders can be found in the Allen Chess Collection, Library Company of Philadelphia.

41. "Curiosities of Mechanism," 296. The editor of the *Franklin Journal,* for instance, reported the rumor that Kempelen's young daughter was the hidden agent when he exhibited the chess-player and that her declining health, caused by "the confinement to which she was subjected," forced Kempelen to stop exhibiting the device. See [Thomas P. Jones], "Observations upon the Automaton Chess Player," *Franklin Journal* 3 (February 1827), 130.

CHAPTER 2: HEAD AND HAND

1. Gulian C. Verplan[c]k, "The Influence of Mechanical Invention on the Improvement of Mankind," *Knickerbocker* 3 (January 1834), 40, 41; Gulian C. Verplanck, *A Lecture, Introductory to the Course of Scientific Lectures, before the Mechanics' Institute of the City of New-York. . . .* (New York, 1833), [1]. For another publication, see Gulian C. Verplanck, "Introductory Address, Delivered before the Mechanics' Institute of the City of New-York, November 27, 1833," *Mechanics' Magazine, and Register of Inventions and Improvements* 3 (January 1834), [47]–56.

2. Typical of the older mechanics' associations was the Salem Charitable Mechanic Association, founded in 1817. In an address before the association in 1821, Joseph Sprague reiterated its purpose: "The object of the Salem Charitable Mechanic Association, is to diffuse the knowledge of their art among its members, by free discussions at the Hall of the society, and by encouraging the members to exercise the high privilege they enjoy in its valuable and increasing library; to stimulate the members and their apprentices, by proper inducements, to a course of honorable conduct and diligent application; to discountenance all dishonorable and underhanded dealings; to encourage the thrifty members to entertain a fellow feeling for those of their craft

whom misfortune or adversity has overtaken, and to extend to the widows and orphans of deceased members such relief as the funds of the society will warrant." See Joseph E. Sprague, *An Address Delivered before the Salem Charitable Mechanic Association on their Fourth Anniversary, July 4, 1821,* . . . (1821), 14–15. On antebellum education reform, see Carl F. Kaestle, *Pillars of the Republic: Common Schools and American Society* (New York, 1983); Lawrence A. Cremin, *American Education: The National Experience, 1783–1876* (New York, 1980); Rush Welter, *Popular Education and Democratic Thought in America* (New York, 1962); and Carl Bode, *The American Lyceum: Town Meeting of the Mind* (New York, 1956).

3. The one monograph is Bruce Sinclair, *Philadelphia's Philosopher Mechanics: A History of the Franklin Institute, 1824–1865* (Baltimore, Md., 1974). For articles, see Stephen P. Rice, "The Mechanics' Institute of the City of New-York and the Conception of Class Authority in Early Industrial America, 1830–1860," *New York History* 81 (July 2000), 269–99; Thomas R. Winpenny, "Those Who Attend Meetings Will Be Excused from Paying Dues: The Lancaster Mechanics' Institute in Search of Mechanics," *Pennsylvania History* 55 (January 1988), 31–41; Donald S. McPherson, "Mechanics' Institutes and the Pittsburgh Workingman, 1830–1840," *Western Pennsylvania Historical Magazine* 56 (April 1973), [155]–69; and Edward N. Clopper, "The Ohio Mechanics Institute: Its 125th Anniversary," *Bulletin of the Historical and Philosophical Society of Ohio* 11 (July 1953), [179]–91. See also Gena Debra Glickman, "A Study of the Role of Women in the Transformation of the Curriculum at the Maryland Institute for the Promotion of Mechanic Arts, from 1825–1875" (Ph.D. diss., University of Maryland, 1992); Arlene Anne Elliott, "The Development of the Mechanics' Institutes and Their Influence upon the Field of Engineering: Pennsylvania, a Case Study, 1824–1860" (Ph.D. diss., University of Southern California, 1972). For a study of young man's institutes, which were similar to mechanics' institutes, see J. Richard Uberti, "Men, Manners, and Machines: The Young Man's Institute in Antebellum Philadelphia" (Ph.D. diss., University of Pennsylvania, 1977). For a study of early-nineteenth-century master mechanics that examines mechanics' associations, see Gary John Kornblith, "From Artisans to Businessmen: Master Mechanics in New England, 1798–1850" (Ph.D. diss., Princeton University, 1983). Finally, see Nina Evelyn Lerman, "From 'Useful Knowledge' to 'Habits of Industry': Gender, Race, and Class in Nineteenth-Century Technical Education" (Ph.D. diss., University of Pennsylvania, 1993).

4. James Madison Porter, *An Address to the Mechanics of Easton, Pennsylvania* (Easton, Penn., 1835), 12, 14–15, [4]. This was not the first time that Porter had urged the founding of a mechanics' association in Easton. In 1829, he wrote a letter to Philadelphia's Franklin Institute, one of the earliest and best known mechanics' institutes in the country, announcing that a group of Easton mechanics had decided to form an association that would aid sick members and their families and diffuse knowledge among craftsmen. "Keeping both the objects, the relief of members in case of sickness—and the promotion of useful knowledge, in view," he wrote, "we shall be able to associate from 100 to 200 mechanics if the terms are not too high, as the most of them are men of but little property." Porter's renewed effort six years later suggests that the earlier group lasted only a short time, if it was organized at all. See James M. Porter to James Ronaldson, March 2, 1829, "Incoming Correspondence, 1824–1848," Archives of the Franklin Institute, Philadelphia.

5. *Charter, Constitution, and By-Laws of the New-York Mechanic and Scientific Institution* (New York, 1822), 3. For a brief discussion of the institution, see Sean Wilentz, *Chants Democratic: New York City and the Rise of the American Working Class, 1788–1850* (New York, 1984), 40–41. The demise of the Mechanic and Scientific Institution occurred at least in part because of differences among members as to the purpose of the organization. For insight into the institution's difficulties, see *Report on a Plan for Extending and More Perfectly Establishing the Mechanic and Scientific Institution of New-York* (1824). In 1828, a group of former members were instrumental in founding the American Institute, which survived for many years as one of New York's premier societies for the promotion of domestic manufactures and the arts. See C.T., "Fairs Generally," *Journal of the American Institute* 4 (January 1839), 215. See also Thomas Bender, *New York Intellect: A History of Intellectual Life in New York City, from 1750 to the Beginnings of Our Own Time* (New York, 1987), 87; Alpheus Cary, *An Address, Delivered before the Massachusetts Charitable Mechanic Association, October 7, 1824, . . .* (Boston, 1824), 18. For an account of the birth of the mechanics' institute movement, see Charles Alpheus Bennett, *History of Manual and Industrial Education up to 1870* (Peoria, Ill., 1926), 301–44. For the mechanics' institute movement in Great Britain, see June Purvis, *Hard Lessons: The Lives and Education of Working-Class Women in Nineteenth-Century England* (Cambridge, 1989); Mabel Tylecote, *The Mechanics' Institutes of Lancashire and Yorkshire before 1851* (Manchester, 1957); James Hole, *An Essay on the History and Management of Literary, Scientific, and Mechanics' Institutions; . . .* (London, 1853); and J[ames] W[illiam] Hudson, *The History of Adult Education, . . .* (London, 1851). Hudson's volume contains an extensive listing of mechanics' and literary institutions in England.

6. Sinclair, *Philadelphia's Philosopher Mechanics*, 13; "Preface," *Mechanics' Magazine, and Register of Inventions and Improvements* 1 (1833), iv–v. Such educational efforts exposed themselves to ridicule, however. In his *Yankee Notions,* the Boston editor Samuel Kettell included a brief parody titled "Proceedings of the Society for the Diffusion of Useless Knowledge." There, various members of the society—meeting in the "asineum"—profess their admiration for some of the popular scientific movements of the day. "Useless knowledge was never more highly prized or more eagerly sought after," proclaims one eager member, "and mortal understandings were never in a more admirable confusion than at present." See Timo[thy] Titterwell [Samuel Kettell], *Yankee Notions: A Medley,* 2nd ed. (Boston, 1838), [183], 186. Redmond Conyngham, speaking before the Lancaster Mechanics' Society in 1835 at what appears to have been the inauguration of a Mechanics' Library Association, noted the potentially ephemeral quality of new associations. "This is a society making age, and societies are easily formed, be their objects what they may, one sometimes dazzles us with the lustre of its light, but becoming gradually more and more dim, it sinks into oblivion, until the revolving year reminds its officers of their existence." Redmond Conyngham, "Address, Delivered before the Mechanics' Society," *Hazard's Register of Pennsylvania* 14 (June 20, 1835), 396–97; [Oliver William Bourne Peabody], "Popular Education," *North American Review* 29 (July 1829), 251; W., "Observations on the Rise and Progress of the Franklin Institute," *American Mechanics' Magazine* 1 (February 1826), 69; Conyngham, "Address, Delivered before the Mechanics' Society," 391.

7. Edgar Needham, "Valedictory," *Catalogue of the First Exhibition of the Kentucky Mechanics' Institute* (Louisville, Ky., 1854), 63; George B. Emerson, *An Address, Delivered at the Opening of the Boston Mechanics' Institution, February 7, 1827* (Boston, 1827), 7, 11; *Constitution and By-Laws of the Mechanics' Institute of the City of New-York* (New York, 1835), 9. Proponents frequently expressed the belief that no one could remain ignorant of the principles of science and expect to get ahead in the modern world. In this way, institutes seeking to ensure broad support called on men from all occupations to enlist in their activities. In a typical statement, a speaker before the Pittsburgh Mechanics' Institute argued in 1830 that "there is no calling or profession in which an acquaintance with Chemistry, Natural History, Mechanical Philosophy, and the other branches of Practical Science can fail of being advantageous." See "Pittsburg Mechanics' Institute," *Register of Pennsylvania* 6 (July 17, 1830), 41.

8. Emerson, *An Address*, 7–8, 18. On the first lectures at the institute, see *The First Annual Report of the Board of Managers of the Boston Mechanics' Institution* (Boston, 1828), 3, 4–5. In early 1833, a Boston clerk, Bradley N. Cumings, recorded his attendance at that season's lecture series. "Wednesday, March 6, 1833. The last lecture before the Mechanics' Institute for this season was delivered by J. Quincy, Jr., and was quite interesting: he spoke of the wonders of gun powder in past times, and told of the probable benefits to be derived from steam in various ways, in days to come—out of this course of lectures, I have heard 13, four by Mr. Pickering, 3 by Prof. Farrar, 2 by Prof. Webster, 2 by E. Everett, 1 by F. C. Gray and 1 by J. Quincy, Jr." Bradley N. Cumings, Journal 1828–1847, 25, Massachusetts Historical Society; L. D. Gale to J. K. Mitchell, May 4, 1835, "Other Mechanics' Institutes and Their Affairs," Archives of the Franklin Institute, Philadelphia; "History and Proceedings of the Mechanics' Institute of the City of New York, from the Corresponding Secretary," *American Journal of Science and Arts* 31 (January 1837), 415, 417. The change might have come in response to the sort of complaint voiced by the editor of the *Mechanics' Magazine* in 1834. Responding to a letter in praise of the efforts of the young organization, the editor concurred that the institute was worthy of support "*even as at present conducted.*" He had, however, several suggestions for improvement. "We have been long of opinion that there is not sufficient of popular science introduced by the lecturers and managers of that institution," he wrote. He also suggested that the institute consider offering "classes for self-instruction in the various sciences," as well as language courses. See "The Mechanics' Institute of the City of New-York," *Mechanics' Magazine, and Register of Improvements* 4 (September 27, 1834), 182; "History and Proceedings of the Mechanics' Institute of the City of New York," 417; for a listing of the lectures delivered at the Maryland Institute from its founding in 1825, see Glickman, "A Study of the Role of Women," Appendix N; "Report of Committee on the State of the Institution," Ohio Mechanics' Institute Collection, Box 4, Board of Directors, Supporting Papers, Archives and Rare Books Department, University of Cincinnati.

9. The figure for the Kentucky Mechanics' Institute is from J. Henry Thomas, "Closing Address," *Report of Exhibition Committee of Kentucky Mechanics' Institute* (Louisville, Ky., 1855), 60; the figure for the Ohio Mechanics' Institute is from Geo[rge] W. Kendall, *A Sketch of the History of the Ohio Mechanics' Institute: And a Statement of its Present Condition* (Cincinnati, Oh., 1853), 23; "History and

Proceedings of the Mechanics' Institute of the City of New York," 415. For a full list of the holdings in the library and reading room of the Mechanics' Institute of the City of New-York in 1835, see *Catalogue of the Library of the Mechanics' Institute of the City of New-York* (New York, 1835). The institute published a second catalogue of its library's holdings in 1844. *Address of the Mechanics' Institute of the City of New-York, to Mechanics and Others; . . .* (New York, 1838), 10; Frederick Fraley, "Address Delivered before the Franklin Institute at the Close of the Eleventh Exhibition of American Manufactures," *Journal of the Franklin Institute* 30 (November 1840), 312. The practice of trading one's own journal for others appears to have been common. When the Chicago Mechanics' Institute launched its *Chicago Magazine* in 1857, it advertised that the journal was founded in part to satisfy a charter provision requiring the institute to found a free public library. The plan was to trade the journal for other newspapers and periodicals, thereby filling the institute's reading room. See the advertisement on the back cover of the *Chicago Magazine: The West As It Is* 1 (March 1857); D. C. Cassat to J. P. Foote, January 20, 1844, Ohio Mechanics' Institute Collection, Box 4, Board of Directors, Supporting Papers, Archives and Rare Books Department, University of Cincinnati.

10. F[rederic] D[an] Huntington, *Hands: Brain: Heart. . . .* (Boston, 1856), 5–6. Huntington waxed eloquent about the nature of mechanics' exhibitions. "We call it an exhibition," he insisted, "but that name does not describe the thing. It is more. It is an educator. The whole scene is a vital, earnest institute of instruction. It is an argument. It is a treatise. It is a poem. It is an illustrated text-book. It is one of the people's quick-witted, extemporized, unencumbered universities." See ibid., 5. For an interesting discussion of the fair of the Ohio Mechanics' Institute, see Steven J. Ross, *Workers on the Edge: Work, Leisure, and Politics in Industrializing Cincinnati, 1788–1890* (New York, 1985), 88–89.

11. *Prairie Farmer* (1843) [printed circular], "Incoming Correspondence, 1824–1848," Archives of the Franklin Institute, Philadelphia; J[ohn] K. Mitchell, "On Some of the Means of Elevating the Character of the Working Classes," *Journal of the Franklin Institute* 14 (August 1834), 107.

12. For an account of the founding of the Rock County organization, as well as copies of its annual proceedings, see Orrin Guernsey and Josiah F. Willard, eds., *History of Rock County, and Transactions of the Rock County Agricultural Society and Mechanics' Institute* (Janesville, Wis., 1856).

13. *Charter, Constitution, and By-Laws of the Mechanics' Institute of the City of Chicago* (Chicago, 1847), 4; *Report of the Eighth Annual Fair of the Chicago Mechanics' Institute* (Chicago, 1856), 6; *Charter of Incorporation, Constitution, and By-Laws of the Franklin Institute of the State of Pennsylvania for the Promotion of the Mechanic Arts* (Philadelphia, 1824), 7; "Pittsburg Mechanics' Institute," 42; William W. Wheildon, *Memoir of Solomon Willard, Architect and Superintendent of the Bunker Hill Monument* ([Boston],1865), 54; *Constitution and By-Laws of the Mechanics' Institute of St. Louis* (St. Louis, Mo., 1843), 3. On the Ohio Mechanics' Institute, see, for instance, the Ohio Mechanics' Institute Collection, vol. 23, Member Records, Minutes 1840–1855, Archives and Rare Books Department, University of Cincinnati.

14. For an account of Horace Greeley's life in the mid 1830s, see Horace Greeley, *Recollections of a Busy Life* (New York, 1868), 91–97. The membership list of

the Mechanics' Institute of the City of New-York, which was published late in 1835, appears in *Constitution and By-Laws of the Mechanics' Institute of the City of New-York,* [17]–36. The list contains 1,176 names. The one hundred names were selected randomly and checked against *Longworth's . . . City Directory* (New York, 1835). In searching the directory, possible variant name spellings were checked. A name from the membership list was considered to be included in the directory in those instances where more than one such name appeared. On the exclusivity of American city directories, see Richard Oestreicher, "The Counted and the Uncounted: The Occupational Structure of Early American Cities," *Journal of Social History* 28 (winter 1994), [351]–61.

   15. Gale to Mitchell, May 4, 1835, and Oliver White to William Hamilton, April 21, 1835, "Incoming Correspondence, 1824–1848," Archives of the Franklin Institute, Philadelphia.

   16. On Windt's dismissal, see Walter Hugins, *Jacksonian Democracy and the Working Class: A Study of the New York Workingmen's Movement, 1829–1837* (Stanford, Ca., 1960), 30. See also Wilentz, *Chants Democratic,* 224–25. On the General Trades' Union in New York City, see Wilentz, *Chants Democratic,* ch. 6. D. K. Minor to Gulian C. Verplanck, December 16, 1833, Gulian Verplanck Papers, Box #5, New-York Historical Society.

   17. Mitchell, "On Some of the Means of Elevating the Character of the Working Classes," 107–108. For another reference to women attending lectures at a mechanics' institute, see "Societies for Promoting Useful Knowledge, in Boston, Mass.," *Mechanics' Magazine, and Register of Inventions and Improvements* 1 (May 1833), 250. But as a speaker at the opening of the first exhibition of the Metropolitan Mechanics' Institute noted in 1853, "Woman's name is scarcely found on the muster-roll of such an institution as this." See Joseph R. Chandler, "Address," *Catalogue of Articles Deposited for Competition and Premium, at the First Annual Exhibition of the Metropolitan Mechanics' Institute* (Washington, 1853), 12. In Britain, some mechanics' institutes did allow women to become members, though limits were usually placed on access to privileges. For a discussion of women and the mechanics' institute movement in England, see chapters 5 and 6 of Purvis, *Hard Lessons.* Ohio Mechanics' Institute Collection, vol. 23, Members Records, Minutes 1840–1855, entry dated October 12, 1847, Archives and Rare Books Department, University of Cincinnati.

   18. Edward Everett, "An Essay on the Importance to Practical Men of Scientific Knowledge, and on the Encouragements to its Pursuit," *American Library of Useful Knowledge* 1 (Boston, 1831), 60; Joseph Story, "A Discourse Delivered before the Boston Mechanics' Institution, at the Opening of their Annual Course of Lectures, November, 1829," *American Library of Useful Knowledge* 1 (Boston, 1831), 35; Porter, *An Address to the Mechanics of Easton,* 10.

   19. E. L. Magoon, *Oration . . . Delivered July 4th, 1848, at the Laying of the Corner Stone of the Ohio Mechanics' Institute, Cincinnati* (Cincinnati, Oh., 1848), 14; Joseph Henry, "Address," *Catalogue of Articles Deposited for Competition and Premium, at the First Annual Exhibition of the Metropolitan Mechanics' Institute* (Washington, 1853), [3].

   20. Walter R. Johnson, *Address Introductory to a Course of Lectures on Mechanics and Natural Philosophy, Delivered before the Franklin Institute, Philadelphia, November 19, 1828* (Boston, 1829), 7; James R. Leib, *Lecture on Scientific Educa-*

tion, *Delivered Saturday, December 18, 1830, before the Members of the Franklin Institute* (Philadelphia, Penn., 1831), 15.

21. Robert Rantoul, Jr., *An Oration, Delivered before the Gloucester Mechanic Association, on the Fourth of July, 1833* (Salem, Mass., 1833), 50; Samuel L. Southard, *Address Delivered before the Newark Mechanics' Association, July 5, 1830* (Newark, N.J., 1830), 21. Worthington Hooker, speaking on the same day as Southard, evoked a similar scene of social and political turmoil that would ensue were "the people" to remain ignorant. "The dangers which threaten [our prosperity], must be looked at in all their breadth and depth; and they must be met with more efficiency than they have ever yet been; or, instead of being removed, they will go on to increase, till they shall burst upon us and involve this nation in ruin. This will be the sure result, if we trust for safety to anything else but the moral intelligence of the people." Worthington Hooker, *An Oration Delivered before the Norwich Lyceum and Mechanics' Institute, on the 5th of July, 1830* (Norwich, Conn., 1830), 16. Conyngham, "Address, Delivered before the Mechanics' Society," 396, 397.

22. Daniel Webster, "Mr. Webster's Introductory Lecture, before the Mechanics' Institution," *The American Library of Useful Knowledge* 1 (Boston, 1831), [38]; John K. Mitchell, *The Value of the Practical Interrogation of Nature* (Philadelphia, Penn., 1834), 16; Walter R. Johnson, *A Lecture on the Mechanical Industry and the Inventive Genius of America* (Baltimore, Md., 1849), 5; "Mechanic Association," *Niles Weekly Register* 33 (October 20, 1827), 118.

23. Daniel Read, *An Address Delivered before the Mechanics' Institute of Bloomington, at the Celebration of Their Anniversary, February 22, 1844* (Bloomington, In., 1844), 5; Needham, "Valedictory," 61–62, 62. While my focus here is on how people enacted class difference in a popular discourse on mechanization, this discourse was constitutive of gender difference as well. Head, hand, and heart indicated distinct areas of activity—the intellectual, the physical, and the moral—in which each individual operated. While balance among all three was the ideal, early-nineteenth-century writers increasingly marked head and hand as masculine domains, and heart as a feminine domain. That the work of the heart would be largely left to women points to a gendered understanding of knowledge that figured the technical and scientific knowledge of the mechanics' institute as distinctly masculine, as opposed to the moral and spiritual learning that was evident in, say, the *Lowell Offering*, published by the female factory operatives at Lowell. On this question of how masculine knowledge and feminine knowledge differed, it is interesting to compare the mechanics' institute periodicals with the *Lowell Offering*. Unlike men who worked with or on machinery, the women at Lowell did not fill the pages of their journal with technical discussions or suggestions for improving the machines they operated. Rex Burns points to one possible explanation for this. In his *Success in America,* Burns notes the complexity of new machines and suggests that few operatives would have been able to grasp the mechanized production process from beginning to end. "Perhaps this helps explain why the Lowell millgirls, whose publications indicate a high level of education, made no known mechanical contributions to their factories." My point is somewhat different. While female operatives may or may not have sought to improve the machines they operated, their public display of learning was most assuredly not of a technical nature. See Rex Burns, *Success in America: The Yeoman Dream and the Industrial Revolution* (Amherst,

Mass., 1976), 108. See also Lerman, "From 'Useful Knowledge' to 'Habits of Industry'"; and Purvis, *Hard Lessons*, ch. 5 and 6.

24. E. D. Mansfield, "The Worth of the Mechanic Arts," *Report of the Annual Fair of the Ohio Mechanics' Institute* (Cincinnati, Oh., 1838), 28; Huntington, *Hands: Brain: Heart*, 17, 18.

25. Mitchell, "On Some of the Means of Elevating the Character of the Working Classes," 95, 97, 98, 99, 102.

26. Ibid., 103, 104.

27. Ibid., 105, 105–106. This address was later printed as a pamphlet and reprinted in other journals.

28. Chandler, *Address*, 5; Neal Dow, *An Oration, Delivered before the Maine Charitable Mechanic Association, at their Triennial Celebration, July 4, 1829* (Portland, Maine, 1829), 10–11; John Neal, "Education," *Mechanic* 3 (June 1834), 186. The *Mechanic* was co-edited by Timothy Claxton, who was a founding member and onetime officer of the Boston Mechanics' Institution; "Evil Effects of the Division of Labor," *Supplement to the Connecticut Courant* 4 (November 2, 1835), 158.

29. On the final disposition of the *Mechanics' Magazine*, see "To Subscribers," *American Railroad Journal, and Mechanics' Magazine* 7 (July 1, 1838), 1. The failure of the *Mechanics' Magazine* was a real blow to the institute. Calling the loss a subject of "great importance," the directors conceded in 1838 that a journal "adapted to the wants of mechanics" was crucial to the life of the institute. "It would introduce the Institute to, and render it familiar with, the scientific world, and give it rank and permanence amongst the Institutions of the day, which it can never obtain without." See *Address of the Mechanics' Institute of the City of New-York*, 11. In early 1840, the institute's corresponding secretary, James J. Mapes, launched a new monthly magazine titled the *American Repertory of Arts, Sciences and Manufactures* to replace the *Mechanics' Magazine* as the official journal of the institute, but it folded after two years. When the *American Repertory* ceased publication in 1842, it merged its subscription list with that of the *Journal of the Franklin Institute*. See Sinclair, *Philadelphia's Philosopher Mechanics*, 283–84; for statistics on the enrollment of the Mechanics' Institute School, see Zadock Pratt, *Address Delivered January 16, 1849, Before the Mechanics' Institute, of the City of New York, . . .* (New York, 1849), Appendix, Table IV.

30. The institute's actuary, Charles Barritt, noted a new sense of optimism in an October 1844 letter to the Franklin Institute thanking its members for inviting a delegation to visit the annual fair in Philadelphia. Barritt wrote that although "the embarrassments of the society" had been "of such a character for the past 3 or 4 years" that the institute had been unable to reciprocate the kindness of the Franklin Institute, he was hopeful that the future would be different. "Our society . . . is fast recovering [from] the depression," he continued, "and during the coming year, we have every assurance that we shall again be in a condition to participate in the glorious work, now so ably labored in by our sister institutes of Philadelphia—Boston—Cincinnati—and our own immediate neighbor the American Institute." See Charles L. Barritt to William Hamilton, October 9, 1844, "Other Mechanics' Institutes and Their Affairs," Archives of the Franklin Institute, Philadelphia; *Proceedings of the Board of Aldermen* 36, part 2 (February 19–May 8, 1849), 629; B. G. Noble, ed., *New York Illustrated* (New York, 1847), 10.

31. James J. Mapes, *Inaugural Address, Delivered Tuesday Evening, Jan. 7, 1845, before the Mechanics' Institute, of the City of New-York* (New York, 1845), 9, 14; On Greeley's comments, see "Mechanics' Institute," *Farmer and Mechanic*, n.s., 4 (December 5, 1850), 585. The following spring, another observer challenged "five thousand of our young mechanics" to become members prior to July 4, noting that if they were to do so they could "keep Independence Day with a clear conscience." See "New York Mechanics' Institute," *Scientific American* 6 (May 17, 1851), 275; "The Mechanics and Men of Literature in New York," *Scientific American* 8 (January 15, 1853), [137]; "Mechanics' Lectures," *Scientific American* 8 (January 8, 1853), 133. On working-class leisure activity in antebellum New York, see Richard B. Stott, *Workers in the Metropolis: Class, Ethnicity, and Youth in Antebellum New York City* (Ithaca, N.Y., 1990), chs. 8–9; and Peter George Buckley, "To the Opera House: Culture and Society in New York City, 1820–1860" (Ph.D. diss., State University of New York at Stony Brook, 1984).

32. Pratt, *Address Delivered before the Mechanics' Institute of the City of New York*, [5]; "The Mechanic's Institute," *Farmer and Mechanic*, n.s., 3 (November 29, 1849), 574; "Mechanics' Institute Rooms, 100 Bowery," *Farmer and Mechanic*, n.s., 4 (June 20, 1850), 298; "New York Mechanics' Institute," 275; James Henry, Jr., *Lecture before the Members of the Mechanics' Institute of the City of New York, December 1, 1853* (New York, 1854), [41].

33. James Henry, Jr., *Lecture before the Members of the Mechanics' Institute*, [1], 9, [19], 20. The subject of the address appears near the bottom of the title page.

34. Ibid., 6, 7, 8, 12, [30].

35. Charles P. Daly, *Origin and History of Institutions for the Promotion of the Useful Arts . . .* (Albany, N.Y., 1864), 30. Daly delivered this lecture at a celebration of the thirty-fifth anniversary of the American Institute on November 11, 1863.

36. Benson J. Lossing, *History of New York City, . . .* (New York, 1884), 2: 483n; *The First Annual Report of the Trustees of the Cooper Union, for the Advancement of Science and Art* (New York, 1860), 9, 28. One newspaper as early as 1854, when construction began on the Cooper Union building, noted the similarity of purpose between the Mechanics' Institute and the Cooper Union. See the excerpt from the *Journal of Commerce* in James Henry, Jr., *Lecture before the Members of the Mechanics' Institute*, 34–35; *The First Annual Report of the Trustees of the Cooper Union*, 30; on the establishment of the library, see *The Second Annual Report of the Trustees of the Cooper Union for the Advancement of Science and Art* (New York, 1861), 21–22. Similarly, no mention of a gift from the Mechanics' Institute is made in the minutes of the trustees' meetings. See "Minutes of the Trustees, Cooper Union for the Advancement of Science and Art," vol. 1, Cooper Union Archives; Preston King to the Cooper Union, January 14, 1860, Library, Various Correspondence (1859–1860), Cooper Union Archives. This collection contains a second letter of transmittal from King, addressed to the Mechanics' Institute and dated January 9, 1860.

CHAPTER 3: HAND AND HEAD

1. "Manual Labor," *American Annals of Education and Instruction*, 3d ser., 3 (June 1833), [241], 242, [241], 242.

2. *First Annual Report of the Board of Trustees of the Manual Labour Academy of Pennsylvania* (Philadelphia, Penn., 1829), 13. For an account of the founding of the Oneida Institute, see *Third Report of the Trustees of the Oneida Institute of Science and Industry* (Utica, N.Y., 1831), 23–25. The *American Annals of Education,* published through the 1820s and 1830s, frequently reported on the founding and activities of manual labor schools. See also Stephen H. Tyng, *The Importance of Uniting Manual Labour with Intellectual Attainments, in a Preparation for the Ministry. . . .* (Philadelphia, Penn., 1830), [20]–32, for the activities of specific schools. On the manual labor school movement in America, see Robert Abzug, *Cosmos Crumbling: American Reform and the Religious Imagination* (New York, 1994), 116–24; Jonathan A. Glickstein, *Concepts of Free Labor in Antebellum America* (New Haven, Conn., 1991), 78–86; Paul Goodman, "The Manual Labor Movement and the Origins of Abolitionism," *Journal of the Early Republic* 13 (fall 1993), [355]–88; Laura Graham, "From Patriarchy to Paternalism: Disestablished Clergymen and the Manual Labor School Movement" (Ph.D. diss., University of Rochester, 1993); and Milton C. Sernett, *Abolition's Axe: Beriah Green, Oneida Institute, and the Black Freedom Struggle* (Syracuse, N.Y., 1986).

3. James Madison Porter, *An Address Delivered before the Literary Societies of Lafayette College at Easton, PA, July 4, 1832* (Easton, Penn., [1832]), 3.

4. William A. Alcott wrote in 1839 that the manual labor system was especially important to "a large proportion of the young men of our country who find their way into the ministry." "We regret, exceedingly," he continued, "that our candidates from the ministry cannot oftener be selected, not from the feeblest of their respective families, but from the more healthy and hardy; and we regret still more that it has never come to be regarded as an imperative duty of those who educate for the gospel ministry to educate the body, as effectually as the mind and soul." See "Labor and Study," *American Annals of Education,* 3d ser., 9 (January 1839), 20. For discussions of the relation between the manual labor school movement and antebellum Protestant reform, see Abzug, *Cosmos Crumbling,* 116–24; and Graham, "From Patriarchy to Paternalism"; P[eter] W[allace] G[allaudet], *A System of Education, on the Principle of Connecting Science with Useful Labour* (n.d.), 7; *Minutes and Proceedings of the First Annual Convention of the People of Colour: . . .* (Philadelphia, Penn., 1831), 5–6. In September 1831, *Hazard's Register of Pennsylvania* reported on a recent meeting in New Haven, attended by "numerous" citizens, in which the "*Mayor, Aldermen, Common Council and Freemen of the City of New-Haven*" passed a resolution stating that they would "resist the establishment of the proposed college in this place, by every lawful means." See "Education of Coloured People," *Hazard's Register of Pennsylvania* 8 (September 24, 1831), 196. See also Russell W. Irvine and Donna Zani Dunkerton, "The Noyes Academy, 1834–35: The Road to the Oberlin Collegiate Institute and the Higher Education of African-Americans in the Nineteenth Century," *Western Journal of Black Studies* 22 (1998), 260–73. The report published as a result of the Pennsylvania state legislature's house resolution was Mr. Matthias, *Report of the Committee on Education, on the Subject of Manual Labor Academies, . . .* (Harrisburg, Penn., 1833). For an enthusiastic response to the report, see "State Manual Labor Academy," *American Annals of Education,* 3d ser., 3 (April 1833), 186–87; T[homas]W. Dyott, *An Exposition of the System of Moral and Mental Labor, Established at the Glass Factory of Dyottville, in the County of*

Philadelphia . . . (Philadelphia, Penn., 1833), 5, 38. Although Dyott's concern was with providing educational opportunities to manual workers rather than with providing manual labor to students, an article appearing in *Hazard's Register of Pennsylvania* in 1833 clearly saw the efforts at his factory to be akin to the manual labor school movement. "In the science of education," he wrote at the opening of his discussion of a recent visit to the Dyottville glassworks, "the problem of connecting simultaneously mental and manual labour has been fortunately made of late the subject of serious discussion." See "Manual and Mental Labor Connected," *Hazards Register of Pennsylvania* 12 (September 14, 1833), 170; Robert Dale Owen, *Circular Addressed to the Friends of Liberal Education in General, and to the Former Readers of the Free Enquirer, in Particular* (1835), 2.

5. *Fellenberg or an Appeal to the Friends of Education on Behalf of Lafayette College* (Easton, Penn., 1835), 7; Goodman, "The Manual Labor Movement and the Origins of Abolitionism," 388.

6. "Reply on Manual Labor Schools," *American Annals of Education*, 3d ser., 4 (April 1834), 158; S. A. Tissot, *An Essay on Diseases Incidental to Literary and Sedentary Persons* . . . (London, 1768); [Chandler Robbins], *Remarks on the Disorders of Literary Men, or an Inquiry into the Means of Preventing the Evils Usually Incident to Sedentary and Studious Habits* (Boston, 1825); George Hayward, *A Lecture on Some of the Diseases of a Literary Life* (Boston, 1833); John Frost, *An Oration, Delivered at Middlebury, before the Associated Alumni of the College, August 19, 1829* (Utica, N.Y., 1829), 7–8; Robley Dunglison, *Human Health;* . . . (Philadelphia, Penn., 1844), 424. Earlier, Dunglison had expressed doubt over the "diseases of a literary life" model: "It has been imagined by many," he wrote, "that literary occupations are positively injurious to health; and that this may occasionally be the case can scarcely be doubted. They are probably, however, less frequently the cause of disease than is imagined." See *Human Health*, 411. For a more typical account showing the "Obvious Effects of Too Much Mental Labor," see J[ohn] L[ee] Comstock, *Outlines of Physiology, both Comparative and Human,* 3d ed., (New York, 1844), 233–34; W[ooster] Beach, *A Treatise on Anatomy, Physiology, and Health, Designed for Students, Schools, and Popular Use* (New York, 1847), 83, 84; B[ela] B. Edwards, *An Address Delivered at the Fourth Anniversary of the Mount Holyoke Female Seminary,* . . . (Andover, N.H., 1841), 25, 26.

7. Charles Caldwell, *Thoughts on Physical Education:* . . . (Boston, 1834), 58. For a discussion of the multiple symptoms ascribed to dyspepsia, see Edward Hitchcock, *Dyspepsy Forestalled and Resisted:* . . . (Amherst, Mass., 1830), 321–47. Charles Caldwell pointed out the short distance between dyspepsia and insanity: "Dyspepsia and mental derangement are among the most grievous maladies that affect the human race," he wrote, "and they are much more nearly allied to each other than they are generally supposed to be. So true is this, that the one is not unfrequently converted into the other, and often alternates with it." See Caldwell, *Thoughts on Physical Education,* 87. Ibid., 94; "Reply on Manual Labor Schools," 159.

8. A writer for the *Journal of Health,* in a passage reprinted in the *New-Harmony Gazette* in December 1826, applauded the new gymnasium in Boston. Of particular interest to him was the "diversity of situations in life" among the gymnasium pupils. "Physicians, lawyers, and clergymen," he wrote, "are intermixed with young men from the counter and the counting-house, and with boys from the public schools."

See "Gymnastics," *New-Harmony Gazette* 2 (December 13, 1826), 85. For a discussion of gymnasia in other communities in the United States, see "Gymnastics," *American Quarterly Review* 3 (March 1828), 126–50; *A Course of Calisthenics for Young Ladies, in Schools and Families* (Hartford, Conn., 1831), 3; "Reply on Manual Labor Schools," 159–60. In September 1830, a writer appearing in the *Supplement to the Connecticut Courant,* in recommending gymnastic exercises to young men, similarly wrote that the gymnasium "is regarded with less interest since its novelty has gone." See "Physical Education," *Supplement to the Connecticut Courant* 2 (September 21, 1830), 283; John C. Warren, *Physical Education and the Preservation of Health* (Boston, 1846), 39. Popular interest in gymnasia began to return by the mid 1850s, however. On this mid-century resurgence, see [Charles G. Leland], "Physical Education," *Graham's Magazine* 53 (December 1858), 495–97. For the history of American interest in exercise and physical fitness, see Harvey Green, *Fit for America: Health, Fitness, Sport and American Society* (New York, 1986). See also John R. Betts, "Mind and Body in Early American Thought," *Journal of American History* 54 (March 1968), 787–805.

9. "Manual Labor Schools," *American Magazine of Useful and Entertaining Knowledge* 1 (May 1835), 392; "Education with Manual Labor," *Register of Pennsylvania* 2 (November 1, 1828), 258; Theodore D. Weld, *First Annual Report of the Society for Promoting Manual Labor in Literary Institutions;* . . . (New York, 1833), 53.

10. "Manual Labor Schools," 392; *Report of a Committee of the Trustees of Allegheny College, on the Manual Labor System* (Meadville, Penn., 1833), [3]; Weld, *First Annual Report,* 103.

11. The information on the Lane Seminary is from "Lane Seminary, Ohio," *American Annals of Education,* 3d ser., 2 (June 1, 1832), 290; Tyng, *The Importance of Uniting Manual Labour with Intellectual Attainments,* 7; "Manual Labor School Society," *Annals of Education,* 3d ser., 2 (January 15, 1832), 93.

12. "Manual Labor Schools at the South," *American Annals of Education,* 3d ser., 5 (September 1835), 426; *Report of a Committee of the Trustees of Allegheny College,* 12; "Manual Labor," *Quarterly Register* 7 (August 1834), 65, 66.

13. "Manual Labor School," *American Annals of Education,* 3d ser., 1 (August 1831), 397. For an account of Weld's activities on behalf of the society, see Benjamin P. Thomas, *Theodore Weld: Crusader for Freedom* (New Brunswick, N.J., 1950), ch. 2.

14. Weld, *First Annual Report,* 18, 27, 39. The phrase "the present system of education" is used in every chapter title for the first section of Weld's report. "Manual Labor," *American Annals of Education,* 242. The Philadelphia printer Mathew Carey hailed Weld's report but worried that, at 120 pages, it was too long to gain the readership it deserved. Consequently, Carey published two substantially abridged versions of the report with the hope of disseminating it further. See [Theodore Weld], *Societies for Promoting Manual Labor in Literary Institutions,* 2d ed. (Philadelphia, Penn., 1833); and [Theodore Weld], *Societies for Promoting Manual Labor in Literary Institutions,* 3d ed. (Philadelphia, Penn., 1834). The gendered language in Weld's report was not uncommon, as the specter of disease and frailty frequently evoked a language of effeminacy among those concerned with the deleterious effects of too little physical activity in American men. A writer appearing in the *Cabinet* in 1831, to cite just one example, in discussing the importance of "a vigorous muscular frame" to "the action of a powerful mind," decried what he called "the taper

fingers of modern effeminacy." See "Gymnastics," *Cabinet* 5 (January 1831), 25, 26. For what is intended to be a humorous depiction of certain gender implications of middle-class life, see Ben Scribbler, "A Scene in 1956," *Graham's Illustrated Magazine* 49 (August 1856), 104. On efforts among some middle-class men to resist this possible fate, see Brian Roberts, *American Alchemy: The California Gold Rush and Middle-Class Culture* (Chapel Hill, N.C., 2000).

15. "Education with Manual Labor," 257. For an account of the academy's founding, see *First Annual Report of the Board of Trustees of the Manual Labour Academy of Pennsylvania*, [7]. For a list of the original trustees, see [John Monteith], *A Report on the Subject of Connecting Manual Labour with Study. . . .* (Philadelphia, Penn., 1828), [2]. Ibid., [5], 6, 13.

16. On the school's first year, see *First Annual Report of the Board of Trustees of the Manual Labour Academy of Pennsylvania*. Passages are on 9, 10, 12, and 9. "Report of the Faculty of the Manual Labor Academy of Penn. to the Board of Trustees," *Register of Pennsylvania* 4 (December 5, 1829), 357.

17. See *Second Annual Report of the Board of Trustees of the Manual Labour Academy of Pennsylvania* (Philadelphia, Penn., 1830); and *Third Annual Report of the Board of Trustees of the Manual Labour Academy of Pennsylvania* (Philadelphia, Penn., 1832).

18. George Junkin, *The Bearings of College Education upon the Welfare of the Whole Community. . . .* (Rossville, Oh., 1843), 18; George Junkin, *A Plea for North-Eastern Pennsylvania: The Tenth Baccalaureate in Lafayette College* (Easton, Penn., 1845), 12.

19. D. X. Junkin, *The Reverend George Junkin, D.D., LL.D.: A Historical Biography* (Philadelphia, Penn., 1871), 143; *Third Annual Report of the Board of Trustees of the Manual Labour Academy of Pennsylvania*, 13.

20. *Memorial to the Legislature of Pennsylvania, for the Incorporation of Lafayette College, at Easton* (1825), [3]; the Historical Society of Pennsylvania (HSP), William Darrach Diary (1832–37), entry for Thursday, November 22, 1832. In their first annual report, published in 1833, the trustees of Lafayette College noted that "in a qualified sense, Lafayette College is a continuation of the Manual Labor Academy of Pennsylvania." See "First Annual Report of the Board of Trustees of Lafayette College," *Hazard's Register of Pennsylvania* 12 (September 21, 1833), 190. For a brief discussion of the demise of the Manual Labor Academy of Pennsylvania and Junkin's move to Lafayette College, see Edward W. Hocker, *Germantown 1683–1933 . . .* (Germantown, Penn., 1933), 173–74.

21. The daily schedule is taken from the Lafayette College Faculty Minutes, May 3, 1834, Special Collections and College Archives, Skillman Library, Lafayette College; Alexander Ramsey to F. Kelker, September 7, 1834, Letters of Alexander Ramsey [typescript of originals held by the Minnesota Historical Society], Lafayette Collection, Special Collections and College Archives, Skillman Library, Lafayette College. Ramsey wrote shortly thereafter that provisions had improved. "Petition of [?] of Northampton County," February 16, 1834, Early Records—1834 Folder, Special Collections and College Archives, Skillman Library, Lafayette College. This accusation of sectarianism appears to have been particularly galling to the leaders of the college. In late February, students passed a resolution calling the charge "utterly groundless, slanderous and false" and pointing out that "the students are by birth or

by profession divided among five different christian denominations"; both Porter and Junkin refuted the accusation in their addresses at Junkin's inauguration in May. On the student resolution, see Lafayette College Board of Trustees Minutes, February 21, 1834, Special Collections and College Archives, Skillman Library, Lafayete College. For Porter and Junkin's responses, see their respective addresses in *Inaugural Charge by J. M. Porter, Esq., President of the Board of Trustees, and Inaugural Address of the Rev. George Junkin, D.D. President of Lafayette College* (1834). My brief account of the first two years of Lafayette College is drawn from the following sources: David Bishop Skillman, *The Biography of a College: Being the History of the First Century of the Life of Lafayette College*, vol. 1 (Easton, Penn., 1932); W. B. Owen, *Historical Sketches of Lafayette College, with an Account of Its Present Organization and Courses of Study* (Easton, Penn., 1876); and D. X. Junkin, *The Reverend George Junkin*. It also draws on the first three annual reports of the Lafayette College Board of Trustees.

22. Matthias, *Report of the Committee on Education*, 6; "Manual Labor Schools," *American Magazine of Useful and Entertaining Knowledge*, 392; *Report of a Committee of the Trustees of Allegheny College*, 13.

23. G[allaudet], *A System of Education*, 2. A writer for Lafayette College in 1835, probably George Junkin, similarly noted of the manual labor program that "whatever has the effect of making manual labor honorable, must operate a happy influence in creating a universal brotherhood in the community. The mass of mankind ought not to be, and cannot be, in moral right, despised, because they must necessarily depend upon physical and not mental labor, as the source of supply and means of usefulness." See *Fellenberg*, 18; Weld, *First Annual Report*, 60; *The Second Annual Report of the Board of Trustees of Lafayette College* (Easton, Penn., 1833), 6; Weld, *First Annual Report*, 60–61, 64.

24. *Lafayette College: The Seventh Annual Report* (Easton, Penn., 1839), 6; *Third Annual Report of the Board of Trustees of the Manual Labor Academy of Pennsylvania*, [14–15]. Other occupations listed are planter, merchant, ice-man, lumber dealer, grocer, and hardware. James Madison Porter to George Kelchner, December 17, 1832, Early Records—1832 Folder, Special Collections and College Archives, Skillman Library, Lafayette College.

25. "First Annual Report of the Board of Trustees of Lafayette College," 191; Weld, *First Annual Report*, 117; George Junkin, *The Bearings of College Education upon the Welfare of the Whole Community . . .* , 6; George Junkin, *A Plea for North-Eastern Pennsylvania*, 13, 15.

26. Weld, *First Annual Report*, 117–18, 112.

27. On Oberlin College, see Graham, "From Patriarchy to Paternalism," 142–54; William Riddle to Reverend J. F. Clark, January 26, 1836, Early Records—1836 Folder, Special Collections and College Archives, Skillman Library, Lafayette College; Alexander Ramsey to R. F. Kelker, September 21, 1834, Letters of Alexander Ramsey [typescript of originals held by the Minnesota Historical Society], Lafayette Collection, Special Collections and College Archives, Skillman Library, Lafayette College; H. M. Borden to James Madison Porter, October 1, 1835, Early Records—1835 Folder, Special Collections and College Archives, Skillman Library, Lafayette College. David Coulter, who was a student at Lafayette in the early 1830s, suggested in his memoir that it was the financial benefit of the manual labor system that drew him to the

school. "I learned that there was a Manual Labor Institution at Easton, Pennsylvania, of which Rev. George Junkin, D.D., was President," he wrote. "I was told that a young man disposed to labor part of his time, might thus defray a considerable portion of his expenses. I therefore wrote to Dr. Junkin, stating my wishes and circumstances." See David Coulter, *Memoir of David Coulter, D.D. with Reminiscences, Letters, Lectures and Sermons* (St. Louis, Mo., n.d.), 36–37.

28. "Manual Labor Schools," *American Magazine of Useful and Entertaining Knowledge* 2 (November 1835), 103; Alcott, "Labor and Study," 19; *Fellenberg*, 11.

29. "Petition to the Senate and House of Representatives of the Commonwealth of Pennsylvania in General Assembly," Early Records—1833 Folder, Special Collections and College Archives, Skillman Library, Lafayette College. The minutes of the Lafayette College Board of Trustees indicate that on December 9, 1833, "a memorial to the legislature for aid was presented by the President which was agreed to and ordered to be forwarded." This is almost certainly a copy of that memorial, and the handwriting appears to be that of Porter, who was the president of the Board of Trustees at the time. See Lafayette College Board of Trustees Minutes, December 9, 1833, Special Collections and College Archives, Skillman Library, Lafayette College.

30. Weld, *First Annual Report*, 40, 40–41, 13.

31. Ibid., 60; "Petition to the Senate and House of Representatives"; *Fellenberg*, 18; Joseph R. Ingersol, *An Address Delivered before the Literary Societies of Lafayette College at Easton, PA, July 4, 1833* (Philadelphia, Penn., 1833), 16.

32. "Manual Labor School Society," 93; Porter, *An Address Delivered before the Literary Societies of Lafayette College*, 15; Thomas S. Grimké, *Correspondence on the Principles of Peace, Manual Labor Schools, Etc.* (Charleston, S.C., 1833), 11, 14.

33. Beriah Green to Theodore Weld, November 17, 1838, in Gilbert H. Barnes and Dwight L. Dumond, eds., *Letters of Theodore Dwight Weld, Angelina Grimké Weld, and Sarah Grimké, 1822–1844*, vol. 2 (New York, 1934), 715. For discussions of the relation between abolitionism and manual labor schools, see Goodman, "The Manual Labor Movement and the Origins of Abolitionism"; and Sernett, *Abolition's Axe*. On the abolitionist activity at the Lane Seminary, and on the history of the school more generally, see Lawrence Thomas Lesick, *The Lane Rebels: Evangelicalism and Antislavery in Antebellum America* (Metuchen, N.J., 1980). James Patterson, *A Sermon, on the Effects of the Hebrew Slavery as Connected with Slavery in this Country. . . .* (Philadelphia, Penn., 1825), 19. Patterson would later become a trustee of the Manual Labor Academy of Pennsylvania. Another future trustee, John H. Kennedy, delivered a sermon on July 4, 1828, titled *Sympathy, Its Foundation and Legitimate Exercise Considered, in Special Relation to Africa: . . .* (Philadelphia, Penn., [1828]), which also expressed strong support for colonization efforts. For colonization addresses given by future officers of the Society for Promoting Manual Labor in Literary Institutions, see Theodore Frelinghuysen, *An Oration: Delivered at Princeton, New Jersey, November 16, 1824, before the New-Jersey Colonization Society* (Princeton, N.J., 1824); and James Milnor, *Plea for the American Colonization Society: A Sermon, Preached in St. George's Church, New-York, on Sunday, July 9, 1826. . . .* (New York, 1826). For a list of the officers of the society, see Weld, *First Annual Report*, viii. On the diversity of ideas about slavery and race among colonization supporters and the shift to radical abolitionism among some of those who supported colonization through the 1820s, see Lawrence J. Friedman, *Gregarious Saints: Self and Community*

in American Abolitionism, 1830–1870 (Cambridge, 1982), ch. 1; and William Jay, *An Inquiry into the Character and Tendency of the American Colonization, and American Anti-Slavery Societies* (New York, 1835), 146. Jay added the italics in quoting from a New York City newspaper article published two years earlier. See "American Colonization Society," *New-York Commercial Advertiser* (October 10, 1833), 2; George Junkin, *The Integrity of Our National Union vs. Abolitionism: . . .* (Cincinnati, Oh., 1843), iv.

34. Beriah Green, *Success: A Valedictory Address, Delivered at the Anniversary of the Oneida Institute, November 1, 1843* (Utica, N.Y., 1843), 16; "Holliston Manual Labor School," *American Annals of Education*, 3d ser., 8 (October 1838), 476; "Worcester County Manual Labor High School," *American Annals of Education*, 3d ser., 8 (November 1838), 522.

35. J. H. Fairchild, *Oberlin: Its Origin, Progress and Results. . . .* (Oberlin, Oh., 1860), 34; Delazon Smith, *A History of Oberlin, or, New Lights of the West: . . .* (Cleveland, Oh., 1837), 15–16, 17. I want to thank Phil Lapsansky at the Library Company of Philadelphia for showing me this remarkable pamphlet. Smith's account of students laboring to excess on behalf of the school's desire to make progress on improving its grounds might have been seconded by students at Lafayette College in 1834. The author of the school's annual report for that year admits that "a very considerable amount of labor, and severe labor" had been performed by students during the previous year, "much more so, than is ordinary or desirable in such an Institution." The work included digging a cistern and cellar in hard rock that "made full experiment of the skill and prowess of our students." See *The Third Annual Report of the Board of Trustees of Lafayette College* ([Easton, Penn.], 1834), 6.

36. Fairchild, *Oberlin*, 34; Emerson Davis, *The Half Century; . . .* (Boston, 1851), 75; untitled printed circular dated November 15, 1836, Early Records—1836 Folder, Special Collections and College Archives, Skillman Library, Lafayette College. Quoted passages are on page 2. *Lafayette College: The Seventh Annual Report,* [5]. This brief account of Lafayette College in the late 1830s draws in part on Skillman, *The Biography of a College.*

37. "Manual Labor Colleges," *American Annals of Education*, 3d ser., 5 (March 1835), 115; William A. Alcott, *The Laws of Health; Or, Sequel to "The House I Live In"* (Boston, 1857), 388.

CHAPTER 4: MIND AND BODY

1. "Physical Development in America," *Scientific American* 14 (January 8, 1859), 145; Amariah Brigham, *Remarks on the Influence of Mental Cultivation upon Health* (Hartford, Conn., 1832), [iii].

2. "Physical Education," *American Monthly Magazine* 1 (November 1829), 542 [misnumbered as 541]; [William A. Alcott], "Physical Education," *Moral Reformer* 1 (January 1835), 21; for Alcott's use of the phrase "the laws of health," see William A. Alcott, *The Laws of Health; or, Sequel to "The House I Live In"* (Boston, 1857).

3. Stephen Nissenbaum, *Sex, Diet, and Debility in Jacksonian America: Sylvester Graham and Health Reform* (Westport, Conn., 1980); Martha H. Verbrugge, *Able-Bodied Womanhood: Personal Health and Social Change in Nineteenth-Century Boston* (New York, 1988), 48; Joan Burbick, *Healing the Republic: The Language of*

Health and the Culture of Nationalism in Nineteenth-Century America (New York, 1994), 5. On health reform in nineteenth-century America, see also James C. Whorton, *Crusaders for Fitness: The History of American Health Reformers* (Princeton, N.J., 1982). On popular ideas about health and the human body in nineteenth-century America, see Michael Sappol, *A Traffic of Dead Bodies: Anatomy and Embodied Social Identity in Nineteenth-Century America* (Princeton, N.J., 2002).

4. For a relatively detailed discussion of the relation between manual occupations and health, see Robley Dunglison, *Human Health* (Philadelphia, 1844), 405–11. See also Alcott, *The Laws of Health,* 34–38, 51–53. For an additional discussion of health and factory work, see John C. Warren, *Physical Education and the Preservation of Health* (Boston, 1846), 64–66.

5. Charles E. Rosenberg, "Catechisms of Health: The Body in the Prebellum Classroom," *Bulletin of the History of Medicine* 69 (summer 1995), 181; Dr. Keagy, "Education of the Stomach," *Moral Reformer* 1 (February 1835), 61; William A. Alcott, "On the Study of Physiology as a Branch of General Education," *American Annals of Education,* 3d ser., 3 (September 1833), 396; Jane Taylor, *Wouldst Know Thyself! or, the Outlines of Human Physiology* (New York, 1858), 64. The best discussion of antebellum popular physiology textbooks is Lamar Riley Murphy, *Enter the Physician: The Transformation of Domestic Medicine, 1760–1860* (Tuscaloosa, Ala., 1991), ch. 5 ("The Pedagogical Crusade").

6. For a lengthy review of Dunglison's book in a popular periodical, see "Dunglison's Physiology," *American Quarterly Review* 13 (June 1833), 375–403. Taylor, *Wouldst Know Thyself!,* front cover.

7. For an outline of Coates's lectures, see Reynell Coates, *Syllabus of a Course of Popular Lectures on Physiology, With an Outline of the Principles Which Govern the Gradual Developement* [sic] *of the Faculties of Mind and Body* (Philadelphia, 1840). See also Reynell Coates, *An Address Introductory to a Popular Course of Lectures on the History of Organic Development, and the Means of Improving the Mental and Physical Faculties; . . .* (Philadelphia, 1839). For an excellent account of Mary Gove Nichols's life and career, see Jean L. Silver-Isenstadt, *Shameless: The Visionary Life of Mary Gove Nichols* (Baltimore, Md., 2002). Lectures on human physiology had been delivered to popular audiences prior to the 1830s. In early 1826, for instance, two Boston physicians offered a twice-weekly series of lectures on physiology in Boston's Pantheon Hall. Their lectures included discussions of digestion, the brain, and sleep. See "Lectures on the Physiology and Natural History of Man," *American Journal of Education* 1 (January 1826), 61.

8. Timo[thy] Titterwell [Samuel Kettell], *Yankee Notions: A Medley,* 2d ed. (Boston, 1838), 171–72. For a defense of Graham against the ridicule he suffered at the hands of several Boston newspaper editors in 1835, see "Mr. Graham," *The Moral Reformer* 1 (October 1835), 322–23. The defense was almost certainly written by William Alcott, who was the editor of *The Moral Reformer.* Graham characterized the leaders of the Portland mob as a particularly dishonorable group. "According to common and accredited report," he wrote on the final page of a volume of his lecture notes, the five rabble-rousers included "an infamous whoremaster" who was said to have seduced two girls the previous winter, a "violent Jackson man" who was not only a "bitter opposer of the temperance cause" but was also probably an atheist, a second infamous whoremaster who was "shut out from society," and a "despised" lawyer who

was "believed to be the father to a molatto [sic] bastard." See Sylvester Graham, Lecture Notes, folio volume, American Antiquarian Society. For an account of the founding of the American Physiological Society, see *First Annual Report of the American Physiological Society* (Boston, 1837), 6–7. The society's membership number comes from the *Third Annual Report of the American Physiological Society* (Boston, 1839), 13. For a social profile of the members of the American Physiological Society, see Nissenbaum, *Sex, Diet, and Debility*, 143–45. For an outline of the society's objectives, see *Constitution of the American Physiological Society . . . To which is Prefixed a Summary Explanation of the Objects of the Society* (Boston, 1837), 3–13. On the gift given to Graham by female members of the society, see the entry for April 7, 1837, "Record of the Proceedings of the Ladies Physiological Society," 1837–1840, Codman-Butterfield Papers, Massachusetts Historical Society. For an extended account of Graham's career, see Nissenbaum, *Sex, Diet, and Debility*.

9. Abel G. Duncan, *Evils of Violating the Laws of Health, and the Remedy. . . .* (Boston, 1838), 6; Calvin Cutter, *Physiology for Children* (Boston, 1846), [3]; George Hayward, *Outlines of Human Physiology; Designed for the Use of the Higher Classes in Common Schools* (Boston, 1834), 4; William A. Alcott, *The House I Live In. . . .* (Boston, 1834), viii; John William Draper, *Human Physiology, Statical and Dynamical; or, the Conditions and Course of the Life of Man* (New York, 1856), vi; Coates, *An Address Introductory to a Popular Course of Lectures*, 21. For another expression of hope that popular physiological knowledge would slow the progress of quackery, see "March of Mind," *American Monthly Magazine* 4 (February 1835), 417–21.

10. Review of Edward Jarvis, *Practical Physiology: For the Use of Schools and Families,* in *Graham's Magazine* 32 (March 1848), 191.

11. Brigham, *Remarks on the Influence of Mental Cultivation upon Health,* 75, 76; "Insanity and Insane Hospitals," *North American Review* 44 (January 1837), 118, 119; Charles Caldwell, *Thoughts on Physical Education: . . .* (Boston, 1834), 89, 90–91, 91, 92.

12. Edward Hitchcock, *Dyspepsy Forestalled and Resisted: . . .* (Amherst, Mass., 1830), 306. "Savages," he continued, "and men whose lives are chiefly spent in active pursuits, in the open air, are rarely troubled with them [nervous maladies] in the slightest degree." Caldwell, *Thoughts on Physical Education,* 27.

13. Reynell Coates, *Popular Medicine or, Family Adviser* (Philadelphia, 1838), 169, 170; "Dyspepsia," *Southern Review* 4 (August 1829), 209; "Gymnastic Exercises," *Journal of Health* 1 (January 13, 1830), 132.

14. Catharine E. Beecher, *Letters to the People on Health and Happiness* (New York, 1855), 91, 88.

15. Brigham, *Remarks on the Influence of Mental Cultivation Upon Health,* [iii]; Coates, *Popular Medicine,* 170. Not everybody agreed that modern social practices were responsible for the debility of the age. John Frost, in a commencement address at Middlebury College in 1829, averred that "all the evils experienced from bodily weakness and disease, are not the fault of students, nor of the present generation." For Frost, the diseases of modern American society were more the result of past indiscretions. "Physical debility, and a predisposition to many diseases," he continued, "are the inheritance left us by our forefathers. Men have not that mental and physical strength and activity which they would have inherited, had their predecessors conformed to the divine will, and strove to be '*temperate in all things.*'" See John

Frost, *An Oration, Delivered at Middlebury, before the Associated Alumni of the College, August 19, 1929* (Utica, N.Y., 1829), 9. In the very next paragraph, however, Frost criticized the current methods for educating children, arguing that they tended to produce delicate and enfeebled adults.

16. [Charles G. Leland], "Physical Education," *Graham's Magazine* 53 (December 1858), 496. The passage quoted is from a *Baltimore Dispatch* editorial that Leland quotes at length. "Exercise," *Supplement to the Connecticut Courant* 2 (December 22, 1829), 168; "Gymnastics," *New-Harmony Gazette* 2 (December 27, 1826), 102; "Progress of Physical Education," *American Journal of Education* 1 (January 1826), 20–21; [Theodore] P[arker], "Thoughts on Labor," *New-Yorker* 11 (May 8, 1841), 119.

17. Beecher, *Letters to the People on Health and Happiness,* 110–11, 111; R[ussell] T. Trall, *The Illustrated Family Gymnasium; . . .* (New York, 1857), 179, 179–80. See also W[ooster] Beach, *A Treatise on Anatomy, Physiology, and Health, Designed for Students, Schools, and Popular Use* (New York, 1847), 82: "Take that city belle, rendered delicate, nervous, sickly, miserable, by excessive nervous and cerebral derangement consequent on novel reading, parties, amusements, and all the excitement of fashionable city life. . . . She is doomed either to wear out a miserable existence, or else to EXERCISE HER MUSCLES; nor can salvation come from any other source." Here Beach is quoting from another work. For a discussion of the class and gender dimensions of promenading in New York in the nineteenth century, see David Scobey, "Anatomy of the Promenade: The Politics of Bourgeois Sociability in Nineteenth-Century New York," *Social History* 17 (May 1992), [203]–27.

18. F[rancis] W[illiam] Bird, *Physiological Reform. An Address, Delivered before the American Physiological Society at their First Annual Meeting, June 1, 1837* (Boston, 1837), 14–15; Coates, *An Address Introductory to a Popular Course of Lectures,* 10–11; Elisha Bartlett, *Obedience to the Laws of Health, a Moral Duty. . . .* (Boston, 1838), 22. This was a lecture that Bartlett gave before the American Physiological Society on January 30, 1838; Alcott, *The Laws of Health,* 13.

19. Bartlett, *Obedience to the Laws of Health,* 7; Bird, *Physiological Reform,* 46.

20. Bird, *Physiological Reform,* 26; T[homas] S[cott] Lambert, *Practical Anatomy, Physiology, and Pathology; Hygiene and Therapeutics* (Portland, Me., 1851), 28; [Oliver Wendell Holmes], "Mechanism of Vital Actions," *North American Review* 85 (July 1857), 53; John H. Griscom, *Animal Mechanism and Physiology . . .* (New York, 1848), 174. Griscom's book was originally published in 1839. The 1848 edition was printed by Harper & Brothers as part of the Harper's Family Library. William. A. Alcott, *The Structure, Uses and Abuses of the Human Hand* (Boston, 1856), 116.

21. Griscom, *Animal Mechanism and Physiology* , [i], [ix], 15; Worthington Hooker, *First Book in Physiology for the Use of Schools and Families. . . .* (New York, 1855), 9, 11–12.

22. Lambert, *Practical Anatomy, Physiology, and Pathology,* [31]; Caldwell, *Thoughts on Physical Education,* 4, 22; Hooker, *First Book in Physiology,* 190; L. N. Fowler [Lydia Folger Fowler], *Familiar Lessons on Phrenology, Designed for the Use of Children and Youth in Schools and Families* (New York, 1848), 14. This is the second volume of Fowler's two-part *Familiar Lessons on Physiology and Phrenology, for Children and Youth . . .* (New York, 1848), which was published as a single volume. Edward Jarvis, *Primary Physiology, for Schools* (Philadelphia, 1848), 156.

23. Edward Jarvis, *Lecture on the Necessity of the Study of Physiology,* . . . (Boston, 1845), 8; J[ohn] L. Arnold, *Arnold's Lectures on Anatomy, Physiology and Hygiene;* . . . (Cincinnati, Oh., 1856), [11].

24. Jarvis, *Lecture on the Necessity of the Study of Physiology,* 54, 54–55; Bird, *Physiological Reform,* 26. Bird returned to this conceit later in his talk: "Suppose a manufacturer should hear some unusual thumping in any part of his machinery; would he be satisfied with saying—'Oh, no matter, the mill is "subject" to such occasional thumps?' and would he wait until half a dozen cogs are broken out, or the fragments of the machinery are flying about his ears? No; if he were wise, he would say at once—'Shut down, and don't start again until you have discovered the cause of the trouble, and have remedied it as far as possible; and in future avoid it.' But when we hear such a thumping in the curious machinery of our frames—when a head-ache, or a stomach-ache or a rheumatic twinge kindly warns us that something is wrong, we take no notion of the monition, until bye and bye down we go, and then we call the doctor, and 'patch up.' " See page 43.

25. William A. Alcott, *Lectures on Life and Health: or, the Laws and Means of Physical Culture* (Boston, 1853), 206, 207, 208. In the same paragraph as the factory metaphor, Alcott compared the microscopic view of a patch of skin to a view from "the top of the famous Crystal Palace in New York," where one could survey the "wonders collected there for public exhibition." He also compared it to "the dissection of a steam engine into its more than five thousand pieces." See page 208. Lambert, *Practical Anatomy, Physiology, and Pathology,* [46], 48. Lambert's book, like a number of books published in the period that were designed for educating children, included at the bottom of each page questions that might be asked of the reader. In Lambert's long discussion of the various functions of the factory, the questions at the bottom suggest the book was as much a primer on the organization of a factory as a primer on the organization of the body: "Why may we compare the body to a machine? Why are shops needed by a factory? *Do most factories have a machine shop connected with them?* Where then must the substance be taken? What is it evident must be furnished to the shop? Why? What is also necessary? Where should the worn-out parts be carried?" and so forth. See pages [46]–47.

26. T[homas] S[cott] Lambert, *Hygienic Physiology* (Portland, 1852), 24; Hooker, *First Book in Physiology,* 96. Hooker also called the brain a "central office." See 11, 181; [Holmes], "Mechanism of Vital Actions," 51.

CHAPTER 5: HUMAN AND MACHINE

1. Joseph Henry, "Address," *Catalogue of Articles Deposited for Competition and Premium, at the First Annual Exhibition of the Metropolitan Mechanics' Institute* (Washington, 1853), 6. The equation of the mind with the soul suggested by Henry was not unusual. "Yet there are many collateral proofs of the spirituality of the mind," wrote a contributor to the *Literary Tablet* in 1833. "I say mind, because there is no distinction between mind and soul,—mind is not intelligence, but it is the thing that knows; it is an intelligent being." See "Mind," *Literary Tablet* 2 (September 14, 1833), 91.

2. William Bross, *Address before the Mechanics' Institute, at the Close of the Sixth Annual Fair, November 14, 1853* (Chicago, 1853), 9.

3. For the most detailed account of the *Moselle* explosion, see *Report of the Committee Appointed by the Citizens of Cincinnati, April 26, 1838, to Enquire into the Causes of the Explosion of the Moselle* (Cincinnati, Oh., 1838). Louis C. Hunter writes that "fully two-thirds of the major disasters by explosion on the western rivers down to 1852 took place as the boat left the bank or, in a few instances, while at a landing." See Louis C. Hunter, *Steamboats on the Western Rivers: An Economic and Technological History* (Cambridge, Mass., 1949), 295. For accounts of the New York City explosion, see *Report of the Special Committee Appointed by the Common Council of the City of New York, Relative to the Catastrophe in Hague Street, . . .* (New York, 1850); "The Late Dreadful Catastrophe," *Farmer and Mechanic*, n.s., 4 (February 14, 1850), 80–81; "Explosions of Steam Boilers," *Scientific American* 5 (February 23, 1850), 181; B., "An Account of the Explosion of a Steam Boiler in Hague St., New York," *Journal of the Franklin Institute* 49 (March 1850), 204–208; and "Terrible Explosion in New York," *Stryker's American Register and Magazine* 4 (July 1850), 135–36.

4. R[obert] M'Lane, *An Examination into the Cause of Explosions by Steam on the Western Waters* (Louisville, Ky., 1839), 8; Amadis De Gaul, "The Age We Live In. No. 1," *Democratic Review* 40 (August 1857), 175.

5. Only a few historians have studied the problem of boiler explosions in the antebellum period. See John G. Burke, "Bursting Boilers and the Federal Power," *Technology and Culture* 7 (winter 1966), 1–23; and Bruce Sinclair, *Early Research at the Franklin Institute: The Investigation into the Causes of Steam Boiler Explosions, 1830–1837* (Philadelphia, Penn., 1966). See also Hunter, *Steamboats on the Western Rivers*, 282–304, 520–46; and Bruce Sinclair, *Philadelphia's Philosopher Mechanics: A History of the Franklin Institute, 1824–1865* (Baltimore, Md., 1974), 170–91. For a recent, more interpretive study, see Julie Wosk, *Breaking Frame: Technology and the Visual Arts in the Nineteenth Century* (New Brunswick, N.J., 1993), esp. the introduction and ch.1, "The Traumas of Transport in Nineteenth-Century Art." On the professionalization of mechanical engineering in America during the nineteenth century, see Monte A. Calvert, *The Mechanical Engineer in America, 1830–1910: Professional Cultures in Conflict* (Baltimore, Md., 1967).

6. "Explosion of the Reindeer," *Gleason's Pictorial Drawing Room Companion* 3 (September 25, 1852), 196.

7. Figures for the period from 1825 to 1830 are from *Letter from the Secretary of the Treasury, Transmitting, in Obedience to a Resolution of the House of the 29th of June Last, Information in Relation to Steam Engines, etc.*, 25th Cong., 3d sess., 1838, H. Exec. Doc. 21, 399–406. Figures for the period from 1848 to 1852 are from Hunter, *Steamboats on the Western Rivers*, 541. Fifty could be low—for a contemporary account that suggests a higher figure, see "Explosions of Steam Boilers—Their Causes and Remedies," *Scientific American* 6 (February 8, 1851), 163. By 1838, the approximate number of steam engines in America was as follows: 1,860 stationary engines, 800 steamboat engines, and 350 locomotive engines. These figures are from Carroll W. Pursell, *Early Stationary Steam Engines in America: A Study in the Migration of a Technology* (Washington, 1969), 73. For discussions of the distribution of high-pressure and low-pressure steam engines in antebellum America, by geographic region and by industry, see Peter Temin, "Steam and Waterpower in the Early Nineteenth Century," *Journal of Economic History* 26 (June

1966), 187–205; and Harlan I. Halsey, "The Choice Between High-Pressure and Low-Pressure Steam Power in America in the Early Nineteenth Century," *Journal of Economic History* 41 (December 1981), 723–44. See also Jeremy Atack, Fred Bateman, and Thomas Weiss, "The Regional Diffusion and Adoption of the Steam Engine in American Manufacturing," *Journal of Economic History* 40 (June 1980), 281–308; and Pursell, *Early Stationary Steam Engines in America,* 113–15. On the efforts of the federal government to pass safety legislation, see Burke, "Bursting Boilers and the Federal Power."

8. "Another Explosion," *New-York Evening Post* (June 8, 1831), 2; "Explosion of Steam Boilers," *Scientific American* 6 (December 28, 1850), 117; James T. Lloyd's *Lloyd's Steamboat Directory, and Disasters on the Western Waters* (Philadelphia, Penn., [1856]) volume was an especially curious blend of the useful and the startling. Interspersed with maps of the Mississippi and Ohio Rivers, factual sketches of the principal western cities, information about railroad lines, and generously illustrated advertisements were detailed accounts of more than fifty boiler explosions (plus another thirty fires, collisions, and other accidents), complete with engravings showing bodies flying apart amidst the wreckage. A fascinating argument about the "cultural work" performed by Lloyd's book is in Ann Fabian, " 'Scenes too horrible for description': James T. Lloyd's Account of Exploding Steamboats," typescript in author's possession.

9. "The Steamboat Union," *New-York Evening Post* (December 28, 1826), 2; "Further Particulars," *New-Yorker* 5 (May 5, 1838), 108; Lloyd, *Lloyd's Steamboat Directory,* 56. For a typical sentimental account of a boiler explosion, see the reporting of the *Ben Sherrod* fire and explosion in "Appalling Calamity," *New-Yorker* 3 (May 27, 1837), 157–58. Perhaps the most sentimental chronicler of boiler explosions was S. A. Howland, author of *Steamboat Disasters and Railroad Accidents in the United States; . . .* (Worcester, Mass., 1840). In his preface, Howland wrote that the object of the book was both to record the history of disasters and to elicit feelings in his readers. He hoped that by perpetuating the memory of those who had suffered so greatly in the past, he would help his readers to be compassionate and charitable when called on in the present. Howland's sentimental design is evident in the poem "Loss of the Pulaski," which he placed at the end of a long account of an explosion that sank the steamship *Pulaski* off the coast of North Carolina in June 1838. After professing that "a scene like this can never be portray'd," the poet (who probably was not Howland) dwelled on the shrieking, praying, crying passengers. "In frantic agony a mother wild, / Clasps to her breast a dear and only child,— / He lifts his hands, and, with imploring eye, / Cries, 'mother, mother, must we, must we die?' " See page 75. For another sentimental treatment of a boiler explosion, see John Stanford, *Aetna: A Discourse, Delivered in the New-York City Hospital, on Lord's Day Morning, May 23, 1824. . . .* (New York, 1824), which was written after the explosion of the steamboat *Aetna.*

10. On the diffusion of steam power in manufacturing in the early nineteenth century, see Pursell, *Early Stationary Steam Engines in America,* ch. 6. The information on Pittsburgh is taken from page 83. Ibid., 87. The 1830 explosion is reported in "Another Disaster from the Use of Steam," [Philadelphia] *National Gazette* (September 28, 1830), 1; "Pratt's Steam Boiler Explosion," *Scientific American* 8 (August 20, 1853), 389.

11. "Appalling Explosion," *Farmer and Mechanic*, n.s., 2 (March 23, 1848), 145; "Another Disaster from the Use of Steam," 1; "The Way of Explosions," *Scientific American* 7 (July 25, 1852), 357.

12. "Pratt's Steam Boiler Explosion," 389; "Care in the Position and Management of Steam Boilers," *Farmer and Mechanic*, n.s., 4 (February 14, 1850), 79; "Fatal Accident," *New-Yorker* 9 (June 20, 1840), 223.

13. "Bursting of Steam Boilers," *Minerva* 2 (February 19, 1825), 312; "Explosion of Steam Boilers," *Scientific American* 6, 117; "Traveling by Steam," *New-Yorker* 5 (September 8, 1838), 393; R.M., "Suggestions of Means Calculated to Promote Safety in Steam-Boat Boilers," *Journal of the Franklin Institute* 17 (June 1836), 372. In the preface to his *Treatise on the Steam Engine*, published in 1830, James Renwick called the steam engine "the most important of the instruments by which the power of man is extended," and he wrote that he hoped his book would "have an influence of bringing into use those precautions and apparatus by which the risk to which human life is exposed, may be lessened." See *Treatise on the Steam Engine* (New York, 1830), iv.

14. J[ohn] L. Arnold, *Arnold's Lectures on Anatomy, Physiology and Hygiene; . . .* (Cincinnati, Oh., 1856), 12, 24; William A. Alcott, *Lectures on Life and Health; or, the Laws and Means of Physical Culture* (Boston, Mass., 1853), 205, 206.

15. "Humorous Description of the Steam Engine," *Boston Daily Advertiser* (June 17, 1828), 2; [James Kirke Paulding], *The Merry Tales of the Three Wise Men of Gotham* (New York, 1826), 28.

16. Joseph H. Moore, "Revolutions," *Herald of Truth* 1 (June 1847), 435, 434, 436, 434.

17. This account draws substantially from Hunter, *Steamboats in the Western Rivers*; Herbert Quick and Edward Quick, *Mississippi Steamboatin': A History of Steamboating on the Mississippi and its Tributaries* (New York, 1926); George Byron Merrick, *Old Times on the Upper Mississippi: The Recollections of a Steamboat Pilot from 1854 to 1863* (Cleveland, Oh., 1909); and [James H. Ward], *Steam for the Million. . . .* (Philadelphia, Penn., 1847).

18. *Steamboats*, 22nd Cong., 1st sess., 1832, House Rept. 478, 45. All steam boilers used during the antebellum period were made of cast iron, wrought iron, or copper. Each material had its own advantages and disadvantages. Copper was easy to work into the desired shape and was less subject to oxidation, but it was considerably more expensive than iron. Cast iron could also be molded with relative ease, but it was more liable to crack from heat, and boilers made from cast iron had to have much thicker walls to sustain the needed pressure. Considering all factors, wrought iron—formed into plates that could be shaped and riveted together—was the best material and the one used in the construction of most fresh-water boilers. For a comparison of these three materials, see James Renwick, *Treatise on the Steam Engine*, 2nd ed. (New York, 1839), 53–55. Many observers of the problem of boiler explosions understood the importance of good, quality boiler plate. In April 1851, for instance, the New Orleans Chamber of Commerce—convinced that many explosions resulted from the use of faulty material—passed a resolution calling on the government to inspect, test, and stamp "all iron to be used in the construction of boilers used in boats, for locomotives, and other purposes." See New Orleans Chamber of Commerce, *Reports and Resolutions Relative to the Causes of the Explosion of Steam*

Boilers, and the Measures Deemed Necessary for Prevention (New Orleans, La., 1851), 13. Samuel Slater, who was a principal founder of the Steam Cotton Manufacturing Company in Providence, Rhode Island in the late 1820s, took considerable care in ensuring that the iron used in the construction of his steam boilers was of high quality. On April 3, 1834, he wrote a letter to an iron manufacturer with whom he had been doing business, rejecting outright a batch of boiler plate that had been delivered the previous day. "This iron will never do for our boilers," he wrote, noting the shoddy workmanship that left the metal brittle and deeply indented. Expressing a desire to "avoid injury to ourselves and others," Slater was clearly concerned that the badly made boiler plate would be dangerous to use in his manufacturing operation. See Samuel Slater to Mackin & Murdock, April 3, 1834, Letterbook (1827–1836), vol. 14, Slater Companies Collection, Baker Library, Harvard Business School. For a brief discussion of some of the techniques used in the manufacture of boiler plate in the early 1830s, see *Steamboats,* House Rept. 478, 44–46.

19. "Steamboat Jackson," *New-York Commercial Advertiser* (June 15, 1831), 2.

20. One of the Fraternity, "Cause of Explosions," *Scientific American* 9 (May 6, 1854), 266. Some suggested that a similar burst of steam and explosion might occur if the engineer allowed the water to fall too low and then pumped more water into the overheated boiler. See, for instance, Thomas Earle, "On the Causes of Some Explosions of Steam Boilers," *Journal of the Franklin Institute* 7 (March 1831), 154–56. A steamboat traveler writing in *The New-Yorker* in 1838, in an account that was previously published in a newspaper in Boston, noted that "in travelling on high pressure boats, when the boat stops, if I can hear the pump going, . . . I feel that all is safe. But if it stops long, and no pump is in motion, it is immaterial how much steam is rattling off,—I yet feel under apprehensions, when the moment comes to shove off—that all may not be right, and take my station as far back in the rear as convenient, till the boat has started and has run a few hundred yards;—when, if she does not explode, the danger will be over." See A.J., "On Steamboat Accidents," *New-Yorker* 5 (May 12, 1838), 124; An Engineer, "Steam Boiler Explosions—Lieut. Hunt Criticised," *Scientific American* 9 (September 24, 1853), 11.

21. Quick and Quick, *Mississippi Steamboatin',* 206; "Steamboat Disaster—Bursting of the Boilers of the General Brown," *Family Magazine* 6 (1839), 299; "The Car of Commerce," *Niles' Weekly Register* 34 (June 7, 1828), 235; "Steamboat Disaster—Bursting of the Boilers of the General Brown," 299. For a fictional account of a boat race that ends with an explosion, see [Frederick William Thomas], "A Steamboat Race on the Ohio," *New-Yorker* 2 (December 10, 1836), 180–82. The account was excerpted from Thomas's novel, *East and West* (Philadelphia, Penn., 1836). See also Mark Twain [Samuel Clemens], *Life on the Mississippi* (London, 1883), ch. 16, "Racing Days." Clemens's younger brother, Henry, was killed in June 1858 when the steamboat Pennsylvania, on which he was clerk, exploded on the Mississippi River near Memphis. Clemens recounted the accident in *Life on the Mississippi,* ch. 20, "A Catastrophe."

22. Louis Hunter notes that in 1848 more than four hundred safety devices for steam engines were reported to have been patented. See Hunter, *Steamboats on the Western Rivers,* 535–36; A., "Remarks on Suggestions, by Mr. Perkins, in regard to the Explosions of Steam Boilers," *Journal of the Franklin Institute* 17 (June 1836), [369]; "Steam Navigation," *Niles' Weekly Register* 13 (November 1, 1817), 151. On

the doubts about the *Etna* engine, see *Report of the Committee on Commerce, Accompanied by a Bill for Regulating of Steam Boats, and for the Security of Passengers Therein,* 18th Cong., 1st sess., 1824, House Rept. 125, 3: "Many respectable mechanics and engineers in this country, for some time considered that the improved boiler, invented by Oliver Evans, obviated the objections to high pressure engines; the late melancholy occurrence on board the Etna, in the waters of New York harbor, must have undeceived them. The Engine in this boat was constructed on the plan of that skilful mechanic, and was furnished with all the guards his ingenuity could devise." Henry Howson, "Safety-Valves," in Oliver Byrne, *The American Engineer, Draftsman, and Machinist's Assistant; . . .* (Philadelphia, Penn., 1853), 61; R.D.H., "Remarks on the Effect of Salt Water in Steam Engine Boilers," *Journal of the Franklin Institute* 7 (May 1831), 291. Another observer later that decade wrote that "a safety valve is of no more relief to a boiler in the instant production of steam, than is the fusehole of a bomb-shell, when a charge of powder is exploded in its cavity." See William H. Hale, "Explosion of Steam-Boat Boilers," *Journal of the American Institute* 3 (July 1838), 532; A.J., "On Steamboat Accidents," 124; "Another Explosion," 2.

23. "Fulton and Steam Engines," *American Magazine of Useful and Entertaining Knowledge* 2 (November 1835), 91; *Opinions and Testimonials in Favor of Barnum's Self Acting Safety Apparatus, for the Prevention of Explosions and Fires on Board of Steam Vessels* [New York, 1848], 3; "Explosion of Steam-Boilers," *Journal of the American Institute* 4 (December 1838), 165; Howson, "Safety-Valves," 56.

24. F., "Causes of the Explosion of Steam Boilers," *Journal of the Franklin Institute* 53 (June 1852), 423; on the "stame" theory, see "Explosions of Steam Boilers—Their Causes and Remedies," 163; *Report of a Joint Committee of the Legislature of the State of Louisiana, on the Petition of J. O. Blair, upon the Subject of Steam Explosion,* 22nd Cong., 1st Sess., 1832, Doc. 226, 7, 8; "Explosions of Steam Boilers—Their Causes and Remedies," 163. This article extracted items from several sources, with this passage coming from the *Mobile Tribune.* The theory that explosions resulted from the accumulation of an explosive gas such as hydrogen suffered both controversy and scorn, however. One writer for the *Journal of the American Institute* in 1838, for instance, dismissed the theory as "nonsense." See Hale, "Explosion of Steam-Boat Boilers," 531. But the theory survived at least through the 1860s. As late as 1868, an inventor in Michigan published a circular arguing that steam boilers exploded when hydrogen gas seeped not only into the boiler, but into the boiler plate, rendering the metal itself explosive. See [Daniel Burns], *Burns' Theory of Boiler Explosions, Their Causes and Prevention* (Detroit, Mi., 1868), 5; See "Hawkins' Steam Engine," *Minerva* 1 (June 26, 1824), 184.

25. *General Report on the Explosion of Steam-Boilers, by a Committee of the Franklin Institute . . .* (Philadelphia, Penn., 1836), 4. This copy is printed in facsimile in Sinclair, *Early Research at the Franklin Institute.* For one post-report pamphlet that rejected the notion that steam pressure caused boilers to explode, and that promoted a vastly different alternative theory, see Jacob Harshman, *The Cause and Preventive of Steam Boiler Explosions* (Dayton, Oh., [1855]). According to Harshman, steam engines exploded when water inside the boiler converted into an "ethereal caloric" state. The "positive pole" of ethereal caloric naturally entered into an explosive reaction with any nearby "absorbing pole," which, in some cases, was the remaining water in the boiler. Harshman argued that his theory could account for

the higher incidence of explosions in western and southern waters, claiming that those regions tended to have higher amounts of "aeriform" ethereal caloric in the atmosphere. On the Franklin Institute study, see Sinclair, *Philadelphia's Philosopher Mechanics*, ch. 7; Sinclair, *Early Research at the Franklin Institute*; and Burke, "Bursting Boilers and the Federal Power."

26. *General Report on the Explosions of Steam-Boilers*, [44]; "New Steamboat Law," *New-Yorker* 5 (August 11, 1838), 334. This discussion of the legislative efforts of the federal government through 1838 is drawn from Hunter, *Steamboats on the Western Rivers*, ch. 13; Sinclair, *Early Research at the Franklin Institute*, part 5; and Burke, "Bursting Boilers and the Federal Power."

27. "Another Shocking Steamboat Accident," *New-Yorker* 11 (May 1, 1841), 108; "Another Terrible Explosion," *Brother Jonathan* 2 (July 16, 1842), 323; the figures for the years between 1841 and 1848 are from Hunter, *Steamboats on the Western Rivers*, 287; *Report of the Committee Appointed by the Citizens of Cincinnati*, 69; "The New Steamboat Law," *American Railroad Journal, and Mechanics' Magazine* 7 (September 1, 1838), 143; "Explosions of Steam Boilers—Their Causes and Remedies," 163.

28. [James M. Higbee], "Steamboat Disasters," *North American Review* 50 (January 1840), 21; Renwick, *Treatise on the Steam Engine*, 2d ed., 87; Cadwallader Evans, *A Treatise on the Causes of Explosions of Steam Boilers, with Practical Suggestions for Their Prevention. . . .* (Pittsburgh, Penn., 1850), [3], 16; A. C. Jones, "An Account of the Explosion of the Steamboat 'Brilliant,' " *Journal of the Franklin Institute* 53 (May 1852), 322.

29. "Explosion of the Steamer Timour," *Scientific American* 10 (December 23, 1854), 118.

30. *Report of the Committee on Commerce*, 2, 3; [Philadelphia] *American Sentinel* (December 28, 1826), 2; "Moral Causes of Recent Disasters," *American Railroad Journal, and Mechanics' Magazine* 7 (August 15, 1838), 126.

31. Jacob Walter, *An Essay on Steam, and Practical Engineering* (Holcomb, 1838), 2; Jones, "An Account of the Explosion of the Steamboat 'Brilliant,' " 322n; [Higbee], "Steamboat Disasters," 28; [Thomas], "A Steamboat Race on the Ohio," 180–82; "Appalling Calamity," *New-Yorker*, 157; "Explosions," *Niles' Weekly Register* 38 (May 1, 1830), 173.

32. [Higbee], "Steamboat Disasters," 40; R.D.H., "Remarks on the Effect of Salt Water in Steam Engine Boilers," 290; *Report of the Committee Appointed by the Citizens of Cincinnati*, 73; F., "Causes of the Explosion of Steam Boilers," 424; [Ward], *Steam for the Million*, 16; Walter, *An Essay on Steam*, 2.

33. Evans, *A Treatise on the Causes of Explosions of Steam Boilers*, 19.

34. A.J., "On Steamboat Accidents," 124; Evans, *A Treatise on the Causes of Explosions of Steam Boilers*, 19; [Higbee], "Steamboat Disasters," 34; "Boiler Explosions," *Scientific American* 7 (June 19, 1852), 320; Evans, *A Treatise on the Causes of Explosions of Steam Boilers*, 19; Walter, *An Essay on Steam*, 3; "Distressing Accident," *New-York American* (May 8, 1826), 2.

35. "Explosions of Steam Boilers," *Journal of the Franklin Institute* 8 (November 1831), 312, 314.

36. "Explosion of Steam Boilers," *Scientific American* 5 (July 20, 1850), 349; [Higbee], "Steamboat Disasters," 40; John Clowes, "Causes of Explosions of Steamboat Boilers—Accidents, Etc.," *Farmer and Mechanic*, n.s., 2 (March 23, 1848), 142.

37. Fulton, "What Constitutes an Engineer?" *Journal of the Franklin Institute* 51 (January 1851), 55. John Clowes, an engineer who wrote a series of articles on boiler explosions for the *Farmer and Mechanic* in 1848, might have been one of the experienced engineers who understood the value of theoretical knowledge that Fulton wrote about. "Some forty years of practical experience with stationary engines," wrote Clowes, "has fully satisfied me, together with many of my scientific associates, that the most effectual way to prevent explosions and accidents to the working gear on board steamboats, is a sound, practical, scientific and mechanical education in the profession of Engineering." See "Causes of Explosions of Steamboat Boilers," 142.

38. M'Lane, *An Examination into the Cause of Explosions by Steam on the Western Waters*, 12, 3, 13–14. M'Lane devoted considerable energy to expressing how little use he had for theoretical knowledge: "I have not the capacity to solve the watery element, nor tell what various materials compose it, . . . nor do I believe that a full investigation of the matter would explain to the most sensitive mind, the reason why boilers burst," he wrote. "But this I know, that the two elements, fire and water, in conjunction form steam; and confine that steam and there is great power in it, and the more it is confined, the greater. So much for my knowledge; and how many are there who know more?" Ibid., 3. Evans, *A Treatise on the Causes of Explosions of Steam Boilers*, 18, [3]. Otto Mayr offers an illuminating discussion of the "polarization" between theorists and "practical" men in the professionalization of American engineering in "Yankee Practice and Engineering Theory: Charles T. Porter and the Dynamics of the High-Speed Engine," *Technology and Culture* 16 (October 1975), 570–602. Monte A. Calvert, in *The Mechanical Engineer in America, 1830–1910*, similarly argues for a prevailing tension between a "shop culture" and a "school culture" in nineteenth-century mechanical engineering.

39. Clowes, "Causes of Explosions of Steamboat Boilers," 142; *Report of the Committee Appointed by the Citizens of Cincinnati*, 73; New Orleans Chamber of Commerce, *Reports and Resolutions Relative to the Causes of the Explosion of Steam Boilers*, 6. John Harley Warner has convincingly argued that physicians in the later decades of the nineteenth century similarly embraced science even before scientific knowledge had a substantial contribution to make to medical practice because the language of science helped physicians—in a time of epistemological crisis—to articulate a shared professional identity. See John Harley Warner, "Ideals of Science and Their Discontents in Late Nineteenth-Century American Medicine," *Isis* 82 (1991), 454–78. See also John Harley Warner, *The Therapeutic Perspective: Medical Practice, Knowledge, and Identity in America, 1820–1885* (Cambridge, Mass., 1986).

40. *An Act to Amend an Act Entitled "An Act to Provide for the Better Security . . . ,"* Statutes at Large 10, ch. 106, 67 (1852); *General Report on the Explosions of Steam-Boilers*, 47; *An Act to Provide for the Better Security of the Lives of Passengers . . . , Statutes at Large* 5, ch. 191, 305 (1838). In its 1836 report, the Franklin Institute admitted that "in the present state of general education" it was not practical "to insist that . . . steam-engineers, should be versed in the scientific principles which regulate the use of steam," and that it was enough for them to have "a thorough practical acquaintance with the steam-engine." See *General Report on the Explosions of Steam-Boilers*, 39; Clowes, "Causes of Explosions of Steamboat Boilers," 142. Without suggesting the metaphorical meanings I am arguing for here, Louis Hunter writes that, with the 1852 law, "engineers and pilots ceased in the eyes of the law to be merely

hired hands and their efforts to attain professional status . . . were materially strengthened." See Hunter, *Steamboats on the Western Rivers*, 538. For an extended discussion of the various efforts at legislative solutions to the problem of steam boiler explosions, see ibid., ch. 13, "The Movement for Steamboat Regulation."

41. The figures for the years 1848 to 1852 are from Hunter, *Steamboats on the
Western Rivers*, 541. The figures for the years from 1844 to 1860 are from Burke,
"Bursting Boilers and the Federal Power," 22. "Workings of the New Steamboat Law,"
Scientific American 10 (March 3, 1855), 195.

42. "Explosions of Steam Boilers," *Scientific American*, 181; "Valuable Communication," *New-York Commercial Advertiser* (February 13, 1832), 2.

EPILOGUE

1. This synopsis of the *Sultana* disaster is drawn from Gene Eric Salecker, *Disaster on the Mississippi: The* Sultana *Explosion, April 27, 1865* (Annapolis, Md.,
1996); and Jerry O. Potter, *The Sultana Tragedy: America's Greatest Maritime Disaster* (Gretna, La., 1992). See also James W. Elliott, *Transport to Disaster* (New York,
1962).

2. Quoted in Coy F. Cross II, *Justin Smith Morrill: Father of the Land-Grant Col-
leges* (East Lansing, Mich., 1999), 88. On the formulation and passage of the 1862
Morrill Act, see ibid., ch. 5. On engineering education in America prior to 1862,
see Terry S. Reynolds, "The Education of Engineers in America before the Morrill
Act of 1862," *History of Education Quarterly* 32 (winter 1992), [459]–82. Monte
Calvert finds that many of the new land grant school engineering programs got off
to a slow start. See Monte A. Calvert, *The Mechanical Engineer in America, 1830–1910:
Professional Cultures in Conflict* (Baltimore, Md., 1967), 47–48.

3. Quoted in William Hannibal Robinson, "The History of Hampton Institute,
1868–1949" (Ph.D. diss., New York University, 1953), 69. My account of Armstrong
and the founding of the Hampton Institute is based on Robinson's discussion. On
Indian boarding schools, see Jacqueline Fear-Segal, "Nineteenth-Century Indian Education: Universalism Versus Evolutionism," *Journal of American Studies* 33 (August
1999), [323]–41; and David Wallace Adams, *Education for Extinction: American Indians and the Boarding School Experience, 1875–1928* (Lawrence, Ks., 1995). The phrase
"off-reservation" is taken from Adams. Both studies discuss in detail the relation
between the Hampton Institute and the postbellum Indian schools.

4. On the principles of thermodynamics, I have depended primarily on John F.
Sandfort, *Heat Engines: Thermodynamics in Theory and Practice* (Garden City, N.J.,
1962); and D. S. L. Cardwell, *From Watt to Clausius: The Rise of Thermodynamics
in the Early Industrial Age* (Ithaca, N.Y., 1971). My thinking about the relation between
the laws of thermodynamics and ideas about work, exhaustion, and the human body
is deeply indebted to Anson Rabinbach's *The Human Motor: Energy, Fatigue, and
the Origins of Modernity* (New York, 1990). See also Mark Seltzer, *Bodies and
Machines* (New York, 1992). For early discussions of the principles of thermodynamics in popular American periodicals, see [Oliver Wendell Holmes], "Mechanism of
Vital Action," *North American Review* 85 (July 1857), 39–77; "What Are We Going
to Make?" *Atlantic Monthly* 2 (June 1858), 90–101; "Dynamical Theory of Heat,"
Eclectic Magazine 62 (June 1864), [129]–43; "The Correlation of Forces," *Lippincott's*

Magazine 1 (March 1868), 306–10, and (April 1868), 371–74; and "The New Theory of Heat," *Harper's New Monthly Magazine* 39 (August 1869), 322–29.

5. [Walter Wells], "Strength, and How to Use It," *Lippincott's Magazine* 2 (October 1868), 417, 418, 420, 419, 421; Walter Wells, "Strength, and How to Use It," *Lippincott's Magazine* 3 (June 1869), 661–62.

6. Wells, "Strength, and How to Use It," *Lippincott's Magazine* 3, 661; [Walter Wells], "Strength, and How to Use It" *Lippincott's Magazine* 2 (November 1868), 552; Walter Wells, "Strength, and How to Use It," *Lippincott's Magazine* 2 (December 1868), 663.

7. Two articles describing neurasthenia appeared in American medical journals in 1869. See George Beard, "Neurasthenia, or Nervous Exhaustion," *Boston Medical and Surgical Journal* 80 (April 29, 1869), [217]–21; and E. H. Van Deusen, "Observations on a Form of Nervous Prostration, (Neurasthenia,) Culminating in Insanity," *American Journal of Insanity* 25 (April 1869), [445]–61. It is clear from chapters 3 and 4, however, that Americans prior to the formulation of neurasthenia as a diagnosis understood there to be an association between modern life and disease. In a discussion of the precedents for the diagnosis of neurasthenia, Charles E. Rosenberg notes that physicians frequently found modern American life to be especially dangerous to health. "Since at least the time of Benjamin Rush," Rosenberg writes, "American physicians had, almost as a matter of course, conceded that the unique pace of American life, its competitiveness, its lack of stability in religion and government, was somehow related to an incidence of mental illness higher than that of other Western countries." See Charles E. Rosenberg, "The Place of George M. Beard in Nineteenth-Century Psychiatry," *Bulletin of the History of Medicine* 36 (May-June 1962), 254. For Beard's discussion of the causes of neurasthenia, see George M. Beard, *American Nervousness: Its Causes and Consequences* (New York, 1881), ch. 3; S. Weir Mitchell, "Wear and Tear," *Lippincott's Magazine* 4 (November 1869), 493. Sales information on Mitchell's book is from Barbara Sicherman, "The Uses of a Diagnosis: Doctors, Patients, and Neurasthenia," in Judith Walzer Leavitt and Ronald L. Numbers, eds., *Sickness and Health in America: Readings in the History of Medicine and Public Health,* 2d ed. (Madison, Wis., 1985), 23. The features of Mitchell's rest cure are most clearly set out in S. Weir Mitchell, *Fat and Blood: And How to Make Them* (Philadelphia, Penn., 1877). Because many of the patients who were placed under the extreme regimen of the rest cure were women, historians have studied the diagnosis and treatment of neurasthenia in terms of the power that male physicians exerted over female patients. See, for example, Suzanne Poirier, "The Weir Mitchell Rest Cure: Doctor and Patients," *Women's Studies* 10 (1983), [15]–40; and Ann Douglas Wood, " 'The Fashionable Diseases': Women's Complaints and Their Treatment in Nineteenth-Century America," *Journal of Interdisciplinary History* 4 (summer 1973), [25]–52.

8. Mitchell, "Wear and Tear," 494. George Beard seemed even more intent than Mitchell on reserving the diagnosis of neurasthenia for brain-workers and the social elite. In *American Nervousness,* Beard held that neurasthenia arose from an evolutionary process whereby those suitable to brain-work are more highly developed—and therefore more sensitive—than those more suited to muscle-work. Consequently, he argued, neurasthenia only occasionally occurred among "the lower orders." Indeed, he wrote, "All that is said here of American nervousness refers only to a fraction of

American society; for in America, as in all lands, the majority of the people are mus-
cle-workers rather than brain-workers; have little education, and are not striving
for honor, or expecting eminence or wealth." See Beard, *American Nervousness,*
96–97. A number of studies have noted this particular class dimension to neurasthenia. See, for example, Sicherman, "The Uses of a Diagnosis"; Howard M. Feinstein, "The Use and Abuse of Illness in the James Family Circle: A View of Neurasthenia as a Social Phenomenon," in Robert J. Brugger, ed., *Our Selves/Our Past:
Psychological Approaches to American History* (Baltimore, Md., 1981), 228–43; Joan
Burbick, *Healing the Republic: The Language of Health and the Culture of Nationalism in Nineteenth-Century America* (New York, 1994), chs. 11 and 12; and Jackson Lears, *No Place of Grace: Antimodernism and the Transformation of American
Culture, 1880–1920* (New York, 1981), 47–58. My list of working-class occupations
is from Francis Gosling's *Before Freud,* which reveals that neurasthenia was much
more widely diagnosed among wage-workers than had previously been thought. In
a study of 217 neurasthenia patients discussed in medical journals between 1870 and
1910 and identified by occupation, Gosling finds that 77—a full 35.5%—were either
laborers or low-wage office workers. See F. G. Gosling, *Before Freud: Neurasthenia
and the American Medical Community, 1870–1910* (Urbana, Ill., 1987), 31–32, and
appendix B, 184–85. Gosling's book offers a fascinating and detailed discussion both
of the prevalence of neurasthenia among men and women who worked for wages,
and of how they were diagnosed and treated differently by doctors.

   9. [Wells], "Strength, and How to Use It" *Lippincott's Magazine* 2 (October 1868),
420. On scientific management, see Daniel Nelson, *Managers and Workers: Origins of the Twentieth-Century Factory System in the United States, 1880–1920,* 2d
ed. (Madison, Wis., 1995); David Montgomery, *The Fall of the House of Labor: The
Workplace, the State, and American Labor Activism, 1865–1925* (New York, 1987);
Daniel Nelson, "The Making of a Progressive Engineer: Frederick W. Taylor," *Penn-
sylvania Magazine of History and Biography* 103 (October 1979), 446–66; and Samuel
Haber, *Efficiency and Uplift: Scientific Management in the Progressive Era, 1890–1920*
(Chicago, 1964). The most recent full biography of Taylor is Robert Kanigel, *The
One Best Way: Frederick Winslow Taylor and the Enigma of Efficiency* (New York,
1997). On the efficiency ideal in early twentieth-century American culture, see Haber,
Efficiency and Uplift; Cecelia Tichi, *Shifting Gears: Technology, Literature, Culture
in Modernist America* (Chapel Hill, N.C., 1987); Martha Banta, *Taylored Lives: Nar-
rative Productions in the Age of Taylor, Veblen, and Ford* (Chicago, 1993); and Seltzer,
Bodies and Machines.

   10. Frank B. Gilbreth and L. M. Gilbreth, *Applied Motion Study: A Collection
of Papers on the Efficient Method to Industrial Preparedness* (New York, 1917), 169.
For the Gilbreths' vision of the efficient workplace, see Frank B. Gilbreth and Lillian
M. Gilbreth, *Fatigue Study: The Elimination of Humanity's Greatest Unnecessary
Waste, A First Step in Motion Study* (New York, 1916). For Frederic Lee's use of the
phrase "human machine," see Frederic S. Lee, *The Human Machine and Industrial
Efficiency* (New York, 1919); Frederic S. Lee, "Physical Exercise from the Standpoint
of Physiology," *Science,* n.s., 29 (April 2, 1909), 522; Frederic S. Lee, "Is the Eight-Hour
Working-Day Rational?" *Science,* n.s., 44 (November 24, 1916), [727], 734. For Lee's
criticism of scientific management, see *The Human Machine and Industrial Efficiency,*
90–95. See also Alan Derickson, "Physiological Science and Scientific Management in

the Progressive Era: Frederic S. Lee and the Committee on Industrial Fatigue," *Business History Review* 68 (winter 1994), [483]–514. On the development of industrial fatigue as a field of study, see ibid.; and Richard Gillespie, "Industrial Fatigue and the Discipline of Physiology," in Gerald L. Geison, ed., *Physiology in the American Context, 1850–1940* (Bethesda, Md., 1987), 237–62.

Bibliography

PRIMARY SOURCES: MANUSCRIPT COLLECTIONS

American Antiquarian Society
    Sylvester Graham, Lecture Notes, folio volume
The Cooper Union
    The Cooper Union Archives
        Library, Various Correspondence
        Minutes of the Trustees
The Franklin Institute Science Museum
    Franklin Institute Archive
Harvard Business School, Baker Library
    Slater Companies Collection
The Historical Society of Pennsylvania
    William Darrach Diary (1832–37)
Lafayette College
    Special Collections and College Archives, Skillman Library
        Early Records
        Lafayette Collection
        Lafayette College Board of Trustees Minutes
        Lafayette College Faculty Minutes
Library Company of Philadelphia
    Allen Chess Collection
Massachusetts Historical Society
    Bradley Newcomb Cumings Journal
    Codman-Butterfield Papers
New-York Historical Society
    Gulian Verplanck Papers
University of Cincinnati

Archives and Rare Books Department
Ohio Mechanics' Institute Collection

PRIMARY SOURCES: PRINTED MATERIAL

A. "Remarks on Suggestions, by Mr. Perkins, in Regard to the Explosions of Steam Boilers." *Journal of the Franklin Institute* 17 (June 1836), [369]–72.

A. J. "On Steamboat Accidents." *New-Yorker* 5 (May 12, 1838), 124.

An Act to Amend an Act Entitled "An Act to Provide for the Better Security . . . ," Statutes at Large 10, ch. 106 (1852).

An Act to Provide for the Better Security of the Lives of Passengers . . . , Statutes at Large 5, ch. 191, (1838).

Address of the Mechanics' Institute of the City of New-York, to Mechanics and Others; . . . New York, 1838.

Alcott, William A. *The House I Live In.* . . . Boston, 1834.

Alcott, W[illia]m A. "Labor and Study." *American Annals of Education,* 3d ser., 9 (January 1839), 17–22.

————. *The Laws of Health; or, Sequel to "The House I Live In."* Boston, 1857.

————. *Lectures on Life and Health; or, the Laws and Means of Physical Culture.* Boston, 1853.

————. "On the Study of Physiology as a Branch of General Education." *American Annals of Education,* 3d ser., 3 (September 1833), [385]–403.

[————]. "Physical Education." *Moral Reformer* 1 (January 1835), 19–21.

————. *The Structure, Uses and Abuses of the Human Hand.* Boston, 1856.

"American Colonization Society." *New-York Commercial Advertiser* (October 10, 1833), 2.

[Philadelphia] *American Sentinel* (December 28, 1826), 2.

"Another Disaster from the Use of Steam." [Philadelphia] *National Gazette* (September 28, 1830), 1.

"Another Explosion." *New-York Evening Post* (June 8, 1831), 2.

"Another Shocking Steamboat Accident." *New-Yorker* 11 (May 1, 1841), 107–108.

"Another Terrible Explosion." *Brother Jonathan* 2 (July 16, 1842), 323.

"Appalling Calamity." *New-Yorker* 3 (May 27, 1837), 157–58.

"Appalling Explosion." *Farmer and Mechanic,* n.s., 2 (March 23, 1848), 145.

Arnold, J[ohn] L. *Arnold's Lectures on Anatomy, Physiology and Hygiene; . . .* Cincinnati, 1856.

"The Automaton." *New-York American* (April 22, 1826), 2.

"Automaton." *New-York Evening Post* (May 27, 1826), 2.

"Automaton Chess-Player." [New York] *Commercial Advertiser* (April 14, 1826), 2.

"The Automaton Chess-Player." [New York] *Commercial Advertiser* (April 21, 1826), 2.

"Automaton Chess-Player." *New-York Evening Post* (April 14, 1826), 2.

"Automaton Chess-Player." *New-York Evening Post* (April 24, 1826), 2.

"The Automaton Chess-Player." [New York] *Truth Teller* (April 22, 1826), 6.

"Automaton Chess Player etc." [Boston] *Columbian Centinel* (September 16, 1826), 2.

"Automaton Exhibition in Julien Hall." [Boston] *Columbian Centinel* (September 20, 1826), 2.

B. "An Account of the Explosion of a Steam Boiler in Hague St., New York." *Journal of the Franklin Institute* 49 (March 1850), 204–208.

"Babbage's Calculating Engine." *American Magazine of Useful and Entertaining Knowledge* 1 (October 1834), 88–96.

Baker, James L. *Men and Things; or, Short Essays on Various Subjects*. Boston, 1858.

[Baldwin, Henry]. "Judge Baldwin's Address." *Register of Pennsylvania* 6 (October 23, 1830), 259–62.

Barnes, Gilbert H., and Dwight L. Dumond, eds. *Letters of Theodore Dwight Weld, Angelina Grimké Weld, and Sarah Grimké, 1822–1844*. 2 vols. New York, 1934.

Bartlett, Elisha. *Obedience to the Laws of Health, a Moral Duty*. . . . Boston, 1838.

Beach, W[ooster]. *A Treatise on Anatomy, Physiology, and Health, Designed for Students, Schools, and Popular Use*. New York, 1847.

Beard, George M. *American Nervousness: Its Causes and Consequences*. New York, 1881.

———. "Neurasthenia, or Nervous Exhaustion." *Boston Medical and Surgical Journal* 80 (April 29, 1869), [217]–21.

Beecher, Catharine E. *Letters to the People on Health and Happiness*. New York, 1855.

Bird, F[rancis] W[illiam]. *Physiological Reform: An Address, Delivered before the American Physiological Society at their First Annual Meeting, June 1, 1837*. Boston, 1837.

"Boiler Explosions." *Scientific American* 7 (June 19, 1852), 320.

[Bradford, Gamaliel]. *The History and Analysis of the Supposed Automaton Chess Player, of M. De Kempelen,* . . . Boston, 1826.

Brigham, Amariah. *Remarks on the Influence of Mental Cultivation Upon Health*. Hartford, Conn., 1832.

Bross, William. *Address before the Mechanics Institute, at the Close of the Sixth Annual Fair, November 14, 1853*. Chicago, 1853.

[Burns, Daniel]. *Burns' Theory of Boiler Explosions, Their Causes and Prevention*. Detroit, Mich., 1868.

Burritt, Elihu. "Why I Left the Anvil." *Supplement to the Courant* 15 (April 20, 1850), 62.

"Bursting of Steam Boilers." *Minerva* 2 (February 19, 1825), 312–13.

C.T. "Fairs Generally." *Journal of the American Institute* 4 (January 1839), 213–15.

Caldwell, Charles. *Thoughts on Physical Education:* . . . Boston, 1834.

"The Car of Commerce." *Niles' Weekly Register* 34 (June 7, 1828), 235.

"Care in the Position and Management of Steam Boilers." *Farmer and Mechanic*, n.s., 4 (February 14, 1850), 79.

[Carlyle, Thomas]. "Signs of the Times." *Edinburgh Review* 49 (June 1829), 439–59.

Cary, Alpheus. *An Address, Delivered before the Massachusetts Charitable Mechanic Association, October 7th 1824,* . . . Boston, 1824.

Catalogue of the Library of the Mechanics' Institute of the City of New-York. New York, 1835.

C[hace], W. S. "Andraud's New System of Railroad Locomotion." *Merchants' Magazine* 17 (July 1847), 40–43.

Chandler, Joseph R. "Address." In *Catalogue of Articles Deposited for Competition and Premium, at the First Annual Exhibition of the Metropolitan Mechanics' Institute,* [3]-14 . Washington, 1853.

Charter, Constitution, and By-Laws of the Mechanics' Institute of the City of Chicago.
    Chicago, 1847.
Charter, Constitution, and By-Laws of the New-York Mechanic and Scientific Insti-
    tution. New York, 1822.
Charter of Incorporation, Constitution and By-Laws of the Franklin Institute of the
    State of Pennsylvania for the Promotion of the Mechanic Arts. Philadelphia, Penn.,
    1824.
"The Chess-Player." [Philadelphia] *American Sentinel* (January 6, 1827), 2.
"The Chess-Player." [New York] *Commercial Advertiser* (April 25, 1826), 2.
"Chess Player." [Boston] *Evening Gazette* (August 17, 1833), 2.
"The Chess Player Discovered." [Washington, D.C.] *Daily National Intelligencer* (June
    4, 1827), 3.
Chester, Burlington. "To the Automaton Chess Player." *Philadelphia Gazette and*
    Daily Advertiser (February 10, 1827), 2.
Chicago Magazine: The West As It Is 1 (March 1857).
Clowes, John. "Causes of Explosions of Steamboat Boilers—Accidents, Etc." *Farmer*
    and Mechanic, n.s., 2 (March 23, 1848), 142.
Coates, Reynell. *An Address Introductory to a Popular Course of Lectures on the*
    History of Organic Development, and the Means of Improving the Mental and
    Physical Faculties, . . . Philadelphia, Penn., 1839.
_____. *Popular Medicine or, Family Adviser* . . . Philadelphia, Penn., 1838.
_____. *Syllabus of a Course of Popular Lectures on Physiology, with an Outline of*
    the Principles which Govern the Gradual Developement [sic] *of the Faculties of*
    Mind and Body. Philadelphia, Penn., 1840.
Comstock, J[ohn] L[ee]. *Outlines of Physiology, Both Comparative and Human;* . .
    . , 3d ed. New York, 1844.
Constitution and By-Laws of the Mechanics' Institute of the City of New-York. New
    York, 1835.
Constitution and By-Laws of the Mechanics' Institute of St. Louis. St. Louis, Mo.,
    1843.
Constitution of the American Physiological Society . . . *To Which Is Prefixed a Sum-*
    mary Explanation of the Objects of the Society. Boston, 1837.
Conyngham, Redmond. "Address, Delivered before the Mechanics' Society." *Hazard's*
    Register of Pennsylvania 14 (June 20, 1835), 391–97.
"The Correlation of Forces." *Lippincott's Magazine* 1 (March 1868), 306–10; (April
    1868), 371–74.
Coulter, David. *Memoir of David Coulter, D.D. with Reminiscences, Letters, Lec-*
    tures and Sermons. St. Louis, Mo., n.d.
A Course of Calisthenics for Young Ladies, in Schools and Families. Hartford, Conn.,
    1831.
"Curiosities of Mechanism." *Scientific American* 3 (June 1848), 296.
Cutter, Calvin. *Physiology for Children.* Boston, 1846.
Daly, Charles P. *Origin and History of Institutions for the Promotion of the Useful*
    Arts. . . . Albany, N.Y., 1864.
Davis, Emerson. *The Half Century;* . . . Boston, 1851.
[DeBow, J. D. B.] "American Legislation, Science, Art, and Agriculture." *Commer-*
    cial Review 2 (September 1846), 76–116.

_____. "Morse's Electro-Magnetic Telegraph." *Commercial Review* 1 (February 1846), 133–42.

De Gaul, Amadis. "The Age We Live In. No. 1." *Democratic Review* 40 (August 1857), 174–76.

"Distressing Accident." *New-York American* (May 8, 1826), 2.

Dow, Neal. *An Oration, Delivered before the Maine Charitable Mechanic Association, at Their Triennial Celebration, July 4, 1829.* Portland, Maine, 1829.

Draper, John William. *Human Physiology, Statical and Dynamical; Or, the Conditions and Course of the Life of Man.* New York, 1856.

Duncan, Abel G. *Evils of Violating the Laws of Health, and the Remedy. . . .* Boston, 1838.

Dunglison, Robley. *Human Health; . . .* Philadelphia, Penn., 1844.

"Dunglison's Physiology." *American Quarterly Review* 13 (June 1833), 375–403.

"Dynamical Theory of Heat." *Eclectic Magazine* 62 (June 1864), [129]–43.

Dyott, T[homas] W. *An Exposition of the System of Moral and Mental Labor, Established at the Glass Factory of Dyottville, in the County of Philadelphia . . .* Philadelphia, Penn., 1833.

"Dyspepsia." *Southern Review* 4 (August 1829), 208–41.

Earle, Thomas. "On the Causes of Some Explosions of Steam Boilers." *Journal of the Franklin Institute* 7 (March 1831), 154–56.

"Education." *American Quarterly Review* 6 (September 1829), 145–71.

"Education of Coloured People." *Hazard's Register of Pennsylvania* 8 (September 24, 1831), 195–96.

"Education with Manual Labor." *Register of Pennsylvania* 2 (November 1, 1828), 257–58.

Edwards, B[ela] B. *An Address Delivered at the Fourth Anniversary of the Mount Holyoke Female Seminary, . . .* Andover, N.H., 1841.

"Effects of Machinery." *North American Review* 34 (January 1832), 220–46.

Emerson, George B. *An Address, Delivered at the Opening of the Boston Mechanics' Institution, February 7, 1827.* Boston, 1827.

An Engineer. "Steam Boiler Explosions—Lieut. Hunt Criticised." *Scientific American* 9 (September 24, 1853), 11.

"Ericsson's Caloric Engine." *Hunt's Merchants' Magazine* 27 (July 1852), 19–28.

Evans, Cadwallader. *A Treatise on the Causes of Explosions of Steam Boilers, with Practical Suggestions for Their Prevention. . . .* Pittsburgh, 1850.

Everett, Edward. "An Essay on the Importance to Practical Men of Scientific Knowledge, and on the Encouragements to its Pursuit." *The American Library of Useful Knowledge* 1 (Boston, 1831), 59–105.

"Evil Effects of the Division of Labor." *Supplement to the Connecticut Courant* 4 (November 2, 1835), 157–59.

Ewbank, Thomas. *Inorganic Forces Ordained to Supercede Human Slavery.* New York, 1860.

"Exercise." *Supplement to the Connecticut Courant* 2 (December 22, 1829), 168.

"Explosion of Steam-Boat Boilers." *Journal of the American Institute* 3 (July 1838), 529–37.

"Explosion of Steam-Boilers." *Journal of the American Institute* 4 (December 1838), 165.

"Explosion of Steam Boilers." *Scientific American* 5 (July 20, 1850), 349.

"Explosion of Steam Boilers." *Scientific American* 6 (December 28, 1850), 117.

"Explosion of the Reindeer." *Gleason's Pictorial Drawing Room Companion* 3 (September 25, 1852), 196.

"Explosion of the Steamer Timour." *Scientific American* 10 (December 23, 1854), 118.

"Explosions." *Niles' Weekly Register* 38 (May 1, 1830), 173.

"Explosions of Steam Boilers." *Journal of the Franklin Institute* 8 (November 1831), 306–15.

"Explosions of Steam Boilers." *Scientific American* 5 (February 23, 1850), 181.

"Explosions of Steam Boilers—Their Causes and Remedies." *Scientific American* 6 (February 8, 1851), 163.

F. "Causes of the Explosion of Steam Boilers." *Journal of the Franklin Institute* 53 (June 1852), 423–32.

Fairchild, J. H. *Oberlin: Its Origin, Progress and Results.* . . . Oberlin, Oh., 1860.

"Fatal Accident." *New-Yorker* 9 (June 20, 1840), 223.

Fellenberg or an Appeal to the Friends of Education on Behalf of Lafayette College. Easton, Penn., 1835.

First Annual Report of the American Physiological Society. Boston, 1837.

The First Annual Report of the Board of Managers of the Boston Mechanics' Institution. Boston, 1828.

"First Annual Report of the Board of Trustees of Lafayette College." *Hazard's Register of Pennsylvania* 12 (September 21, 1833), 190–92.

First Annual Report of the Board of Trustees of the Manual Labour Academy of Pennsylvania. Philadelphia, Penn., 1829.

The First Annual Report of the Trustees of the Cooper Union, for the Advancement of Science and Art. New York, 1860.

"For the American." *New-York American* (May 2, 1826), 2.

Fowler, L. N. [Lydia Folger Fowler]. *Familiar Lessons on Physiology and Phrenology, for Children and Youth* . . . New York, 1848.

Fraley, Frederick. "Address Delivered before the Franklin Institute at the Close of the Eleventh Exhibition of American Manufactures." *Journal of the Franklin Institute* 30 (November 1840), 308–15.

Fraser, Charles. "The Moral Influence of Steam." *Hunt's Merchants' Magazine* 14 (June 1846), 499–515.

Frelinghuysen, Theodore. *An Oration: Delivered at Princeton, New Jersey, November 16, 1824, before the New-Jersey Colonization Society.* Princeton, N.J., 1824.

French, Benjamin Brown. *Witness to the Young Republic: A Yankee's Journal, 1828–1870.* Ed. Donald B. Cole and John J. McDonough. Hanover, N.H.: University Press of New England, 1989.

"From the Baltimore Gazette." *Southern Literary Messenger* 2 (July 1836), 518–19.

"From the United States Gazette." *Southern Literary Messenger* 2 (July 1836), 522.

Frost, John. *An Oration, Delivered at Middlebury, before the Associated Alumni of the College, August 19, 1829.* Utica, N.Y., 1829.

Fulton. "What Constitutes an Engineer?" *Journal of the Franklin Institute* 51 (January 1851), 55–56.

"Fulton and Steam Engines." *American Magazine of Useful and Entertaining Knowledge* 2 (November 1835), [89]–91.

"Further Particulars." *New-Yorker* 5 (May 5, 1838), 108.

G[allaudet], P[eter] W[allace]. *A System of Education, on the Principle of Connecting Science with Useful Labour.* N.d.

Gayarré, Charles. *Influence of the Mechanic Arts on the Human Race.* . . . New York, 1854.

General Report on the Explosions of Steam-Boilers, by a Committee of the Franklin Institute . . . Philadelphia, Penn., 1836.

Gilbreth, Frank B., and L. M. Gilbreth. *Applied Motion Study: A Collection of Papers on the Efficient Method to Industrial Preparedness.* New York, 1917.

Gilbreth, Frank B., and Lillian M. Gilbreth. *Fatigue Study: The Elimination of Humanity's Greatest Unnecessary Waste, a First Step in Motion Study.* New York, 1916.

Gilmor, Robert. "The Diary of Robert Gilmor." *Maryland Historical Magazine* 17 (September 1922), 231–68; (December 1922), 319–47.

[Goodrich, Samuel Griswold]. *Enterprise, Industry, and Art of Man,* . . . Philadelphia, Penn., [1845].

Greeley, Horace. "Labor—Elegant Extract." *Supplement to the Courant* 10 (January 11, 1845), 8.

————. *Recollections of a Busy Life.* New York, 1868.

Green, Beriah. *Success: A Valedictory Address, Delivered at the Anniversary of the Oneida Institute, November 1, 1843.* Utica, N.Y., 1843.

Grimké, Thomas S. *Correspondence on the Principles of Peace, Manual Labor Schools, Etc.* Charleston, S.C., 1833.

Griscom, John H. *Animal Mechanism and Physiology* . . . New York, 1848.

Guernsey, Orrin, and Josiah F. Willard, eds. *History of Rock County, and Transactions of the Rock County Agricultural Society and Mechanics' Institute.* Janesville, Wis., 1856.

"Gymnastic Exercises." *Journal of Health* 1 (January 13, 1830), 132.

"Gymnastics." *American Quarterly Review* 3 (March 1828), 126–50.

"Gymnastics." *Cabinet* 5 (January 1831), 25–26.

"Gymnastics." *New-Harmony Gazette* 2 (December 13, 1826), 85.

"Gymnastics." *New-Harmony Gazette* 2 (December 27, 1826), 102–103.

Hale, William H. "Explosion of Steamboat Boilers." *Journal of the American Institute* 1 (October 1835), 54.

————. "Explosion of Steam-Boat Boilers." *Journal of the American Institute* 3 (July 1838), 529–37.

"Hannington's Diorama." *Journal of the American Institute* 2 (June 1837), 504.

Harshman, Jacob. *The Cause and Preventive of Steam Boiler Explosions.* Dayton, Oh., [1855].

"Hawkins' Steam Engine." *Minerva* 1 (June 26, 1824), 183–84.

Hayward, George. *A Lecture on Some of the Diseases of a Literary Life.* Boston, 1833.

————. *Outlines of Human Physiology; Designed for the Use of the Higher Classes in Common Schools.* Boston, 1834.

Henry, James, Jr. *Lecture before the Members of the Mechanics' Institute of the City of New-York, December 1, 1853.* New York, 1854.

Henry, Joseph. "Address." In *Catalogue of Articles Deposited for Competition and Premium, at the First Annual Exhibition of the Metropolitan Mechanics' Institute,* [3]-11. Washington, 1853.

[Higbee, James M]. "Steamboat Disasters." *North American Review* 50 (January 1840), 19–42.

"History and Proceedings of the Mechanics' Institute of the City of New York, from the Corresponding Secretary." *American Journal of Science and Arts* 31 (January 1837), 415–17.

Hitchcock, Edward. *Dyspepsy Forestalled and Resisted; . . .* Amherst, Mass., 1830.

"Holliston Manual Labor School." *American Annals of Education,* 3d ser., 8 (October 1838), 476.

[Holmes, Oliver Wendell]. "Mechanism of Vital Actions." *North American Review* 85 (July 1857), 39–77.

Hooker, Worthington. *First Book in Physiology for the Use of Schools and Families. . . .* New York, 1855.

_____. *An Oration Delivered before the Norwich Lyceum and Mechanics' Institute, on the 5th of July, 1830.* Norwich, Conn., 1830.

[Howland, S. A.] *Steamboat Disasters and Railroad Accidents in the United States; . . .* Worcester, Mass., 1840.

Howson, Henry. "Safety-Valves." In Oliver Byrne, *The American Engineer, Draftsman, and Machinist's Assistant; . . .* Philadelphia, Penn., 1853.

"The Human Mind." *Bouquet: Flowers of Polite Literature* 1 (September 24, 1831), 62.

"Humorous Description of the Steam Engine." *Boston Daily Advertiser* (June 17, 1828), 2.

Huntington, F[rederic] D[an]. *Hands: Brain: Heart. . . .* Boston, 1856.

"Improvements in Mechanics." *Farmer and Mechanic,* n.s., 4 (February 21, 1850), 90.

"Influence of the Telegraph upon Literature." *Democratic Review* 22 (May 1848), 409–13.

Ingersol, Joseph R. *An Address Delivered before the Literary Societies of Lafayette College at Easton, PA, July 4, 1833.* Philadelphia, Penn., 1833.

"Insanity and Insane Hospitals." *North American Review* 44 (January 1837), 91–121.

"The Iron Horse." *Knickerbocker* 14 (November 1839), 413–15.

Jarvis, Edward. *Lecture on the Necessity of the Study of Physiology, . . .* Boston, 1845.

_____. *Primary Physiology, for Schools.* Philadelphia, Penn., 1848.

Jay, William. *An Inquiry into the Character and Tendency of the American Colonization, and American Anti-Slavery Societies.* New York, 1835.

"John Maelzel." *American Magazine of Useful and Entertaining Knowledge* 3 (February 1837), 196–98.

Johnson, James. "The Rail-road Steamer." *Journal of the American Institute* 3 (June 1838), 490–93.

Johnson, Walter R. *Address Introductory to a Course of Lectures on Mechanics and Natural Philosophy, Delivered before the Franklin Institute, Philadelphia, November 19, 1828.* Boston, 1829.

_____. *A Lecture on the Mechanical Industry and the Inventive Genius of America. . . .* Baltimore, Md., 1849.

Jones, A. C. "An Account of the Explosion of the Steamboat 'Brillant.'" *Journal of the Franklin Institute* 53 (May 1852), 322–24.

Jones, Thomas P. *An Address on the Progress of Manufactures and Internal Improvement, in the United States; . . .* Philadelphia, Penn., 1827.

[_____]. "Observations upon the Automaton Chess Player." *Franklin Journal* 3 (February 1827), 125–32.

Junkin, D. X. *The Reverend George Junkin, D.D., LL.D. a Historical Biography.* Philadelphia, Penn., 1871.

Junkin, George. *The Bearings of College Education upon the Welfare of the Whole Community. . . .* Rossville, Oh., 1843.

_____. "Inaugural Address of President Junkin." In *Inaugural Charge by J. M. Porter, Esq. President of the Board of Trustees, and Inaugural Address of the Rev. George Junkin, D.D. President of Lafayette College,* [8]-16. 1834.

_____. *The Integrity of our National Union vs. Abolitionism: . . .* Cincinnati, Oh., 1843.

_____. *A Plea for North-Eastern Pennsylvania: The Tenth Baccalaureate in Lafayette College.* Easton, Penn., 1845.

Juvenis. "Empire of Mind." *Hartford Pearl and Literary Gazette* 4 (August 20, 1834), 7–8.

Keagy (Dr.). "Education of the Stomach." *Moral Reformer* 1 (February 1835), 61.

Kendall, Geo[rge] W. *A Sketch of the History of the Ohio Mechanic's Institute; And a Statement of its Present Condition.* Cincinnati, 1853.

Kennedy, John H. *Sympathy, Its Foundation and Legitimate Exercise Considered, in Special Relation to Africa: . . .* Philadelphia, Penn., [1828].

Lafayette College: The Seventh Annual Report. Easton, Penn., 1839.

Lambert, T[homas] S[cott]. *Hygienic Physiology.* Portland, Maine, 1852.

_____. *Practical Anatomy, Physiology, and Pathology; Hygiene and Therapeutics.* Portland, Maine, 1851.

"Lane Seminary, Ohio." *American Annals of Education,* 3d ser., 2 (June 1, 1832), 290.

"The Late Dreadful Catastrophe." *Farmer and Mechanic,* n.s., 4 (February 14, 1850), 80–81.

"Lectures on the Physiology and Natural History of Man." *American Journal of Education* 1 (January 1826), 61.

Lee, Frederic S. *The Human Machine and Industrial Efficiency.* New York, 1919.

_____. "Is the Eight-Hour Working-Day Rational?" *Science,* n.s., 44 (November 24, 1916), [727]–35.

_____. "Physical Exercise from the Standpoint of Physiology." *Science,* n.s., 29 (April 2, 1909), [521]–27.

Leib, James R. *Lecture on Scientific Education, Delivered Saturday, December 18, 1830, before the Members of the Franklin Institute.* Philadelphia, Penn., 1831.

_____. *Lecture on the Nature and Objects of the Modern Philosophy . . .* Philadelphia, Penn., 1830.

[Leland, Charles G.] "Physical Education," *Graham's Magazine* 53 (December 1858), 495–97.

Leonard, Benjamin G. *An Introductory Discourse, Delivered before the Chillicothe Lyceum and Mechanics' Institute, on the 1st of November, 1833.* Chillicothe, Oh., 1834.

Letter from the Secretary of the Treasury, Transmitting, in Obedience to a Resolution of the House of the 29th of June Last, Information in Relation to Steam Engines, Etc. 25th Cong., 3rd sess., 1838, H. Exec. Doc. 21.

Lloyd, James T. *Lloyd's Steamboat Directory, and Disasters on the Western Waters.* Philadelphia, Penn., [1856].

Longworth's . . . City Directory. New York, 1835.

Lossing, Benson J. *History of New York City, . . .* 2 vols. New York, 1884.

"Lowell: And Its Manufactures." *Merchants' Magazine* 16 (April 1847), 356–62.

Luther, Seth. *An Address Delivered before the Mechanics and Working-Men, of the City of Brooklyn, . . .* Brooklyn, N.Y., 1836.

————. *An Address to the Working-Men of New-England, on the State of Education, and on the Condition of the Producing Classes in Europe and America: . . .* Boston, 1832.

Maccoun, Robert T. "The Atlantic Telegraph." *Knickerbocker* 52 (August 1858), 187.

"Machinery and Hand Labor." *Scientific American* 10 (August 18, 1855), 387.

"Machinery, for Machine Making." *Graham's Magazine* 41 (November 1852), 469–76.

"Maelzel's Automatons." *New-York Evening Post* (April 14, 1826), 2.

Magoon, E. L. *Oration . . . Delivered July 4th, 1848, at the Laying of the Corner Stone of the Ohio Mechanics' Institute, Cincinnati.* Cincinnati, Oh., 1848.

Mansfield, E. D. "The Worth of the Mechanic Arts." In *Report of the Annual Fair of the Ohio Mechanics' Institute,* [27]–48. Cincinnati, Oh., 1838.

"Manual and Mental Labor Connected." *Hazard's Register of Pennsylvania* 12 (September 14, 1833), 170–72.

"Manual Labor." *American Annals of Education,* 3d ser., 3 (June 1833), [241]–46.

"Manual Labor." *Quarterly Register* 7 (August 1834), 64–67.

"Manual Labor Colleges." *American Annals of Education,* 3d ser., 5 (March 1835), 114–16.

"Manual Labor School." *American Annals of Education,* 3d ser., 1 (August 1831), 396–97.

"Manual Labor School Society." *Annals of Education,* 3d. ser., 2 (January 15, 1832), 92–94.

"Manual Labor Schools." *American Magazine of Useful and Entertaining Knowledge* 1 (May 1835), 392.

"Manual Labor Schools." *American Magazine of Useful and Entertaining Knowledge* 2 (November 1835), 103.

"Manual Labor Schools at the South." *American Annals of Education,* 3d ser., 5 (September 1835), 426.

"Manufactory of Pins." *New-Yorker* 7 (May 25, 1839), 158.

"Manufactory of Pins." *Supplement to the Connecticut Courant* 5 (April 27, 1839), 255.

Mapes, James J. *Inaugural Address, Delivered Tuesday Evening, Jan. 7, 1845, before the Mechanics' Institute, of the City of New-York.* New York, 1845.

"March of Mind." *American Monthly Magazine* 4 (February 1835), 417–21.

Marsh, George P. *Address Delivered before the Burlington Mechanics Institute, . . .* Burlington, Vt., 1843.

Mathias (Mr.). *Report of the Committee on Education, on the Subject of Manual Labor Academies, . . .* Harrisburg, Penn., 1833.

"Mechanic Association." *Niles' Weekly Register* 33 (October 20, 1827), 118.

"The Mechanics and Men of Literature in New York." *Scientific American* 8 (January 15, 1853), 137.

"Mechanics' Institute." *Farmer and Mechanic*, n.s., 3 (June 7, 1849), 274.

"The Mechanics' Institute." *Farmer and Mechanic*, n.s., 3 (November 29, 1849), 574.

"Mechanics' Institute." *Farmer and Mechanic*, n.s., 4 (December 5, 1850), 584.

"The Mechanics' Institute of the City of New-York." *Mechanics' Magazine, and Register of Improvements* 4 (September 27, 1834), 180–82.

"Mechanics' Institute Rooms, 100 Bowery." *Farmer and Mechanic*, n.s., 4 (June 20, 1850), 298.

"Mechanics' Lectures." *Scientific American* 8 (January 8, 1853), 133.

"Mechanism." *New-Harmony Gazette* 2 (December 6, 1826), 77–78.

[Melville, Herman]. "The Paradise of Bachelors and the Tartarus of Maids." *Harper's New Monthly Magazine* 10 (April 1855), 670–78.

Memorial to the Legislature of Pennsylvania, for the Incorporation of LaFayette College, at Easton. 1825.

[Miles, Henry Adolphus]. "The Cotton Manufacture." *North American Review* 52 (January 1841), 31–56.

Milnor, James. *Plea for the American Colonization Society: A Sermon, Preached in St. George's Church, New-York, on Sunday, July 9, 1826*. . . . New York, 1826.

"Mind." *Literary Tablet* 2 (September 14, 1833), 91–92.

Minutes and Proceedings of the First Annual Convention of the People of Colour: . . . Philadelphia, Penn., 1831.

Mitchell, J[ohn] K. "On Some of the Means of Elevating the Character of the Working Classes." *Journal of the Franklin Institute* 14 (August 1834), 94–109.

———. *The Value of the Practical Interrogation of Nature;* . . . Philadelphia, Penn., 1834.

[Mitchell, Silas Weir]. "The Last of a Veteran Chess Player." *Chess Monthly* 1 (February 1857), 40–45.

Mitchell, S. Weir. *Fat and Blood: And How to Make Them*. Philadelphia, Penn., 1877.

———. "Wear and Tear." *Lippincott's Magazine* 4 (November 1869), 493–502.

M'Lane, R[obert]. *An Examination into the Cause of Explosions by Steam on the Western Waters*. Louisville, Ky., 1839.

[Monteith, John]. *A Report on the Subject of Connecting Manual Labour with Study* . . . . Philadelphia, Penn., 1828.

Moore, Joseph H. "Revolutions." *Herald of Truth* 1 (June 1847), 433–37.

"Moral Causes of Recent Disasters." *American Railroad Journal, and Mechanics' Magazine* 7 (August 15, 1838), 125–27.

"Morals of Manufacturing Towns." *Merchants' Magazine* 19 (December 1848), 661–62.

"Mr. Graham." *Moral Reformer* 1 (October 1835), 322–23.

Neal, John. "Education." *Mechanic* 3 (June 1834), 184–86.

Needham, Edgar. "Valedictory." In *Catalogue of the First Exhibition of the Kentucky Mechanics' Institute*, [61]–63. Louisville, Ky., 1854.

New Orleans Chamber of Commerce. *Reports and Resolutions Relative to the Causes of the Explosion of Steam Boilers, and the Measures Deemed Necessary for Prevention*. New Orleans, La., 1851.

"The New Steamboat Law." *American Railroad Journal, and Mechanics' Magazine* 7 (September 1, 1838), 141–44.

"New Steamboat Law." *New-Yorker* 5 (August 11, 1838), 334.

"The New Theory of Heat." *Harper's New Monthly Magazine* 39 (August 1869), 322–29.

"New York Mechanics' Institute." *Scientific American* 6 (May 17, 1851), 275.

Noble, B. G., ed. *New-York Illustrated*. New York, 1847.

"Ollapodiana." *Literary Harvester* 2 (February 15, 1843), 160.

"On the Probable Application of Steam Power to Various Purposes." *Mechanics' Magazine, and Register of Inventions and Improvements* 1 (March 1833), 118–19.

"On the Strength of Men and Animals." *Mechanics' Magazine, and Register of Inventions and Improvements* 1 (February 1833), 81–82.

One of the Fraternity. "Cause of Explosions." *Scientific American* 9 (May 6, 1854), 266.

Opinions and Testimonials in Favor of Barnum's Self-Acting Safety Apparatus, for the Prevention of Explosions and Fires on Board of Steam Vessels. [New York, 1848].

Owen, Robert. "The Social System." *New-Harmony Gazette* 2 (February 7, 1827), 145–46.

Owen, Robert Dale. *Circular Addressed to the Friends of Liberal Education in General, and to the Former Readers of the Free Enquirer, in Particular*. 1835.

———. "Labor: Its History and Prospects." *Herald of Truth* 3 (March 1848), 169–203.

———. "Wealth and Misery." *Popular Tracts* 11 (1830), 1–16.

P[arker, Theodore]. "Thoughts on Labor." *Dial* 1 (April 1841), 497–519.

———. "Thoughts on Labor." *New-Yorker* 11 (May 8, 1841), 119–20.

Patterson, James. *A Sermon, on the Effects of the Hebrew Slavery As Connected with Slavery in This Country*. . . . Philadelphia, Penn., 1825.

[Paulding, James Kirke]. *The Merry Tales of the Three Wise Men of Gotham*. New York, 1826.

[Peabody, Andrew Preston]. "The Future of Labor." *North American Review* 74 (April 1852), 445–63.

[Peabody, Oliver William Bourne]. "Popular Education." *North American Review* 29 (July 1829), 241–58.

Philadelphia Gazette and Daily Advertiser (March 17, 1827), 2.

"Physical Development in America." *Scientific American* 14 (January 8, 1859), 145.

"Physical Education." *American Monthly Magazine* 1 (November 1829), 541–46.

"Physical Education." *Supplement to the Connecticut Courant* 2 (September 21, 1830), 81–283.

"Pittsburg Mechanics' Institute." *Register of Pennsylvania* 6 (July 17, 1830), 41–42.

[Poe, Edgar Allan]. "Maelzel's Chess-Player." *Southern Literary Messenger* 2 (April 1836), 318–26.

"Popular Education." *North American Review* 23 (July 1826), 49–67.

"Portable Steam Engine." *Scientific American* 9 (December 3, 1853), [89].

Porter, James Madison. *An Address Delivered before the Literary Societies of Lafayette College, at Easton, PA, July 4, 1832*. Easton, Penn., [1832].

———. *An Address to the Mechanics of Easton, Pennsylvania*, . . . Easton, Penn., 1835.

Porter, J[ames] M[adison]. "Address and Charge." In *Inaugural Charge by J. M. Porter, Esq. President of the Board of Trustees, and Inaugural Address of the Rev. George Junkin, DD. President of Lafayette College*, [5]–7. 1834.

Pratt, Zadock. *Address Delivered January 16, 1849, before the Mechanics' Institute, of the City of New York*, . . . New York, 1849.

"Pratt's Steam Boiler Explosion." *Scientific American* 8 (August 20, 1853), 389.
Proceedings of the Board of Aldermen 36, part 2 (February 19–May 8, 1849).
"Progress of Physical Education." *American Journal of Education* 1 (January 1826), 19–23.
Quill, Charles [James Waddel Alexander]. *The Working-Man*. Philadelphia, Penn., 1843.
R.D.H. "Remarks on the Effect of Salt Water in Steam Engine Boilers." *Journal of the Franklin Institute* 7 (May 1831), 289–92.
R.M. "Suggestions of Means Calculated to Promote Safety in Steam-Boat Boilers." *Journal of the Franklin Institute* 17 (June 1836), 372–74.
"The Railway System in Europe." *American Review* 4 (November 1846), 485–96.
Rantoul, Robert, Jr. *An Oration, Delivered before the Gloucester Mechanic Association, on the Fourth of July, 1833*. Salem, Mass., 1833.
Read, Daniel. *An Address Delivered before the Mechanics Institute of Bloomington, at the Celebration of their Anniversary, February 22, 1844*. Bloomington, In., 1844.
Renwick, James. *Treatise on the Steam Engine*. New York, 1830.
_____. *Treatise on the Steam Engine*, 2d ed. New York, 1839.
"Reply on Manual Labor Schools." *American Annals of Education*, 3d ser., 4 (April 1834), 158–61.
Report of a Committee of the Trustees of Allegheny College, on the Manual Labor System. Meadville, Penn., 1833.
Report of a Joint Committee of the Legislature of the State of Louisiana, on the Petition of J. O. Blair, upon the Subject of Steam Explosion. 22nd Cong., 1st sess., 1832, Doc. 226.
Report of the Committee Appointed by the Citizens of Cincinnati, April 26, 1838, to Enquire into the Causes of the Explosion of the Moselle. Cincinnati, Oh., 1838.
Report of the Committee on Commerce, Accompanied by a Bill for Regulating of Steam Boats, and for the Security of Passengers Therein. 18th Cong., 1st sess., 1824, House Rept. 125.
Report of the Eighth Annual Fair of the Chicago Mechanics' Institute. Chicago, 1856.
"Report of the Faculty of the Manual Labor Academy of Penn. to the Board of Trustees." *Register of Pennsylvania* 4 (December 5, 1829), 356–58.
Report of the First Annual Fair of the Ohio Mechanics' Institute. Cincinnati, Oh., 1838.
Report of the Special Committee Appointed by the Common Council of the City of New York, Relative to the Catastrophe in Hague Street, . . . New York, 1850.
Report on a Plan for Extending and More Perfectly Establishing the Mechanic and Scientific Institution of New-York. 1824.
Review of *Appleton's Dictionary of Machines, Mechanics, Engine-Work and Engineering*. *New Englander* 9 (November 1851), 625.
Review of Edward Jarvis, *Practical Physiology: For the use of Schools and Families*. *Graham's Magazine* 32 (March 1848), 191.
[Robbins, Chandler]. *Remarks on the Disorders of Literary Men, or an Inquiry into the Means of Preventing the Evils Usually Incident to Sedentary and Studious Habits*. Boston, 1825.
Scribbler, Ben. "A Scene in 1956." *Graham's Illustrated Magazine* 49 (August 1856), 104.
Second Annual Report of the American Physiological Society. Boston, 1838.

The Second Annual Report of the Board of Trustees of Lafayette College. Easton, Penn., 1833.

Second Annual Report of the Board of Trustees of the Manual Labour Academy of Pennsylvania. Philadelphia, Penn., 1830.

The Second Annual Report of the Trustees of the Cooper Union for the Advancement of Science and Art. New York, 1861.

Smith, Delazon. *A History of Oberlin, or, New Lights of the West:* . . . Cleveland, Oh., 1837.

"Societies for Promoting Useful Knowledge, in Boston, Mass." *Mechanics' Magazine, and Register of Inventions and Improvements* 1 (May 1833), 250–52.

Southard, Samuel L. *Address Delivered before the Newark Mechanics' Association, July 5, 1830.* Newark, N.J., 1830.

Sprague, Joseph E. *An Address Delivered before the Salem Charitable Mechanic Association, on their Fourth Anniversary, July 4, 1821,* . . . 1821.

Stanford, John. *Aetna: A Discourse, Delivered in the New-York City Hospital, on Lord's Day Morning, May 23, 1824.* . . . New York, 1824.

Stanton, Fred P. "Address." In *A Record of the Third Exhibition of the Metropolitan Mechanics' Institute.* Washington, 1857.

"State Manual Labor Academy." *American Annals of Education,* 3d ser., 3 (April 1833), 186–87.

"Statues Made by Steam." *Supplement to the Courant* 12 (July 31, 1847), 118.

"Steam." *Harper's New Monthly Magazine* 1 (June 1850), 50.

"Steam." *Niles' Weekly Register* 28 (June 25, 1825), 258.

"Steam and Its Effects." *American Monthly Magazine* 1 (May 1833), 179–80.

"Steam and Other Matters." *Pearl and Literary Gazette* 3 (January 4, 1834), 90–91.

"The Steam-Engine." *American Quarterly Review* 6 (December 1829), 408–37.

"Steam Navigation." *Niles' Weekly Register* 13 (November 1, 1817), 150–51.

"Steamboat Disaster—Bursting of the Boilers of the General Brown." *Family Magazine* 6 (1839), 299.

"Steamboat Jackson." *New-York Commercial Advertiser* (June 15, 1831), 2.

Steamboat Law. 32nd Congress, 1st sess., 1852, ch. 106.

"The Steamboat Union." *New-York Evening Post* (December 28, 1826), 2.

Steamboats. 22nd Cong., 1st sess., 1832, House Rept. 478.

Story, Joseph. "A Discourse Delivered Before the Boston Mechanics' Institution, at the Opening of Their Annual Course of Lectures, November, 1829." *The American Library of Useful Knowledge* 1 (Boston, 1831), 3–37.

Sui Generis [Thomas Man]. *Picture of a Factory Village:* . . . Providence, R.I., 1833.

T.S.K. "A Visit to Lowell." *Supplement to the Courant* 10 (April 5, 1845), 50–51.

Taylor, Jane. *Wouldst Know Thyself! Or, the Outlines of Human Physiology.* New York, 1858.

"Terrible Explosion in New York." *Stryker's American Register and Magazine* 4 (July 1850), 135–36.

Third Annual Report of the American Physiological Society. Boston, 1839.

The Third Annual Report of the Board of Trustees of Lafayette College. [Easton, Penn.], 1834.

Third Annual Report of the Board of Trustees of the Manual Labour Academy of Pennsylvania. Philadelphia, Penn., 1832.

Third Report of the Trustees of the Oneida Institute of Science and Industry. Utica, N.Y., 1831.

[Thomas, Frederick William]. *East and West.* Philadelphia, Penn., 1836.

———. "A Steamboat Race on the Ohio." *New-Yorker* 2 (December 10, 1836), 180–82.

Thomas, J. Henry. "Closing Address." In *Report of Exhibition Committee of Kentucky Mechanics' Institute,* 60–63. Louisville, 1855.

Throstle, T. "Factory Life in New-England." *Knickerbocker* 30 (December 1847), 511–18.

Tissot, S. A. *An Essay on Diseases Incidental to Literary and Sedentary Persons. . . .* London, 1768.

Titterwell, Timo[thy] [Samuel Kettell]. *Yankee Notions: A Medley.* 2d ed. Boston, 1838.

"To Subscribers." *American Railroad Journal, and Mechanics' Magazine* 7 (July 1, 1838), 1.

Trall, R[ussell] T. *The Illustrated Family Gymnasium; . . .* New York, 1857.

"Traveling by Steam." *New-Yorker* 5 (September 8, 1838), 393.

[Tucker, George]. "Progress of Population and Wealth in the United States, in Fifty Years." *Merchants' Magazine* 9 (July 1843), 47–58.

Tuckerman, Henry T. "Robert Fulton." *Graham's Magazine* 38 (March 1851), 233–38.

Twain, Mark [Samuel Clemens]. *Life on the Mississippi.* London, 1883.

Tyng, Stephen H. *The Importance of Uniting Manual Labour with Intellectual Attainments, in a Preparation for the Ministry. . . .* Philadelphia, Penn., 1830.

Uncle Sam's Comic Almanack for 1837. Wheeling, Va. [1837].

"Valuable Communication." *New-York Commercial Advertiser* (February 13, 1832), 2.

Van Deusen, E. H. "Observations on a Form of Nervous Prostration, (Neurasthenia,) Culminating in Insanity." *American Journal of Insanity* 25 (April 1869), [445]–61.

Verplanck, Gulian C. "Introductory Address, Delivered before the Mechanics' Institute of the City of New-York, November 27, 1833." *Mechanics' Magazine, and Register of Inventions and Improvements* 3 (January 1834), [47]–56.

———. *A Lecture, Introductory to the Course of Scientific Lectures, before the Mechanics' Institute of the City of New-York. . . .* New York, 1833.

Verplan[c]k, Gulian C. "The Influence of Mechanical Invention on the Improvement of Mankind." *Knickerbocker* 3 (January 1834), 40–54.

W. "Observations on the Rise and Progress of the Franklin Institute." *American Mechanics' Magazine* 1 (February 1826), 66–71.

[Walker, Timothy]. "Defence of Mechanical Philosophy." *North American Review* 33 (July 1831), 122–36.

Walter, Jacob. *An Essay on Steam, and Practical Engineering.* Holcomb, 1838.

[Ward, James H.] *Steam for the Million. . . .* Philadelphia, Penn., 1847.

Warren, John C. *Physical Education and the Preservation of Health.* Boston, 1846.

"The Way of Explosions." *Scientific American* 7 (July 25, 1852), 357.

Webster, Daniel. "Mr. Webster's Introductory Lecture before the Mechanics' Institution." *The American Library of Useful Knowledge* 1 (Boston, 1831), 38–58.

———. "Second Speech on the Sub-Treasury Bill, Delivered in the Senate of the United States, March 12, 1838." In Daniel Webster, *Speeches and Forensic Arguments,* vol. 3 (Boston, 1843), 277–339.

Weld, Theodore D. *First Annual Report of the Society for Promoting Manual Labor in Literary Institutions, . . .* New York, 1833.

[Weld, Theodore D.] *Societies for Promoting Manual Labor in Literary Institutions,* 2d ed. Philadelphia, Penn., 1833.

[_____]. *Societies for Promoting Manual Labor in Literary Institutions,* 3d ed. Philadelphia, Penn., 1834.

[Wells, Walter]. "Strength, and How to Use It." *Lippincott's Magazine* 2 (October 1868), 416–25; (November 1868), 548–54.

Wells, Walter. "Strength, and How to Use It." *Lippincott's Magazine* 2 (December 1868), 657–68; 3 (June 1869), 649–62.

"What Are We Going to Make?" *Atlantic Monthly* 2 (June 1858), 90–101.

"What Shall Be Done for the Laborer?" *New-Yorker* 11 (July 24, 1841), 297–98.

Wheildon, William W. *Memoir of Solomon Willard, Architect and Superintendent of the Bunker Hill Monument.* [Boston], 1865.

"Worcester County Manual Labor High School." *American Annals of Education,* 3d ser., 8 (November 1838), 522.

"Workings of the New Steamboat Law." *Scientific American* 10 (March 3, 1855), 195.

SECONDARY SOURCES

Abzug, Robert H. *Cosmos Crumbling: American Reform and the Religious Imagination.* New York: Oxford University Press, 1994.

Adams, David Wallace. *Education for Extinction: American Indians and the Boarding School Experience, 1875–1928.* Lawrence: University Press of Kansas, 1995.

A[llen], G[eorge]. "The History of the Automaton Chess-Player in America." In *The Book of the First American Chess Congress,* ed. Daniel Willard Fisk, 420–84. New York: Rudd & Carlton, 1859.

Arrington, Joseph Earl. "John Maelzel, Master Showman of Automata and Panoramas." *Pennsylvania Magazine of History and Biography* 84 (January 1960): 56–92.

Atack, Jeremy, Fred Bateman, and Thomas Weiss. "The Regional Diffusion and Adoption of the Steam Engine in American Manufacturing." *Journal of Economic History* 40 (June 1980): 281–308.

Banta, Martha. *Taylored Lives: Narrative Productions in the Age of Taylor, Veblen, and Ford.* Chicago: University of Chicago Press, 1993.

Beckert, Sven. "Propertied of a Different Kind: Bourgeoisie and Lower Middle Class in the Nineteenth-Century United States." In *The Middling Sorts: Explorations in the History of the American Middle Class,* ed. Burton J. Bledstein and Robert D. Johnston, [285]–95. New York: Routledge, 2001.

Bender, Thomas. *New York Intellect: A History of Intellectual Life in New York City, from 1750 to the Beginnings of Our Own Time.* New York: Alfred A. Knopf, 1987.

Bennett, Charles Alpheus. *History of Manual and Industrial Education up to 1870.* Peoria, Ill.: Manual Arts Press, 1926.

Berlanstein, Lenard R., ed. *Rethinking Labor History: Essays on Discourse and Class Analysis.* Urbana: University of Illinois Press, 1993.

Betts, John R. "Mind and Body in Early American Thought." *Journal of American History* 54 (March 1968): 787–805.

Bledstein, Burton. "Introduction: Storytellers to the Middle Class." In *The Middling Sorts: Explorations in the History of the American Middle Class,* ed. Burton J. Bledstein and Robert D. Johnston, [1]–25. New York: Routledge, 2001.

Bledstein, Burton J. *The Culture of Professionalism: The Middle Class and the Development of Higher Education in America.* New York: W. W. Norton and Company, 1976.

Blumin, Stuart M. *The Emergence of the Middle Class: Social Experience in the American City, 1760–1900.* New York: Cambridge University Press, 1989.

Bode, Carl. *The American Lyceum, Town Meeting of the Mind.* New York: Oxford University Press, 1956.

Bromell, Nicholas K. *By the Sweat of the Brow: Literature and Labor in Antebellum America.* Chicago: University of Chicago Press, 1993.

Brown, JoAnne. "Professional Language: Words That Succeed." *Radical History Review* 34 (January 1986): [33]–51.

Buckley, Peter George. "To the Opera House: Culture and Society in New York City, 1820–1860." Ph.D. diss., State University of New York at Stony Brook, 1984.

Burbick, Joan. *Healing the Republic: The Language of Health and the Culture of Nationalism in Nineteenth-Century America.* New York: Cambridge University Press, 1994.

Burke, John G. "Bursting Boilers and the Federal Power." *Technology and Culture* 7 (winter 1966): 1–23.

Burke, Martin J. *The Conundrum of Class: Public Discourse on the Social Order in America.* Chicago: University of Chicago Press, 1995.

Burns, Rex. *Success in America: The Yeoman Dream and the Industrial Revolution.* Amherst: University of Massachusetts Press, 1976.

Bushman, Richard L. *The Refinement of America: Persons, Houses, Cities.* New York: Alfred A. Knopf, 1992.

Calvert, Monte A. *The Mechanical Engineer in America, 1830–1910: Professional Cultures in Conflict.* Baltimore, Md.: Johns Hopkins Press, 1967.

Cardwell, D. S. L. *From Watt to Clausius: The Rise of Thermodynamics in the Early Industrial Age.* (Ithaca, N.Y.: Cornell University Press, 1971).

Carey, James W. "Technology and Ideology: The Case of Telegraphy." *Prospects* 8 (1983): 303–25.

Carroll, Charles Michael. *The Great Chess Automaton.* New York: Dover Publications, 1975.

Channell, David F. *The Vital Machine: A Study of Technology and Organic Life.* New York: Oxford University Press, 1991.

Clopper, Edward N. "The Ohio Mechanics Institute: Its 125th Anniversary." *Bulletin of the Historical and Philosophical Society of Ohio* 11 (July 1953): [179]–91.

Cook, James W. *The Arts of Deception: Playing with Fraud in the Age of Barnum.* Cambridge, Mass.: Harvard University Press, 2001.

Cook, James W., Jr. "From the Age of Reason to the Age of Barnum: The Great Automaton Chess-Player and the Emergence of Victorian Cultural Illusionism." *Winterthur Portfolio* 30 (winter 1995): 231–57.

Cooper, Carolyn C. *Shaping Invention: Thomas Blanchard's Machinery and Patent Management in Nineteenth-Century America, 1820–1870.* New York: Columbia University Press, 1991.

Cremin, Lawrence A. *American Education: The National Experience, 1783–1876.* New York: Harper & Row Publishers, 1980.

Cross, Coy F. II. *Justin Smith Morrill: Father of the Land-Grant Colleges.* East Lansing: Michigan State University Press, 1999.

Dabakis, Melissa. *Visualizing Labor in American Sculpture: Monuments, Manliness, and the Work Ethic, 1880–1935.* New York: Cambridge University Press, 1999.

Derickson, Alan. "Physiological Science and Scientific Management in the Progressive Era: Frederic S. Lee and the Committee on Industrial Fatigue." *Business History Review* 68 (winter 1994): [483]–514.

Dublin, Thomas. *Women at Work: The Transformation of Work and Community in Lowell, Massachusetts, 1826–1860.* New York: Columbia University Press, 1979.

Dunwell, Steve. *The Run of the Mill: A Pictorial Narrative of the Expansion, Dominion, Decline, and Enduring Impact of the New England Textile Industry.* Boston: David R. Godine, 1978.

Elliott, Arlene Anne. "The Development of the Mechanics' Institutes and Their Influence upon the Field of Engineering: Pennsylvania, a Case Study, 1824–1860." Ph.D. diss., University of Southern California, 1972.

Elliott, James W. *Transport to Disaster.* New York: Holt, Rinehart and Winston, 1962.

Evans, Henry Ridgely. *Edgar Allan Poe and Baron von Kempelen's Chess Playing Automaton.* Kenton, Oh.: International Brotherhood of Magicians, 1939.

Fabian, Ann. " 'Scenes too horrible for description:' James T. Lloyd's Account of Exploding Steamboats." Typescript in author's possession.

Faler, Paul G. *Mechanics and Manufacturers in the Early Industrial Revolution: Lynn, Massachusetts, 1780–1860.* Albany: State University of New York Press, 1981.

Fear-Segal, Jacqueline. "Nineteenth-Century Indian Education: Universalism Versus Evolutionism." *Journal of American Studies* 33 (August 1999): [323]–41.

Feinstein, Howard M. "The Use and Abuse of Illness in the James Family Circle: A View of Neurasthenia as a Social Phenomenon." In *Our Selves/Our Past: Psychological Approaches to American History,* ed. Robert J. Brugger, 228–43. Baltimore, Md.: Johns Hopkins University Press, 1981.

Forman, Ezekial. "Amusements and Politics in Philadelphia, 1794." *Pennsylvania Magazine of History and Biography* 10 (1886): 182–87.

Friedman, Lawrence J. *Gregarious Saints: Self and Community in American Abolitionism, 1830–1870.* Cambridge: Cambridge University Press, 1982.

Gilkeson, John S., Jr. *Middle-Class Providence, 1820–1940.* Princeton, N.J.: Princeton University Press, 1986.

Gillespie, Richard. "Industrial Fatigue and the Discipline of Physiology." In *Physiology in the American Context, 1850–1940,* ed. Gerald L. Geison, 237–62. Bethesda, Md.: American Physiological Society, 1987.

Glickman, Gena Debra. "A Study of the Role of Women in the Transformation of the Curriculum at the Maryland Institute for the Promotion of Mechanic Arts, from 1825–1875." Ph.D. diss., University of Maryland, 1992.

Glickstein, Jonathan A. *Concepts of Free Labor in Antebellum America.* New Haven, Conn.: Yale University Press, 1991.

Goodman, Paul. "The Manual Labor Movement and the Origins of Abolitionism." *Journal of the Early Republic* 13 (fall 1993): [355]–88.

Gosling, F. G. *Before Freud: Neurasthenia and the American Medical Community, 1870–1910*. Urbana: University of Illinois Press, 1987.

Graham, Laura. "From Patriarchy to Paternalism: Disestablished Clergymen and the Manual Labor School Movement." Ph.D. diss., University of Rochester, 1993.

Green, Harvey. *Fit for America: Health, Fitness, Sport and American Society*. New York: Pantheon Books, 1986.

Haber, Samuel. *Efficiency and Uplift: Scientific Management in the Progressive Era, 1890–1920*. Chicago: University of Chicago Press, 1964.

Halsey, Harlan I. "The Choice Between High-Pressure and Low-Pressure Steam Power in America in the Early Nineteenth Century." *Journal of Economic History* 41 (December 1981): 723–44.

Halttunen, Karen. *Confidence Men and Painted Women: A Study of Middle-Class Culture in America, 1830–1870*. New Haven, Conn.: Yale University Press, 1982.

Harris, Neil. *Humbug: The Art of P. T. Barnum*. Chicago: University of Chicago Press, 1973.

Hocker, Edward W. *Germantown 1683–1933* . . . Germantown, Penn.: published by the author, 1933.

Hole, James. *An Essay on the History and Management of Literary, Scientific, and Mechanics' Institutions;* . . . London: Longman, Brown, Green & Longmans, 1853.

Hudson, J[ames] W[illiam]. *The History of Adult Education,* . . . London: Longman, Brown, Green & Longmans, 1851.

Hugins, Walter. *Jacksonian Democracy and the Working Class: A Study of the New York Workingmen's Movement, 1829–1837*. Stanford, Ca.: Stanford University Press, 1960.

Hunter, Louis C. *Steamboats on the Western Rivers: An Economic and Technological History*. Cambridge, Mass.: Harvard University Press, 1949; rpt. New York: Octagon Books, 1969.

Irvine, Russell W., and Donna Zani Dunkerton. "The Noyes Academy, 1834–35: The Road to the Oberlin Collegiate Institute and the Higher Education of African-Americans in the Nineteenth Century." *Western Journal of Black Studies* 22 (1998): 260–73.

Irwin, John T. "Handedness and the Self: Poe's Chess Player." *Arizona Quarterly* 45 (spring 1989): 1–28.

Johnson, Paul E. *A Shopkeeper's Millennium: Society and Revivals in Rochester, New York, 1815–1837*. New York: Hill and Wang, 1978.

Joyce, Patrick. *Visions of the People: Industrial England and the Question of Class 1848–1914*. Cambridge: Cambridge University Press, 1991.

Kaestle, Carl F. *Pillars of the Republic: Common Schools and American Society*. New York: Hill and Wang, 1983.

Kanigel, Robert. *The One Best Way: Frederick Winslow Taylor and the Enigma of Efficiency*. New York: Viking, 1997.

Kasson, John F. *Civilizing the Machine: Technology and Republican Values in America, 1776–1900*. New York: Grossman Publishers, 1976.

———. *Rudeness and Civility: Manners in Nineteenth-Century Urban America*. New York: Hill and Wang, 1990.

Kornblith, Gary John. "From Artisans to Businessmen: Master Mechanics in New England, 1798–1850." Ph.D. diss., Princeton University, 1983.

Laurie, Bruce. *Artisans into Workers: Labor in Nineteenth-Century America*. New York: Hill and Wang, 1989.

Lears, Jackson. *No Place of Grace: Antimodernism and the Transformation of American Culture, 1880–1920*. New York: Pantheon Books, 1981.

Lears, T. J. Jackson. "The Concept of Cultural Hegemony: Problems and Possibilities." *American Historical Review* 90 (June 1985): 567–93.

Lerman, Nina Evelyn. "From 'Useful Knowledge' to 'Habits of Industry': Gender, Race, and Class in Nineteenth-Century Technical Education." Ph.D. diss., University of Pennsylvania, 1993.

Lesick, Lawrence Thomas. *The Lane Rebels: Evangelicalism and Antislavery in Antebellum America*. Metuchen, N.J.: Scarecrow Press, 1980.

Levitt, Gerald M. *The Turk, Chess Automaton*. Jefferson, N.C.: McFarland, 2000.

Licht, Walter. *Industrializing America: The Nineteenth Century*. Baltimore, Md.: Johns Hopkins University Press, 1995.

Mahoney, Timothy R. *Provincial Lives: Middle-Class Experience in the Antebellum Middle West*. New York: Cambridge University Press, 1999.

Marx, Leo. *The Machine in the Garden: Technology and the Pastoral Ideal in America*. New York: Oxford University Press, 1964.

Mayfield, David, and Susan Thorne. "Social History and its Discontents: Gareth Stedman Jones and the Politics of Language." *Social History* 17 (May 1992): [165]–88.

Mayr, Otto. *Authority, Liberty, and Automatic Machinery in Early Modern Europe*. Baltimore, Md.: Johns Hopkins University Press, 1986.

_____. "Yankee Practice and Engineering Theory: Charles T. Porter and the Dynamics of the High-Speed Engine." *Technology and Culture* 16 (October 1975): 570–602.

Mazlish, Bruce. *The Fourth Discontinuity: The Co-Evolution of Humans and Machines*. New Haven, Conn.: Yale University Press, 1993.

McGaw, Judith A. *Most Wonderful Machine: Mechanization and Social Change in Berkshire Paper Making, 1801–1885*. Princeton, N.J.: Princeton University Press, 1987.

McPherson, Donald S. "Mechanics' Institutes and the Pittsburgh Workingman, 1830–1840." *Western Pennsylvania Historical Magazine* 56 (April 1973): [155]–69.

Meier, Hugo A. "Technology and Democracy, 1800–1860." *Mississippi Valley Historical Review* 43 (March 1957): 618–40.

Merrick, George Byron. *Old Times on the Upper Mississippi: The Recollections of a Steamboat Pilot from 1854 to 1863*. Cleveland, Oh.: A. H. Clark, 1909.

Montgomery, David. *The Fall of the House of Labor: The Workplace, the State, and American Labor Activism, 1865–1925*. New York: Cambridge University Press, 1987.

Murphy, Lamar Riley. *Enter the Physician: The Transformation of Domestic Medicine 1760–1860*. Tuscaloosa: University of Alabama Press, 1991.

Nelson, Daniel. "The Making of a Progressive Engineer: Frederick W. Taylor." *Pennsylvania Magazine of History and Biography* 103 (October 1979): 446–66.

_____. *Managers and Workers: Origins of the Twentieth-Century Factory System in the United States, 1880–1920, 2d ed.* Madison: University of Wisconsin Press, 1995.

Nissenbaum, Stephen. *Sex, Diet, and Debility in Jacksonian America: Sylvester Graham and Health Reform*. Westport, Conn.: Greenwood Press, 1980.

Odell, George C. D. *Annals of the New York Stage*. 15 vols. New York, 1927–1949.

Oestreicher, Richard. "The Counted and the Uncounted: The Occupational Structure of Early American Cities." *Journal of Social History* 28 (winter 1994): [351]–61.

O'Malley, Michael. "Specie and Species: Race and the Money Question in Nineteenth-Century America." *American Historical Review* 99 (April 1994): 369–95.

Owen, W. B. *Historical Sketches of Lafayette College, with an Account of Its Present Organization and Courses of Study*. Easton, Penn., 1876.

Palmer, Bryan D. *Descent into Discourse: The Reification of Language and the Writing of Social History*. Philadelphia, Penn.: Temple University Press, 1990.

Poirier, Suzanne. "The Weir Mitchell Rest Cure: Doctor and Patients." *Women's Studies* 10 (1983): [15]–40.

Potter, Jerry O. *The Sultana Tragedy: America's Greatest Maritime Disaster*. Gretna, La.: Pelican Publishing, 1992.

Pursell, Carroll W. *Early Stationary Steam Engines in America: A Study in the Migration of a Technology*. Washington: Smithsonian Institution Press, 1969.

Purvis, June. *Hard Lessons: The Lives and Education of Working-Class Women in Nineteenth-Century England*. Cambridge: Polity Press, 1989.

Quick, Herbert, and Edward Quick. *Mississippi Steamboatin': A History of Steamboating on the Mississippi and Its Tributaries*. New York: H. Holt, 1926.

Rabinbach, Anson. *The Human Motor: Energy, Fatigue, and the Origins of Modernity*. New York: Basic Books, 1990.

Reynolds, Terry S. "The Education of Engineers in America before the Morrill Act of 1862." *History of Education Quarterly* 32 (winter 1992): [459]–82.

Rice, Stephen P. "Making Way for the Machine: Maelzel's Automaton Chess-Player and Antebellum American Culture." *Proceedings of the Massachusetts Historical Society* 106 (1994): 1–16.

_____. "The Mechanics' Institute of the City of New-York and the Conception of Class Authority in Early Industrial America, 1830–1860." *New York History* 81 (July 2000): 269–99.

Rigal, Laura. *The American Manufactory: Art, Labor, and the World of Things in the Early Republic*. Princeton, N.J.: Princeton University Press, 1998.

Roberts, Brian. *American Alchemy: The California Gold Rush and Middle-Class Culture*. Chapel Hill: University of North Carolina Press, 2000.

Robinson, William Hannibal. "The History of Hampton Institute, 1868–1949." Ph.D. diss., New York University, 1953.

Rodgers, Daniel T. *Contested Truths: Keywords in American Politics since Independence*. New York: Basic Books, 1987.

_____. *The Work Ethic in Industrial America, 1850–1920*. Chicago: University of Chicago Press, 1978.

Roediger, David R. *The Wages of Whiteness: Race and the Making of the American Working Class*. New York: Verso, 1991.

Rosenberg, Charles E. "Catechisms of Health: The Body in the Prebellum Classroom." *Bulletin of the History of Medicine* 69 (summer 1995): 175–97.

_____. "The Place of George M. Beard in Nineteenth-Century Psychiatry." *Bulletin of the History of Medicine* 36 (May–June 1962): 245–59.

Ross, Steven J. *Workers on the Edge: Work, Leisure, and Politics in Industrializing Cincinnati, 1788–1890*. New York: Columbia University Press, 1985.

Ryan, Mary P. *Cradle of the Middle Class: The Family in Oneida County, New York, 1790–1865.* New York: Cambridge University Press, 1981.

Salecker, Gene Eric. *Disaster on the Mississippi: The Sultana Explosion, April 27, 1865.* Annapolis, Md.: Naval Institute Press, 1996.

Sandfort, John F. *Heat Engines: Thermodynamics in Theory and Practice.* Garden City, N.J.: Anchor Books, 1962.

Sappol, Michael. *A Traffic of Dead Bodies: Anatomy and Embodied Social Identity in Nineteenth-Century America.* Princeton, N.J.: Princeton University Press, 2002.

Scobey, David. "Anatomy of the Promenade: The Politics of Bourgeois Sociability in Nineteenth-Century New York." *Social History* 17 (May 1992): [203]–27.

Scott, Joan Wallach. "On Language, Gender, and Working-Class History." In *Gender and the Politics of History.* New York: Columbia University Press, 1988.

Scranton, Philip. *Proprietary Capitalism: The Textile Manufacture at Philadelphia, 1800–1885.* New York: Cambridge University Press, 1983.

Seltzer, Mark. *Bodies and Machines.* New York: Routledge, 1992.

Sernett, Milton C. *Abolition's Axe: Beriah Green, Oneida Institute, and the Black Freedom Struggle.* Syracuse, N.Y.: Syracuse University Press, 1986.

Shelton, Cynthia. *The Mills of Manayunk: Industrialization and Social Conflict in the Philadelphia Region, 1787–1837.* Baltimore, Md.: Johns Hopkins University Press, 1986.

Sicherman, Barbara. "The Uses of a Diagnosis: Doctors, Patients, and Neurasthenia." In *Sickness and Health in America: Readings in the History of Medicine and Public Health,* ed. Judith Walter Leavitt and Ronald L. Numbers, 2d ed., 22–35. Madison: University of Wisconsin Press, 1985.

Silver-Isenstadt, Jean L. *Shameless: The Visionary Life of Mary Gove Nichols.* Baltimore, Md.: Johns Hopkins University Press, 2002.

Sinclair, Bruce. *Early Research at the Franklin Institute: The Investigation into the Causes of Steam Boiler Explosions, 1830–1837.* Philadelphia: Franklin Institute of the State of Pennsylvania, 1966.

———. *Philadelphia's Philosopher Mechanics: A History of the Franklin Institute, 1824–1865.* Baltimore, Md.: Johns Hopkins University Press, 1974.

Siracusa, Carl. *A Mechanical People: Perceptions of the Industrial Order in Massachusetts, 1815–1880.* Middletown, Conn.: Wesleyan University Press, 1979.

Skillman, David Bishop. *The Biography of a College: Being the History of the First Century of the Life of Lafayette College.* 2 vols. Easton, Penn.: Lafayette College, 1932.

Standage, Tom. *The Turk: The Life and Times of the Famous Eighteenth-Century Chess-Playing Machine.* New York: Walker, 2002.

Stedman Jones, Gareth. *Languages of Class: Studies in English Working Class History, 1832–1982.* Cambridge: Cambridge University Press, 1983.

Stott, Richard B. *Workers in the Metropolis: Class, Ethnicity, and Youth in Antebellum New York City.* Ithaca, N.Y.: Cornell University Press, 1990.

Temin, Peter. "Steam and Waterpower in the Early Nineteenth Century." *Journal of Economic History* 26 (June 1966): 187–205.

Thomas, Benjamin P. *Theodore Weld: Crusader for Freedom.* New Brunswick, N.J.: Rutgers University Press, 1950.

Thompson, E. P. *The Making of the English Working Class.* New York: Vintage Books, 1966.

Tichi, Cecelia. *Shifting Gears: Technology, Literature, Culture in Modernist America.* Chapel Hill: University of North Carolina Press, 1987.

Tucker, Barbara M. *Samuel Slater and the Origins of the American Textile Industry, 1790–1860.* Ithaca, N.Y.: Cornell University Press, 1984.

Tylecote, Mabel. *The Mechanics' Institutes of Lancashire and Yorkshire before 1851.* Manchester: Manchester University Press, 1957.

Uberti, J. Richard. "Men, Manners, and Machines: The Young Man's Institute in Antebellum Philadelphia." Ph.D. diss., University of Pennsylvania, 1977.

Verbrugge, Martha H. *Able-Bodied Womanhood: Personal Health and Social Change in Nineteenth-Century Boston.* New York: Oxford University Press, 1988.

Wallace, Anthony F. C. *Rockdale: The Growth of an American Village in the Early Industrial Revolution.* New York: W. W. Norton, 1978.

Warner, John Harley. "Ideals of Science and Their Discontents in Late Nineteenth-Century American Medicine." *Isis* 82 (1991): 454–78.

———. *The Therapeutic Perspective: Medical Practice, Knowledge, and Identity in America, 1820–1885.* Cambridge, Mass.: Harvard University Press, 1986.

Welter, Rush. *Popular Education and Democratic Thought in America.* New York: Columbia University Press, 1962.

Whorton, James C. *Crusaders for Fitness: The History of American Health Reformers.* Princeton, N.J.: Princeton University Press, 1982.

Wilentz, Sean. *Chants Democratic: New York City and the Rise of the American Working Class, 1788–1850.* New York: Oxford University Press, 1984.

Williams, Raymond. *Keywords: A Vocabulary of Culture and Society.* New York: Oxford University Press, 1983.

Wimsatt, W. K., Jr. "Poe and the Chess Automaton." *American Literature* 11 (March 1939–January 1940): 138–51.

Winpenny, Thomas R. "Those Who Attend Meetings will be Excused from Paying Dues: The Lancaster Mechanics' Institute in Search of Mechanics." *Pennsylvania History* 55 (January 1988): 31–41.

Wood, Ann Douglas. " 'The Fashionable Diseases': Women's Complaints and Their Treatment in Nineteenth-Century America." *Journal of Interdisciplinary History* 4 (summer 1973): [25]–52.

Wosk, Julie. *Breaking Frame: Technology and the Visual Arts in the Nineteenth Century.* New Brunswick, N.J.: Rutgers University Press, 1993.

Zonderman, David A. *Aspirations and Anxieties: New England Workers and the Mechanized Factory System, 1815–1850.* New York: Oxford University Press, 1992.

Index

Compositor:	IBT Global
Indexer:	Sharon Sweeney
Text:	10/13 Sabon
Display:	Sabon
Printer and Binder:	IBT Global